ISBN 978-1-330-23673-4
PIBN 10060131

1 MONTH OF
FREE
READING

at
www.ForgottenBooks.com

By purchasing this book you are eligible for one month membership to ForgottenBooks.com, giving you unlimited access to our entire collection of over 1,000,000 titles via our web site and mobile apps.

To claim your free month visit:

www.forgottenbooks.com/free60131

English
Français
Deutsche
Italiano
Español
Português

www.forgottenbooks.com

Mythology Photography **Fiction**
Fishing Christianity **Art** Cooking
Essays Buddhism Freemasonry
Medicine **Biology** Music **Ancient
Egypt** Evolution Carpentry Physics
Dance Geology **Mathematics** Fitness
Shakespeare **Folklore** Yoga Marketing
Confidence Immortality Biographies
Poetry **Psychology** Witchcraft
Electronics Chemistry History **Law**
Accounting **Philosophy** Anthropology
Alchemy Drama Quantum Mechanics
Atheism Sexual Health **Ancient History**
Entrepreneurship Languages Sport
Paleontology Needlework Islam
Metaphysics Investment Archaeology
Parenting Statistics Criminology
Motivational

A LIBRARY OF THE

WORLD'S BEST LITERATURE

ANCIENT AND MODERN

CHARLES DUDLEY WARNER

EDITOR

**HAMILTON WRIGHT MABIE   LUCIA GILBERT RUNKLE
GEORGE HENRY WARNER**

ASSOCIATE EDITORS

FORTY-FIVE VOLUMES

VOL. XL.

NEW YORK
THE INTERNATIONAL SOCIETY
MDCCCXCVII

Edition de Luxe

THE ADVISORY COUNCIL

COPYRIGHT NOTICE

F. L. Hosmer: The Indwelling God.

Mrs. Ellen R. Houghton.—George Houghton: The Legend of Walbach

Harper & Brothers.—Will Carleton: Betsey and I Are Out; How Be
    Made Up. Amélie Rives: Unto the Least of These Little Ones.

Houghton, Mifflin & Co.—(Annie Lazarus) Emma Lazarus: Cho
    Cranes of Ibycus; Critic and Poet; The South; Gifts; The Worl
    The Banner of the Jew; The Crowing of the Red Cock. Frank
    Sherman: Pepita. Margaret E. Sangster: Are the Children at Ho
    Perry: After the Ball. John James Piatt: The Blackberry Fa
    M. B. Piatt: The Witch in the Glass; After Wings. Adeline D. T
    Our Mother. Frances L. Mace: A Burmese Parable. Eliza Scu
    Find Out God; No More Sea. Phœbe Cary: Nearer Home. Maur
    son: Wild Honey; Atalanta. Christopher Pearse Cranch: Tho
    American Pantheon. Lizette Woodworth Reese: A Rhyme of D
    Rachel; April Weather. Lucy Larcom: Hannah Binding Shoe
    Longfellow: The Golden Sunset; Greeting; Vesper Hymn. Carolir
    Mason: The Voyage. Alice Cary: Lyra, a Lament. William
    Nightfall. Lilian Clarke: After Ruckert; The Shelter against
    Rain. Edna Dean Proctor: O Lord, I Cannot Lose Heaven.
    Preston: The Boy Van Dyke; The Mystery of Cro-a-tan. Ja
    Roche: The Kearsarge. James Freeman Clarke: A Hymn of 1
    Witch—from Bürger. H. W. Longfellow: Into the Silent Land
    Salis; Beware (Folk Song Tr.); The Two Locks of Hair—fi
    Bayard Taylor: The Haste of Love—from Martin Opitz; The Gi
    from Hebel. William Roscoe Thayer: The Last Hunt. Mrs.
    Tomson: Ephemeron.

George P. Lathrop: The Star to Its Light; The Heart of a Song.

«Life» Publishing Co.—W. P. Bourke: When My Cousin Comes to To
    Romaine: All on One Side. Samuel Minturn Peck: Priscilla. El
    Hall: A Modern Psyche.

Augusta Larned: Perfect Peace.

Lippincott's Magazine: The House of Hate.

Longmans, Green & Co.—T. W. Higginson: The Things I Miss.

Lamson, Wolffe & Co.—Ethelwyn Wetherald: The House of the Trees;
    King; Out of Doors; The Woodside Way; Twilight; The Wind o
    The Wind of Death. Edna Proctor Clarke: The Opal.

William James Linton: Love and Youth.

James Herbert Morse: The Power of Beauty.

Ernest McGaffey: A Dancer.

Mrs. V. H. McKnight.—Geo. McKnight: Though Naught They May to

R. K. Munkittrick: The Root's Dream.

Lloyd Mifflin: The Frontier.

Louise Chandler Moulton: Help Thou My Unbelief; Shall I Look Back.

Emma Huntington Nason: Body and Soul.

Samuel Minturn Peck: Dolly.

Charles Ray Palmer.—Ray Palmer: My Faith Looks Up to Thee.

Charles Henry Phelps: Dorothy.

«Puck.»—Schuyler King: The Poster Knight to His Lady.

L. C. Page & Co.—Albion Fellows Mason: The Time of Day. Ann
    Johnston: The Old Church. Burton Egbert Stevenson: After the

G. P. Putnam's Sons.— John Antrobus: The Cowboy.
Robert Cameron Rogers: The Rosary; À Outrance.
Charles F. Richardson: Justice.
William Carman Roberts: For all his Poems.
James Jeffrey Roche: The V-A-S-E.
Roberts Bros.— Susan Marr Spalding: An Antique Intaglio;
  The Second Place. Frederick H. Hedge: The Morning S
The A. D. F. Randolph Company.— Harriet McEwen Kimball: T
Clinton Scollard: The Book Stall.
George Santayana: Faith.
Montgomery Schuyler: Carlyle and Emerson.
Frank Sewall: Roll Out, O Song.
Minot J. Savage: The Age of Gold; Mystery.
Frederick A. Stokes Company.— Frank Dempster Sherman: Bac
Charles Scribner's Sons.— Julia C. R. Dorr: The Apple-Tree; Se
Herbert S. Stone & Co.: The Marine, a Folk Song. (Trans.)
J. T. Trowbridge: The Vagabonds.
L. Frank Tooker: He Bringeth Them into Their Desired Have
Jean Wright: The Epicurean.
Charles Henry Webb: With a Nantucket Shell.

TABLE OF CONTENTS

VOLUME XL

FULL-PAGE ILLUSTRATIONS

VOLUME XL

SONGS HYMNS AND LYRICS

THE OLD CONTINENTALS

(CARMEN BELLICOSUM)

IN THEIR ragged regimentals
  Stood the old Continentals,
    Yielding not,
When the grenadiers were lunging,
And like hail fell the plunging
    Cannon shot;
    When the files
    Of the isles
From the smoky night encampment bore the banner of the rampant
    Unicorn,
And grummer, grummer, grummer, rolled the roll of the drummer
    Through the morn!

  But with eyes to the front all,
  And with guns horizontal,
    Stood our sires:
  And the balls whistled deadly,
  And in streams flashing redly
    Blazed the fires;
    As the swift
    Billows' drift
Drove the dark battle breakers o'er the green sodded acres
    Of the plain,
And louder, louder, louder, cracked the black gunpowder,
    Cracking amain!

  Now like smiths at their forges
  Labored red St. George's
    Cannoneers,
  And the "villainous saltpetre"
  Rang a fierce discordant metre
    Round their ears;
    Like the roar
    On a shore,

Rose the Horse Guards' clangor, as they rode in roaring anger
On our flanks:
Then higher, higher, higher, burned the old-fashioned fire
Through the ranks!

And the old-fashioned colonel
Galloped through the white infernal
Powder cloud;
His broadsword was swinging
And his brazen throat was ringing,
Trumpet loud:
Then the blue
Bullets flew,
And the trooper jackets reddened at the touch of the leaden
Rifle breath,
And rounder, rounder, rounder; roared the iron six-pounder,
Hurling death!

GUY HUMPHREY McMASTER.

THE HADLEY WEATHERCOCK

ON HADLEY steeple proud I sit,
Steadfast and true; I never flit:
Summer and winter, night and day,
The merry winds around me play;
And far below my gilded feet
The generations come and go
In one unceasing ebb and flow,
Year after year in Hadley street.
I nothing care — I only know
God sits above, he wills it so;
While roundabout, and roundabout, and roundabout I go,
The way o' the wind, the changing wind, the way o' the wind to show.

The hands that for me paid the gold
A century since have turned to mold;
And all the crowds who saw me new
In seventeen hundred fifty-two,
(A noble town was Hadley then,
And beautiful as one could find,)
Dead, long years dead, and out of mind,
Those stately dames and gallant men!

But I abide, while they are low.
God ruleth all, he wills it so:
And roundabout, and roundabout, and roundabout I go,
The way o' the wind, the changing wind, the way o' the wind to show.

The wind blew south, the wind blew north;
I saw an army marching forth;
And when the wind was hushed and still,
I heard them talk of Bunker Hill.
From Saratoga, bold Burgoyne
  (His sullen redcoats, past the town,
  To Aqua Vitæ's plain marched down)
In Hadley mansion stopped to dine.
The new State comes! The King must go!
Glory to God who wills it so!
And roundabout, and roundabout, and roundabout I go,
The way o' the wind, the changing wind, the way o' the wind to show.

The wind blows east, the wind blows west,
In Hadley street the same unrest.
On every breeze that hither comes,
I hear the rolling of the drums,
And well do I know the warning;
  The wind blows north, the wind blows south,
  The ball has left the cannon's mouth,
And the land is filled with mourning.
In Freedom's name they struck the blow!
The Land is One, God wills it so.
And roundabout, and roundabout, and roundabout I go,
The way o' the wind, the changing wind, the way o' the wind to show.

Though all things change upon the ground,
Unchanging, sure, I'm ever found.
In calm or tempest, sun or rain,
No eye inquires of me in vain.
Though many a man betray his trust,
  Though some may honor sell, or buy,
  Like Peter some their Lord deny,
Yet here I preach till I am rust:
Blow high, blow low, come weal, or woe,
God sits above, he wills it so.
Then roundabout, and roundabout, and roundabout I go,
The way o' the wind, the changing wind, the way o' the wind to show.

JULIA TAFT BAYNE.

JUST A MULTITUDE OF CURLS

JUST a multitude of curls
    Weighing down a little head;
    Two wide eyes not blue nor gray,
Like the sky 'twixt night and day;
Small red mouth — and all to say
        Has been said.

Just a saucy word or glance,
    And a hand held out to kiss;
Just a curl — a ribbon through —
Just a flower, fresh and blue —
And to think what men will do
        Just for this!

                            CORA FABBRI.

THE ROSE OF KENMARE

I'VE been soft in a small way
    On the girleens of Galway,
And the Limerick lasses have made me feel quare;
    But there's no use denyin',
    No girl I've set eye on
Could compate wid Rose Ryan of the town of Kenmare.

            Oh, where
        Can her like be found?
            No where,
        The country round,
        Spins at her wheel
            Daughter as true,
        Sets in the reel
            Wid a slide of the shoe,
            a slinderer,
            tinderer,
            purtier,
    wittier colleen than you,
            Rose, aroo!

Her hair mocks the sunshine,
And the soft silver moonshine
Neck and arm of the colleen completely eclipse;

Whilst the nose of the jewel
Slants straight as Carran Tual
From the heaven in her eye to her heather-sweet lip.

Oh, where, etc.

Did your eyes ever follow
The wings of the swallow
Here and there, light as air, o'er the meadow field glance?
For if not, you've no notion
Of the exquisite motion
Of her sweet little feet as they dart in the dance.

Oh, where, etc.

If y' inquire why the nightingale
Still shuns th' invitin' gale
That wafts every song-bird but her to the west,
Faix she knows, I suppose,
Ould Kenmare has a Rose
That would sing any bulbul to sleep in her nest.

Oh, where, etc.

When her voice gives the warnin'
For the milkin' in the mornin',
Ev'n the cow known for hornin' comes runnin' to her pail;
The lambs play about her,
And the small bonneens snout her
Whilst their parints salute her wid a twisht of the tail.

Oh, where, etc.

When at noon from our labor
We draw neighbor wid neighbor
From the heat of the sun to the shelter of the tree,
Wid spuds fresh from the bilin',
And new milk, you come smilin',
All the boys' hearts beguilin', alannah machree!

Oh, where, etc.

But there's one sweeter hour
When the hot day is o'er,
And we rest at the door wid the bright moon above,
And she's sittin' in the middle;
When she's guessed Larry's riddle,
Cries, "Now for your fiddle, Shiel Dhuv, Shiel Dhuv."

Oh, where
Can her like be found?
No where,
The country round,
Spins at her wheel
Daughter as true,
Sets in the reel,
Wid a slide of the shoe,
a slinderer,
tinderer,
purtier,
wittier colleen than you,
Rose, aroo!

ALFRED PERCIVAL GRAVES.

IRISH LULLABY

I'D ROCK my own sweet childie to rest in a cradle of gold on a
bough of the willow,
To the shoheen ho of the wind of the west and the lulla lo of the
soft sea billow.
Sleep, baby dear,
Sleep without fear:
Mother is here beside your pillow.

I'd put my own sweet childie to sleep in a silver boat on the beauti-
ful river,
Where a shoheen whisper the white cascades, and a lulla lo the
green flags shiver.
Sleep, baby dear,
Sleep without fear:
Mother is here with you for ever.

Lulla lo! to the rise and fall of mother's bosom 'tis sleep has bound
you,
And oh, my child, what cosier nest for rosier rest could love have
found you?
Sleep, baby dear,
Sleep without fear:
Mother's two arms are clasped around you.

ALFRED PERCIVAL GRAVES.

THE NUT-BROWN MAID

B<small>E IT</small> ryght or wrong, these men among
 On women do complayne:
Affyrmynge this, how that it is
 A labour spent in vayne
To love them wele; for never a dele
 They love a man agayne:
For late a man do what he can,
 Theyr favour to attayne,
Yet yf a newe do them persue,
 Theyr first true lover than
Laboureth for nought; for from her thought
 He is a banyshed man.

I say nat nay, but that all day
 It is bothe writ and sayd
That woman's faith is, as who sayth,
 All utterly decayd;
But neverthelesse ryght good wytnésse
 In this case might be layd,
That they love true and continúe:
 Recorde the Not-browne Mayd,—
Which, when her love came, her to prove,
 To her to make his mone,
Wold nat depart; for in her hart
 She loved but hym alone.

Than betwaine us late us dyscus
 What was all the manere
Betwayne them two: we wyll also
 Tell all the payne and fere
That she is in. Now I begyn
 So that ye me answére;
Wherfore all ye that present be
 I pray you gyve an ere:—
I am the knyght: I come by nyght,
 As secret as I can;
Sayinge, "Alas! thus standeth the case:
 I am a banyshed man."

SHE

And I your wyll for to fulfyll
 In this wyll nat refuse;

Trustying to shewe, in wordès fewe,
    That men have an yll use
(To theyr own shame) women to blame,
    And causelesse them accuse:
Therfore to you I answere nowe,
    All women to excuse,—
Myne owne hart dere, with what you chere
    I pray you, tell anone;
For in my mynde, of all mankynde
    I love but you alone.

HE

It standeth so,—a dede is do
    Whereof grete harme shall growe:
My destiny is for to dy
    A shamefull deth, I trowe;
Or elles to fle: the one must be.
    None other way I knowe,
But to withdrawe as an outlawe,
    And take me to my bowe.
Wherfore, adue, my owne hart true!
    None other rede I can;
For I must to the grene wode go
    Alone, a banyshed man.

SHE

O Lord, what is thys worldys blysse,
    That changeth as the mone!
My somers day in lusty May
    Is derked before the none.
I here you say farewell: nay, nay,
    We départ nat so sone.
Why say ye so? wheder wyll ye go?
    Alas! what have ye done?
All my welfáre to sorrowe and care
    Sholde chaunge, yf ye were gone;
For in my mynde, of all mankynde
    I love but you alone.

HE

I can beleve it shall you greve,
    And somewhat you dystrayne:
But aftyrwarde, your paynes harde
    Within a day or twayne

Shall some aslake; and ye shall take
 Comfort to you agayne.
Why sholde ye ought? for to make thought,
 Your labour were in vayne.
And thus I do; and pray you to
 As hartely as I can:
For I must to the grene wode go
 Alone, a banyshed man.

SHE

Now, syth that ye have shewed to me
 The secret of your mynde,
I shall be playne to you agayne,
 Lyke as ye shall me fynde.
Syth it is so, that ye wyll go,
 I wolle not leve behynde:
Shall never be sayd, the Not-browne Mayd
 Was to her love unkynde.
Make you redy, for so am I,
 Allthough it were anone;
For in my mynde, of all mankynde
 I love but you alone.

HE

Yet I you rede to take good hede
 What men wyll thynke and say:
Of yonge and olde it shall be tolde,
 That ye be gone away,
Your wanton wyll for to fulfyll,
 In grene wode you to play;
And that ye myght from your delyght
 No lenger make delay.
Rather than ye sholde thus for me
 Be called an yll womán,
Yet wolde I to the grene wode go
 Alone, a banyshed man.

SHE

Though it be songe of old and yonge,
 That I sholde be to blame,
Theyrs be the charge, that speke so large
 In hurtynge of my name:
For I wyll prove that faythfulle love
 It is devoyd of shame;

In your dystresse and hevynesse,
 To part with you, the same:
And sure all tho, that do not so,
 True lovers are they none;
For in my mynde, of all mankynde
 I love but you alone.

HE

I counceyle you, remember howe
 It is no maydens lawe,
Nothynge to dout, but to renne out
 To wode with an outláwe:
For ye must there in your hand bere
 A bowe, redy to drawe;
And as a thefe, thus must you lyve,
 Ever in drede and awe:
Wherby to you grete harme myght growe;
 Yet had I lever than
That I had to the grene wode go
 Alone, a banyshed man.

SHE

I thinke nat nay, but as ye say,
 It is no maidens lore:
But love may make me for your sake,
 As I have sayd before,
To come on fote, to hunt, and shote,
 To gete us mete in store;
For so that I your company
 May have, I aske no more:
From which to part, it maketh my hart
 As colde as ony stone;
For in my mynde, of all mankynde
 I love but you alone.

HE

For an outlawe this is the lawe,
 That men hym take and bynde;
Without pyté, hangèd to be,
 And waver with the wynde.
If I had nede, (as God forbede!)
 What rescous coude ye fynde?
Forsoth, I trowe, ye and your bowe
 For fere wolde drawe behynde:

And no mervayle; for lytell avayle
　　Were in your counceyle than:
Wherfore I wyll to the grene wode go
　　Alone, a banyshed man.

SHE

Right wele know ye, that woman be
　　But feble for to fyght;
No womenhede it is indede
　　To be bolde as a knyght:
Yet in such fere yf that ye were
　　With enemyes day or nyght,
I wolde withstande, with bowe in hande,
　　To greve them as I myght,
And you to save; as women have
　　From deth, men many one:
For in my mynde, of all mankynde
　　I love but you alone.

HE

Yet take good hede; for ever I drede
　　That ye coude nat sustayne
The thornie wayes, the deep valléies,
　　The snowe, the frost, the rayne,
The colde, the hete: for dry or wete,
　　We must lodge on the playne;
And, us above, none other rofe
　　But a brake bush, or twayne:
Which some sholde greve you, I beleve;
　　And ye wolde gladly than
That I had to the grene wode go
　　Alone, a banyshed man.

SHE

Syth I have here bene partynére
　　With you of joy and blysse,
I must also part of your wo
　　Endure, as reson is;
Yet am I sure of one plesúre
　　And shortely, it is this:
That where ye be, me semeth, pardé,
　　I could not fare amysse.
Without more speche, I you beseche
　　That we were sone agone;

For in my mynde, of all mankynde
    I love but you alone,

HE

If ye go thyder, ye must consyder,
    Whan ye have lust to dyne,
There shall no mete be for you gete,
    Nor drinke, bere, ale, ne wyne.
No schetès clene, to lye betwene,
    Made of threde and twyne;
None other house but leves and bowes,
    To cover your hed and myne.
O myne harte swete, this evyll dyéte
    Sholde make you pale and wan;
Wherfore I wyll to the grene wode go
    Alone, a banyshed man.

SHE

Amonge the wild dere, such an archére
    As men say that ye be
Ne may nat fayle of good vitayle,
    Where is so grete plentè;
And water clere of the ryvére
    Shall be full swete to me:
With which in hele I shall ryght wele
    Endure, as ye shall see;
And, or we go, a bedde or two
    I can provyde anone:
For in my mynde, of all mankynde
    I love but you alone.

HE

Lo! yet, before, ye must do more,
    Yf ye wyll go with me:
As cut your here up by your ere,
    Your kyrtel by the kne;
With bowe in hande, for to withstande
    Your enemyes, yf nede be:
And this same nyght, before daylight,
    To wode-warde wyll I fle.
Yf that ye wyll all this fulfill,
    Do it shortely as ye can;
Els wyll I to the grene wode go
    Alone, a banyshed man.

SHE

I shall as nowe do more for you
    Than longeth to womanhede;
To shote my here, a bowe to bere,
    To shote in tyme of nede.
O my swete mother, before all other
    For you I have most drede:
But nowe adue! I must ensue
    Where fortune doth me lede.
All this make ye: now let us fle;
    The day cometh fast upon:
For in my mynde, of all mankynde
    I love but you alone.

HE

Nay, nay, nat so; ye shall nat go,
    And I shall tell ye why:
Your appetyght is to be lyght
    Of love, I wele espy;
For lyke as ye have sayd to me,
    In lyke wyse hardely
Ye wolde answére whosoever it were,
    In way of company.
It is sayd of olde, Sone hot, sone colde;
    And so is a womán.
Wherfore I to the wode wyll go
    Alone, a banyshed man.

SHE

Yf ye take hede, it is no nede
    Such wordes to say by me:
For oft ye prayed, and longe assayed,
    Or I you loved, pardè;
And though that I of auncestry
    A barons daughter be,
Yet have you proved howe I you loved,
    A squyer of lowe degre:
And ever shall, whatso befall
    To dy therfore anone;
For in my mynde, of all mankynde
    I love but you alone.

HE

A barons chylde to be begylde!
    It were a cursèd dede;

To be feláwe with an outlawe!
    Almighty God forbede!
Yet better were the pore squyére
    Alone to forest yede,
Than ye sholde say another day,
    That, by my cursèd dede,
Ye were betrayed; wherfore, good mayd,
    The best rede that I can,
Is, that I to the grene wode go
    Alone, a banyshed man.

SHE

Whatever befall, I never shall
    Of this thyng you upbrayd;
But yf ye go, and leve me so,
    Then have ye me betrayd.
Remember you wele, howe that ye dele:
    For yf ye, as ye sayd,
Be so unkynde, to leve behynde
    Your love, the Not-browne Mayd,
Trust me truly, that I shall dy
    Sone after ye be gone;
For in my mynde, of all mankynde
    I love but you alone.

HE

Yf that ye went, ye sholde repent:
    For in the forest nowe
I have purvayed me of a mayd,
    Whom I love more than you;
Another fayrére than ever ye were,
    I dare it wele avowe:
And of ye bothe eche sholde be wrothe
    With other, as I trowe.
It were myne ese, to lyve in pese;
    So wyll I, yf I can:
Wherfore I to the wode wyll go
    Alone, a banyshed man.

SHE

Though in the wode I undyrstode
    Ye had a paramour,
All this may nought remove my thought,
    But that I will be your:

And she shall fynde me soft, and kynde,
    And courteys every hour;
Glad to fulfyll all that she wyll
    Commaunde me to my power:
For had ye, lo, an hundred mo,
    Of them I wolde be one;
For in my mynde, of all mankynde
    I love but you alone.

HE

Myne owne dere love, I se the prove
    That ye be kynde and true;
Of mayd and wyfe, in all my lyfe,
    The best that ever I knewe.
Be mery and glad, be no more sad,
    The case is chaungèd newe;
For it were ruthe, that for your truthe
    Ye sholde have cause to rewe.
Be nat dismayed: whatsoever I sayd
    To you whan I began,
I wyll nat to the grene wode go,—
    I am no banyshed man.

SHE

These tydings be more gladd to me
    Than to be made a quene,
Yf I were sure they sholde endure;
    But it is often sene,
Whan men wyll breke promyse, they speke
    The wordes on the splene.
Ye shape some wyle me to begyle,
    And stele from me, I wene:
Than were the case worse than it was,
    And I more wo-begone;
For in my mynde, of all mankynde
    I love but you alone.

HE

Ye shall nat nede further to drede;
    I will nat dysparáge
You, (God forfend!) syth ye descend
    Of so grete a lynáge.
Nowe undyrstande: to Westmarlande,
    Which is myne herytage,

I wyll you brynge, and with a rynge
    By way of maryage
I wyll you take, and lady make,
    As shortely as I can;
Thus have you won an erlys son
    And not a banyshed man.

AUTHOR

Here may ye se that women be
    In love, meke, kynde, and stable:
Late never man reprove them than,
    Or call them variable.
But rather, pray God that we may
    To them be comfortable;
Which sometyme proveth such, as he loveth,
    Yf they be charytable.
For syth men, wolde that women sholde
    Be meke to them each one,
Moche more ought they to God obey,
    And serve but hym alone.

PILGRIMAGE

GIVE me my scallop-shell of quiet,
    My staffe of faith to lean upon,
    My scrip of joye — immortal diet —
    My bottle of salvatión,
My gown of glory, hope's true gage; —
And thus I take my pilgrimage.

Blood must be my body's balmer,
While my soul, like peaceful palmer,
Traveleth towards the land of heaven;
Other balm will not be given.

Over the silver mountains,
Where spring the nectar fountains,
    There will I kiss
    The bowle of blisse,
And drink mine everlasting fill
Upon every milken-hill:
My soul will be a-dry before;
But after that will thirst no more.

SIR WALTER RALEIGH.

LOVE WILL FIND OUT THE WAY

OVER the mountains
  And over the waves;
Under the fountains
  And under the graves;
Under floods that are deepest,
  Which Neptune obey;
Over rocks that are steepest,—
  Love will find out the way.

Where there is no place
  For the glow-worm to lye;
Where there is no space
  For receipt of a fly;
Where the midge dares not venture,
  Lest herself fast she lay,—
If love come he will enter,
  And soon find out his way.

You may esteem him
  A child for his might;
Or you may deem him
  A coward from his flight:
But if she whom love doth honor
  Be concealed from the day,
Set a thousand guards upon her,
  Love will find out the way.

Some think to lose him
  By having him confined;
And some do suppose him,
  Poor thing, to be blind:
But if ne'er so close ye wall him,
  Do the best that you may,
Blind love, if so ye call him,
  Will find out his way.

You may train the eagle
  To stoop to your fist;
Or you may inveigle
  The phœnix of the East;
The lioness ye may move her
  To give o'er her prey:
But you'll ne'er stop a lover,—
  He will find out his way.

Author Unknown

LOVE ME LITTLE, LOVE ME LONG

LOVE me little, love me long!
    Is the burden of my song:
    Love that is too hot and strong
Burneth soon to waste.
Still I would not have thee cold—
Not too backward, nor too bold:
Love that lasteth till 'tis old
    Fadeth not in haste.
Love me little, love me long!
Is the burden of my song.

If thou lovest me too much,
'Twill not prove as true a touch;
Love me little more than such—
    For I fear the end.
I'm with little well content,
And a little from thee sent
Is enough, with true intent
    To be steadfast, friend.

Say thou lovest me, while thou live
I to thee my love will give,
Never dreaming to deceive
    While that life endures;
Nay, and after death, in sooth,
I to thee will keep my truth,
As now when in my May of youth:
    This my love assures.

Constant love is moderate ever,
And it will through life persever:
Give me that with true endeavor,—
    I will it restore.
A suit of durance let it be,
For all weathers,—that for me,—
For the land or for the sea;
    Lasting evermore.

Winter's cold or summer's heat,
Autumn's tempests on it beat;
It can never know defeat,
    Never can rebel;

Such the love that I would gain,
Such the love, I tell thee plain,
Thou must give, or woo in vain:
So to thee — farewell!

Author Unknown.

THE SHAN VAN VOCHT*

OH THE French are on the sea,
Says the *shan van vocht;*
The French are on the sea,
Says the *shan van vocht:*
Oh the French are in the bay,
They'll be here without delay,
And the Orange will decay,
Says the *shan van vocht.*

Chorus

Oh the French are in the bay,
They'll be here by break of day,
And the Orange will decay,
Says the *shan van vocht.*

And their camp it shall be where?
Says the *shan van vocht;*
Their camp it shall be where?
Says the *shan van vocht:*
On the Currach of Kildare,
The boys they will be there,
With their pikes in good repair,
Says the *shan van vocht.*

Chorus

To the Currach of Kildare
The boys they will repair,
And Lord Edward will be there,
Says the *shan van vocht.*

* *An t-sean bean bochd,* "the poor old woman," — another name for Ireland. The versions of this song are numberless; but that here given is considered the best. The date of its composition is 1797, the period at which the French fleet arrived in Bantry Bay.

Then what will the yeomen do?
　Says the *shan van vocht;*
What *will* the yeomen do?
　Says the *shan van vocht :*
What *should* the yeomen do
But throw off the red and blue,
And swear that they'll be true
　To the *shan van vocht?*

Chorus

　What *should* the yeomen do
　But throw off the red and blue,
　And swear that they'll be true
　　To the *shan van vocht?*

And what color will they wear?
　Says the *shan van vocht;*
What color will they wear?
　Says the *shan van vocht :*
What color should be seen
Where our fathers' homes have been,
But our own immortal Green?
　Says the *shan van vocht.*

Chorus

　What color should be seen
　Where our fathers' homes have been,
.　But our own immortal Green?
　　Says the *shan van vocht.*

And will Ireland then be free?
　Says the *shan van vocht;*
Will Ireland then be free?
　Says the *shan van vocht :*
Yes! Ireland SHALL be free,
From the centre to the sea;
Then hurrah for Liberty!
　Says the *shan van vocht.*

Chorus

　Yes! Ireland SHALL be free,
　From the centre to the sea
　Then hurrah for Liberty!
　Says the *shan van vocht.*

Street Ballad, 1797.

A DEATH-BED

HER suffering ended with the day,
   Yet lived she at its close;
And breathed the long, long night away
   In statue-like repose.

But when the sun, in all his state,
   Illumed the eastern skies,
She passed through Glory's morning gate,
   And walked in Paradise!

JAMES ALDRICH.

ON A QUIET LIFE

SMALL fields are mine; a small and guiltless rent:
   In both I prize the quiet of content.
My mind maintains its peace, from feverish dread
Secure, and fear of crimes that sloth has bred.
Others let toilsome camps or curule chairs
Invite, and joys which vain ambition shares.
May I, my lot among the people thrown,
Live to myself, and call my time my own!

AVIENUS.

Translation of Charles Abraham Elton.

THE BLUE AND THE GRAY

BY THE flow of the inland river,
   Whence the fleets of iron have fled,
Where the blades of the grave-grass quiver,
   Asleep are the ranks of the dead;—
     Under the sod and the dew,
       Waiting the Judgment Day:
     Under the one, the Blue;
      Under the other, the Gray.

These in the robings of glory,
   Those in the gloom of defeat,
All with the battle-blood gory,
   In the dusk of eternity meet;—
     Under the sod and the dew,
       Waiting the Judgment Day:
     Under the laurel, the Blue;
      Under the willow, the Gray.

From the silence of sorrowful hours
  The desolate mourners go,
Lovingly laden with flowers
  Alike for the friend and the foe;—
    Under the sod and the dew,
      Waiting the Judgment Day:
    Under the roses, the Blue;
      Under the lilies, the Gray.

So with an equal splendor
  The morning sun-rays fall,
With a touch impartially tender,
  On the blossoms blooming for all;—
    Under the sod and the dew,
      Waiting the Judgment Day:
    'Broidered with gold, the Blue;
      Mellowed with gold, the Gray.

So, when the summer calleth,
  On forest and field of grain
With an equal murmur falleth
  The cooling drip of the rain;—
    Under the sod and the dew,
      Waiting the Judgment Day:
    Wet with the rain, the Blue;
      Wet with the rain, the Gray.

Sadly, but not with upbraiding,
  The generous deed was done;
In the storm of the years that are fading,
  No braver battle was won;—
    Under the sod and the dew,
      Waiting the Judgment Day:
    Under the blossoms, the Blue;
      Under the garlands, the Gray.

No more shall the war-cry sever,
  Or the winding rivers be red;
They banish our anger forever
  When they laurel the graves of our dead!
    Under the sod and the dew,
      Waiting the Judgment Day:
    Love and tears for the Blue;
      Tears and love for the Gray.

FRANCIS MILES FINCH.

ABRAHAM LINCOLN

THE ATONEMENT OF MR. PUNCH

You lay a wreath on murdered Lincoln's bier:
   You, who with mocking pencil wont to trace,
Broad for the self-complaisant British sneer,
   His length of shambling limb, his furrowed face,

His gaunt, gnarled hands, his unkempt bristling hair,
   His garb uncouth, his bearing ill at ease,
His lack of all we prize as debonair,
   Of power or will to shine, or art to please;

You, whose smart pen backed up the pencil's laugh,
   Judging each step as though the way were plain;
Reckless, so it could point its paragraph,
   Of chief's perplexity or people's pain,—

Beside this corpse, that bears for winding-sheet
   The Stars and Stripes he lived to rear anew,
Between the mourners at his head and feet,
   Say, scurrile jester, is there room for *you?*—

Yes: he had lived to shame me from my sneer,
   To lame my pencil and confute my pen;
To make me own this hind of princes peer,
   This rail-splitter a true-born king of men.

My shallow judgment I had learned to rue,
   Noting how to occasion's height he rose;
How his quaint wit made home-truth seem more true;
   How, iron-like, his temper grew by blows;

How humble, yet how hopeful he could be;
   How in good fortune and in ill the same:
Nor bitter in success, nor boastful he,
   Thirsty for gold, nor feverish for fame.

He went about his work,—such work as few
   Ever had laid on head and heart and hand,—
As one who knows, where there's a task to do,
   Man's honest will must Heaven's good grace command;

Who trusts the strength will with the burden grow,
   That God makes instruments to work his will,
If but that will we can arrive to know,
   Nor tamper with the weights of good and ill.

So he went forth to battle, on the side
    That he felt clear was Liberty's and Right's,
As in his pleasant boyhood he had plied
    His warfare with rude Nature's thwarting mights:

The uncleared forest, the unbroken soil,
    The iron bark that turns the lumberer's axe,
The rapid that o'erbears the boatman's toil,
    The prairie hiding the mazed wanderer's tracks,

The ambushed Indian, and the prowling bear,—
    Such were the deeds that helped his youth to train;
Rough culture, but such trees large fruit may bear,
    If but their stocks be of right girth and grain.

So he grew up, a destined work to do,
    And lived to do it: four long-suffering years'
Ill fate, ill feeling, ill report lived through;
    And then he heard the hisses change to cheers,

The taunts to tribute, the abuse to praise,
    And took both with the same unwavering mood,—
Till, as he came on light, from darkling days,
    And seemed to touch the goal from where he stood,

A felon hand, between the goal and him,
    Reached from behind his back, a trigger prest,
And those perplexed and patient eyes were dim,
    Those gaunt, long-laboring limbs were laid to rest.

The words of mercy were upon his lips,
    Forgiveness in his heart and on his pen,
When this vile murderer brought swift eclipse
    To thoughts of peace on earth, good-will to men.

The Old World and the New, from sea to sea,
    Utter one voice of sympathy and shame.
Sore heart, so stopped when it at last beat free!
    Sad life, cut short just as its triumph came!

A deed accursed! Strokes have been struck before
    By the assassin's hand, whereof men doubt
If more of horror or disgrace they bore!
    But thy foul crime, like Cain's, stands darkly out,

Vile hand, that brandest murder on a strife,
    Whate'er its grounds, stoutly and nobly striven,
And with the martyr's crown crownest a life
    With much to praise, little to be forgiven.

                              TOM TAYLOR.

A MIRROR

THOU art a mountain stately and serene,
　　Rising majestic o'er each earthly thing,
　　And I a lake that round thy feet do cling,
Kissing thy garment's hem, unknown, unseen.
I tremble when the tempests darkly screen
　　Thy face from mine. I smile when sunbeams fling
Their bright arms round thee. When the blue heavens lean
　　Upon thy breast, I thrill with bliss, O King!
Thou canst not stoop,—we are too far apart;
I may not climb to reach thy mighty heart
　　Low at thy feet I am content to be.
But wouldst thou know how great indeed thou art,
　　Bend thy proud head, my mountain love, and see
　　How all thy glories shine again in me!

SUSAN MARR SPALDING.

THE DAY AFTER THE BETROTHAL

"WHAT troubleth thee, Sweetheart?
　　　　For thine eyes are filled with tears."—
　　I have dwelt in Arcadia, Love,
　　　　So many, many years!

"Is Arcadia fair, Sweetheart?
　　When I called, wert thou loth to go?"—
Nay, ask me not that, I pray,
　　For truly I do not know.

"Is Arcadia dear, Sweetheart,
　　That thine eyes are so heavy and wet?"—
Dear? O Love, how dear
　　I may not tell thee yet!

"Wouldst fain go back, Sweetheart?
　　It's only a step to take."—
No, no! not back! but hold me close,
　　For my heart is like to break.

Not for Arcadia lost—
　　Ah, Love, have I not thee?
But oh, the scent of those wind-swept hills
　　And the salt breath of that sea!

EVA L. OGDEN LAMBERT.

TWICKENHAM FERRY

A HOY! and Oho! and it's who's for the ferry?"
    (The brier's in bud and the sun going down;)
  "And I'll row ye so quick and I'll row ye so steady, •
    And 'tis but a penny to Twickenham Town."
The ferryman's slim and the ferryman's young,
With just a soft tang in the turn of his tongue:
And he's fresh as a pippin and brown as a berry,
    And 'tis but a penny to Twickenham Town.

"Ahoy! and Oho! and it's I'm for the ferry;"
    (The brier's in bud and the sun going down;)
"And it's late as it is, and I haven't a penny:
    Oh, how can I get me to Twickenham Town?"
She'd a rose in her bonnet, and oh! she looked sweet
As the little pink flower that grows in the wheat,
With her cheeks like a rose and her lips like a cherry—
    "And sure, but you're welcome to Twickenham Town."

"Ahoy! and Oho!—" You're too late for the ferry;
    (The brier's in bud and the sun has gone down;)
And he's not rowing quick and he's not rowing steady,—
    It seems quite a journey to Twickenham Town.
"Ahoy! and Oho!" you may call as you will:
The young moon is rising o'er Petersham Hill;
And with Love like a rose in the stern of the wherry,
    There's danger in crossing to Twickenham Town.

                              THÉOPHILE MARZIALS.

DOLLIE

S HE sports a witching gown,
    With a ruffle up and down
        On the skirt:
She is gentle, she is shy,
But there's mischief in her eye,—
        She's a flirt!

She displays a tiny glove,
And a dainty little love
        Of a shoe;
And she wears her hat a-tilt
Over bangs that never wilt
        In the dew.

'Tis rumored chocolate creams
Are the fabrics of her dreams—
          But enough!
I know beyond a doubt
That she carries them about
          In her muff.

With her dimples and her curls
She exasperates the girls
          Past belief:
They hint that she's a cat,
And delightful things like that,
          In their grief.

It is shocking, I declare!
But what does Dollie care
          When the beaux
Come flocking to her feet
Like the bees around a sweet
          Little rose!

                    SAMUEL MINTURN PECK.

DOROTHY

THEY tell me 'tis foolish to prate of love
     In the sweet and olden way:
They say I should sing of loftier things,
     For Love has had his day.
          But when Dorothy comes
               I cannot choose,—
          I must follow her
               Though the world I lose;
          My very soul
               Pours forth in song
          When dainty Dorothy
               Trips along.

It is all very well to say to me
     That Browning's noble strain
Rises and swells with the tide of thought
     Or throbs with the pulse of pain;
          But if Dorothy once
               Had crossed his path,

    Her radiance such
      A witchery hath
  That across the world   .
    Would not seem long
  To follow Dorothy
    With his song.

CHARLES HENRY PHELPS.

RENOUNCEMENT

I MUST not think of thee; and, tired yet strong,
  I shun the thought that lurks in all delight.—
  The thought of thee — and in the blue heaven's height,
And in the sweetest passage of a song.
Oh, just beyond the fairest thoughts that throng
  This breast, the thought of thee waits, hidden yet bright;
  But it must never, never come in sight:
I must stop short of thee the whole day long.

But when sleep comes to close each difficult day,
  When night gives pause to the long watch I keep,
  And all my bonds I needs must loose apart,
Must doff my will as raiment laid away,—
  With the first dream that comes with the first sleep
  I run, I run, I am gathered to thy heart.

ALICE MEYNELL.

THE WITCH IN THE GLASS

"MY MOTHER says I must not pass
    Too near that glass:
    She is afraid that I will see
A little witch that looks like me,
With red, red mouth to whisper low
The very thing I should not know!"

"Alack for all your mother's care!
    A bird of the air,
A wistful wind, or (I suppose,
Sent by some hapless boy) a rose,
With breath too sweet, will whisper low
The very thing you should not know!"

SARAH M. B. PIATT.

IF I COULD ONLY WRITE

AND will you write a letter for me, padre?" —
　　"Yes, child — no need to tell me the address!"
　"Do you know whom it's for because on that dark
　　　evening
　　You saw us walking?" — "Yes."

"Pardon! forgive!" — "Oh no, I don't reproach you!
　The night, the chance — they tempted you, I know.
　Pass me the pen and paper — I will begin, then —"
　　　My own Antonio!

"'My own'?" — "Why, yes, I have it written;
　But if you like, I'll —" — "Oh no, no, go on!"
How sad I am — "Is that it?" — "Yes, of course, sir!"
　　　How sad I am alone!

Now that I'm writing you, I feel so troubled! —
　　　"How do you know so well?" —
"The secrets of a young girl's heart, my daughter,
　　　The old can always tell."

What is this world alone?　A vale of tears, love!
　　　With you — a happy land!
"Be sure you write it *plainly*, won't you, padre?
　　　So that he'll understand."

The kiss I gave you on the eve of marching —
　　　"Why, how did you find out?" —
"Oh, when young people come and go together,
　　　Always — nay, do not pout!"

And if your love can't bring you back here quickly,
　　　'Twill make me suffer — I —
"Suffer! and nothing more?　No, no, dear padre,
　　　Tell him 'twill make me die!"

"Die! child, do you know that offends our Father?"
　　　"But still, padre, write *die!*"
"I will not write 'die.'" — "What a man of iron!
　　　If I could only try!

"Oh no, it is no use, you dear good padre:
　　　'Twill never perfect be
If in these signs you cannot lay before him
　　　The very heart of me.

"Write him, I pray you, that my soul without him
 Would gladly mourn and die,
But that this lonely heartache does not kill me
 Because I've learned to cry.

"And that my lips, the roses of my love's breath,
 Will never ope again;
That they forget the very art of smiling,
 By dint of so much pain.

"And that my eyes he always thought so lovely,—
 No longer clear and bright,
Since there is no dear face to mirror in them,—
 Forever shun the light.

"And that of all the torments ever suffered,
 Parting's most hard to bear;
That like a dream the echo of his voice is ringing
 Forever in my ear.

"But since it is for his dear sake I suffer,
 My heavy heart grows light;—
Goodness! how many things I'd like to tell him
 If I could only write!

"But, padre"—"Bravo, Amor! I'll copy and conclude there.
 Our learning should be meek.
'Tis clear that one needs for this style of writing
 Small Latin and less Greek."

CAMPOAMOR (Spanish).

Translation of Ellen Watson.

LOVE AND YOUTH

Two wingèd genii in the air
 I greeted as they passed me by:
The one a bow and quiver bare,
 The other shouted joyously.
Both I besought to stay their speed,
But never Love nor Youth had heed
 Of my wild cry.

As swift and careless as the wind,
 Youth fled, nor ever once looked back;

LUCIA DI LAMMERMOOR.

Photogravure from a painting by Vely.

A moment Love was left behind,
But followed soon his fellow's track.
Yet, loitering at my heart, he bent
His bow, then smiled with changed intent:
The string was slack.

WILLIAM JAMES LINTON.

HOW TO LOVE

LOVE me, but let me never know
That I the limit of your love may touch;
Always beyond my reach, below, above,
I want to feel that I may find your love.
Love me, but—not too much.

Paint it in quiet, tender tints:
The fragrant flowers of spring wear such,
And summer lies beyond them. In a blaze
Of brilliant hues the fall flowers end their days.
Love me, but—not too much.

Let it be like the soft blue sky,
That folds the earth around with gentle touch:
Not like the crimson clouds at set of sun,
For darkness follows them, and day is done.
Love me, but—not too much.

Like the new moon I want your love:
My life will brighten 'neath its pure white touch.
The full moon gives great floods of silver light,
And then—it fades from out the starry night.
Love me, but—not too much.

But like the ivy, let love grow
Steadily, slowly, reaching wide and high,
Till it embraces all in its strong grasp,
And holds with true, unfading, living clasp.
So love me till I die!

BESSIE CHANDLER PARKER.

IN THE DARK, IN THE DEW

IN THE dark, in the dew,
　I am smiling back to you;
　　But you cannot see the smile,
And you're thinking all the while
How I turn my face from you
　In the dark, in the dew.

In the dark, in the dew,
All my love goes out to you,
Flutters like a bird in pain,
Dies and comes to life again;
While you whisper, "Sweetest, hark:
Some one's sighing in the dark,
　In the dark, in the dew!"

In the dark, in the dew,
All my heart cries out to you,
As I cast it at your feet,
Sweet indeed, but not too sweet;
Wondering will you hear it beat,
Beat for you, and bleed for you,
　In the dark, in the dew!

MARY NEWMARCH PRESCOTT.

BIRD SONG FROM 'ALEXANDER AND CAMPASPE'

WHAT bird so sings, yet does so wail?
　Oh, 'tis the ravished nightingale;
　　"Jug, jug—jug, jug—teren," she cries,
And still her woes at midnight rise.

Brave prick-song! who is't now we hear?
None but the lark so shrill and clear;
Now at heaven's gates she claps her wings,—
The morn not waking till she sings.

Hark, hark! with what a pretty throat
Poor Robin Redbreast tunes his note!
Hark, how the jolly cuckoos sing
"Cuckoo," to welcome in the spring.

JOHN LYLY.

SONG TO GABRIELLE

Morning bright,
     Rise to sight,—
Glad am I thy face to see:
     One I love,
     All above,
Has a ruddy cheek like thee.

     Fainter far
     Roses are,
Though with morning dew-drops bright;
     Ne'er was fur
     Soft like her,
Milk itself is not so white.

     When she sings,
     Soon she brings
Listeners out from every cot;
     Pensive swains
     Hush their strains,—
All their sorrows are forgot.

     She is fair
     Past compare;
One small hand her waist can span.
     Eyes of light —
     Stars, though bright,
Match those eyes you never can.

     Hebe blest
     Once the best
Food of gods before her placed:
     When I sip
     Her red lip,
I can still the nectar taste.

                        KING HENRY IV. OF FRANCE.

NELLY OF THE TOP-KNOTS

Dear God! were I fisher and
     Back in Binédar,
     And Nelly a fish who
     Would swim in the bay there,

I would privately set there
  My net there to catch her:
In Erin no maiden
  Is able to match her.

And Nelly, dear God!
  Why! you should not thus flee me:
I long to be near thee
  And hear thee and see thee;
My hand on the Bible,
  And I swearing and kneeling,
And giving thee part
  Of the heart you are stealing.

I've a fair yellow casket
  And it fastened with crystal,
And the lock opens not
  To the shot of a pistol.
To Jesus I pray,
  And to Columbkill's Master,
That Mary may guide thee
  Aside from disaster.

We may be, O maiden
  Whom none may disparage,
Some morning a-hearing
  The sweet mass of marriage;
But if fate be against us,
  To rend us and push us,
I shall mourn as the blackbird
  At eve in the bushes.

O God! were she with me
  Where the gull flits and tern,
Or in Paris the smiling,
  Or an isle in Loch Erne,
I would coax her so well,
  I would tell her my story,
And talk till I won her,—
  My sunshine of glory!

DOUGLAS HYDE.

THE SEA-FOWLER

THE baron hath the landward park, the fisher hath the sea;
But the rocky haunts of the sea-fowl belong alone to me.

The baron hunts the running deer, the fisher nets the brine;
But every bird that builds a nest on ocean-cliffs is mine.

Come on then, Jock and Alick, let's to the sea-rocks bold:
I was trained to take the sea-fowl ere I was five years old.

The wild sea roars, and lashes the granite crags below,
And round the misty islets the loud strong tempests blow.

And let them blow! Roar wind and wave, they shall not me
          dismay:
I've faced the eagle in her nest and snatched her young away.

The eagle shall not build her nest, proud bird although she be,
Nor yet the strong-winged cormorant, without the leave of me.

The eider-duck has laid her eggs, the tern doth hatch her young,
And the merry gull screams o'er her brood; but all to me belong.

Away, then, in the daylight, and back again ere eve:
The eagle could not rear her young unless I gave her leave.

The baron hath the landward park, the fisher hath the sea;
But the rocky haunts of the sea-fowl belong alone to me.

MARY HOWITT.

PACK, CLOUDS, AWAY

PACK, clouds, away; and welcome, day;
    With night we banish sorrow:
  Sweet air, blow soft; mount, lark, aloft,
    To give my love good-morrow.
Wings from the wind to please her mind,
  Notes from the lark I'll borrow:
Bird, prune thy wing; nightingale, sing,
  To give my love good-morrow.
  To give my love good-morrow,
  Notes from them all I'll borrow.

Wake from thy nest, robin redbreast;
  Sing, birds, in every furrow;

And from each hill let music shrill
   Give my fair love good-morrow!
Blackbird and thrush in every bush,
   Stare, linnet, and cock-sparrow,
You pretty elves, amongst yourselves,
   Sing my fair love good-morrow.
To give my love good-morrow,
   Sing, birds, in every furrow.

THOMAS HEYWOOD.

ANNIE LAURIE

MAXWELTON braes are bonnie
   Where early fa's the dew,
   And it's there that Annie Laurie
Gie'd me her promise true;—
Gie'd me her promise true,
   Which ne'er forgot will be:
And for bonnie Annie Laurie
   I'd lay me doune and dee.

Her brow is like the snaw-drift;
   Her throat is like the swan;
Her face it is the fairest
   That e'er the sun shone on;—
That e'er the sun shone on—
   And dark-blue is her ee:
And for bonnie Annie Laurie
   I'd lay me doune and dee.

Like dew on the gowan lying
   Is the fa' o' her fairy feet;
Like the winds in summer sighing,
   Her voice is low and sweet;—
Her voice is low and sweet,
   And she's a' the world to me:
And for bonnie Annie Laurie
   I'd lay me doune and dee.

WILLIAM DOUGLAS of Kirkcudbright.

THE POOR CLERK

(AR C'HLOAREK PAOUR)

MY WOODEN shoes I've lost them, my naked feet I've torn,
A-following my sweeting through field and brake of thorn:
The rain may beat, and fall the sleet, and ice chill to the bone,
But they're no stay to hold away the lover from his own.

My sweeting is no older than I that love her so,—
She's scarce seventeen; her face is fair, her cheeks like roses glow.
In her eyes there is a fire; sweetest speech her lips doth part;
Her love it is a prison where I've locked up my heart.

Oh, to what shall I liken her, that a wrong it shall not be?
To the pretty little white rose, that is called Rose-Marie?
The pearl of girls; the lily when among the flowers it grows,—
The lily newly opened, among flowers about to close.

When I came to thee a-wooing, my sweet, my gentle May,
I was as is the nightingale upon the hawthorn spray:
When he would sleep, the thorns they keep a-pricking in his breast;
That he flies up perforce and sings upon the tree's tall crest.

I am as is the nightingale, or as a soul must be
That in the purgatory fires lies, longing to be free;
Waiting the blessed time when I unto your house shall come,
All with the marriage-messenger bearing his branch of broom.

Ah me! my stars are froward; 'gainst nature is my state:
Since in this world I came I've dreed a dark and dismal fate;
I have nor living kin nor friends, mother nor father dear,—
There is no Christian on earth to wish me happy here.

There lives no one hath had to bear so much of grief and shame
For your sweet sake as I have, since in this world I came;
And therefore on my bended knees, in God's dear name I sue,
Have pity on your own poor clerk, that loveth only you!

Mediæval Breton.

Translation of Tom Taylor.

CUPID'S CURSE

ŒNONE

F AIR and fair and twice so fair,
   As fair as any may be,—
The fairest shepherd on our green,
   A love for any ladie!

PARIS

Fair and fair and twice so fair,
   As fair as any may be,—
Thy love is fair for thee alone,
   And for no other ladie!

ŒNONE

My love is fair, my love is gay,
As fresh as been the flowers in May;
And of my love my roundelay,
My merry merry merry roundelay,
   Concludes with Cupid's Curse—
They that do change old love for new,
   Pray gods they change for worse!

Both sing

They that do change old love for new,
   Pray gods they change for worse!

ŒNONE

Fair and fair and twice so fair,
   As fair as any may be,—
· The fairest shepherd on our green,
   A love for any ladie!

PARIS

Fair and fair and twice so fair,
   As fair as any may be,—
Thy love is fair for thee alone,
   And for no other ladie!

ŒNONE

My love can pipe, my love can sing,
My love can many a pretty thing,
And of his lovely praises ring
My merry merry roundelays:
   Amen to Cupid's Curse!

They that do change old love for new,
Pray gods they change for worse!

PARIS

They that do change old love for new,
Pray gods they change for worse!

GEORGE PEELE.

THE AVARICIOUS SHEPHERDESS

(L'AVARICIEUSE)

PHILLIS, somewhat hard by nature,
Would not an advantage miss:
She asked Damon—greedy creature!—
Thirty sheep for one small kiss.

Lovely Phillis, on the morrow,
Cannot her advantage keep:
She gives Damon, to her sorrow,
Thirty kisses for one sheep.

On the morrow grown more tender,
Phillis, ah! has come to this:
Thirty sheep she will surrender
For a single loving kiss.

Now another day is over,
Damon sheep and dog might get
For the kiss which he—the rover!
Gave for nothing to Lizette.

CHARLES RIVIÈRE DUFRESNY.

AN UNMARKED FESTIVAL

THERE's a feast undated yet:
Both our true lives hold it fast,—
The first day we ever met.
What a great day came and passed!—
Unknown then, but known at last.

And we met: You knew not me,
Mistress of your joys and fears;

Held my hand that held the key
    Of the treasure of your years,
    Of the fountain of your tears.

For you knew not it was I,
    And I knew not it was you.
We have learnt, as days went by:
    But a flower struck root and grew
    Underground, and no one knew.

Day of days! Unmarked it rose,
    In whose hours we were to meet;
And forgotten passed. Who knows,
    Was earth cold or sunny, Sweet,
    At the coming of your feet?

One mere day, we thought; the measure
    Of such days the year fulfills.
Now, how dearly would we treasure
    Something from its fields, its rills
    And its memorable hills;—

But one leaf of oak or lime,
    Or one blossom from its bowers,
No one gathered at the time.
    Oh, to keep that day of ours
    By one relic of its flowers!

                    ALICE MEYNELL.

A SONG OF LIFE

Did I seek life? Not so: its weight was laid upon me;
    And yet of my burden sore I may not set myself free.
    Two love, and lo, at love's call, a hapless soul must wake:
Like a slave it is called to the world, to bear life, for their love's
        sake.

Did I seek love? Not so: love led me along by the hand.
Love beguiled me with songs and caresses, while I took no note of
        the land.
And lo, I stood in a quicksand, but Love had wings, and he fled:
Ah fool, for a mortal to venture where only a god may tread!

                    ANNE REEVE ALDRICH.

DISAPPOINTMENT

THE bard has sung, God never formed a soul
   Without its own peculiar mate, to meet
Its wandering half, when ripe to crown the whole
   Bright plan of bliss most heavenly, most complete.

But thousand evil things there are that hate
   To look on happiness: these hurt, impede,
And leagued with time, space, circumstance, and fate,
   Keep kindred heart from heart, to pine and pant and bleed.

And as the dove to far Palmyra flying
   From where her native founts of Antioch beam,
Weary, exhausted, longing, panting, sighing,
   Lights sadly at the desert's bitter stream,—

So many a soul, o'er life's drear desert faring,
   Love's pure congenial spring unfound, unquaffed,
Suffers—recoils—then, thirsty and despairing
   Of what it would, descends and sips the nearest draught!

      MARIA GOWEN BROOKS ("Maria del Occidente").

FATE

TWO shall be born the whole wide world apart,
   And speak in different tongues, and have no thought
   Each of the other's being, and no heed:
And these o'er unknown seas, to unknown lands,
Shall cross, escaping wreck, defying death;
And all unconsciously shape every act
And bend each wandering step to this one end,—
That one day out of darkness they shall meet
And read life's meaning in each other's eyes.
And two shall walk some narrow way of life,
So nearly side by side that should one turn
Ever so little space to left or right,
They needs must stand acknowledged face to face;
And yet with wistful eyes that never meet,
With groping hands that never clasp, and lips
Calling in vain to ears that never hear,
They seek each' other all their weary days,
And die unsatisfied.—And this is Fate.

      SUSAN MARR SPALDING.

LAMENT OF THE IRISH EMIGRANT

I'M SITTIN' on the stile, Mary,
    Where we sat side by side
On a bright May mornin' long ago,
    When first you were my bride:
The corn was springin' fresh and green,
    And the lark sang loud and high;
And the red was on your lip, Mary,
    And the love-light in your eye.

The place is little changed, Mary:
    The day is bright as then;
The lark's loud song is in my ear,
    And the corn is green again:
But I miss the soft clasp of your hand,
    And your breath, warm on my cheek;
And I still keep listenin' for the words
    You nevermore will speak.

'Tis but a step down yonder lane,
    And the little church stands near,—
The church where we were wed, Mary;
    I see the spire from here.
But the grave-yard lies between, Mary,
    And my step might break your rest,—
For I've laid you, darling, down to sleep,
    With your baby on your breast.

I'm very lonely now, Mary,
    For the poor make no new friends;
But, oh, they love the better still
    The few our Father sends!
And you were all I had, Mary,—
    My blessin' and my pride;
There's nothing left to care for now,
    Since my poor Mary died.

Yours was the good, brave heart, Mary,
    That still kept hoping on,
When the trust in God had left my soul,
    And my arm's young strength was gone;
There was comfort ever on your lip,
    And the kind look on your brow,—
I bless you, Mary, for that same,
    Though you cannot hear me now.

I thank you for the patient smile
    When your heart was fit to break,—
When the hunger pain was gnawin' there,
    And you hid it for my sake;
I bless you for the pleasant word,
    When your heart was sad and sore;—
Oh, I'm thankful you are gone, Mary,
    Where grief can't reach you more!

I'm biddin' you a long farewell,
    My Mary—kind and true!
But I'll not forget you, darling,
    In the land I'm goin' to;
They say there's bread and work for all,
    And the sun shines always there,
But I'll not forget old Ireland,
    Were it fifty times as fair!

And often in those grand old woods
    I'll sit, and shut my eyes,
And my heart will travel back again
    To the place where Mary lies;
And I'll think I see the little stile
    Where we sat side by side,
And the springin' corn, and the bright May morn,
    When first you were my bride.

                  LADY DUFFERIN.

THE REVEL

(TIME OF THE FAMINE AND PLAGUE IN INDIA)

WE MEET 'neath the sounding rafter,
    And the walls around are bare;
    As they shout back our peals of laughter,
      It seems that the dead are there.
Then stand to your glasses, steady!
    We drink in our comrades' eyes:
One cup to the dead already—
    Hurrah for the next that dies!

Not here are the goblets glowing,
    Not here is the vintage sweet;
'Tis cold as our hearts are growing,
    And dark as the doom we meet.

But stand to your glasses, steady!
   And soon shall our pulses rise:
A cup to the dead already—
   Hurrah for the next that dies!

There's many a hand that's shaking,
   And many a cheek that's sunk;
But soon, though our hearts are breaking,
   They'll burn with the wine we've drunk.
Then stand to your glasses, steady!
   'Tis here the revival lies:
Quaff a cup to the dead already—
   Hurrah for the next that dies!

Time was when we laughed at others;
   We thought we were wiser then:
Ha! ha! let them think of their mothers,
   Who hope to see them again.
No! stand to your glasses, steady!
   The thoughtless is here, the wise:
One cup to the dead already—
   Hurrah for the next that dies!

Not a sigh for the lot that darkles,
   Not a tear for the friends that sink;
We'll fall, 'midst the wine-cup's sparkles,
   As mute as the wine we drink.
Come, stand to your glasses, steady!
   'Tis this that the respite buys:
A cup to the dead already—
   Hurrah for the next that dies!

There's a mist on the glass congealing,
   'Tis the hurricane's sultry breath;
And thus does the warmth of feeling
   Turn ice in the grasp of Death.
But stand to your glasses, steady!
   For a moment the vapor flies:
Quaff a cup to the dead already—
   Hurrah for the next that dies!

Who dreads to the dust returning?
   Who shrinks from the sable shore,
Where the high and haughty yearning
   Of the soul can sting no more?

No! stand to your glasses, steady!
   The world is a world of lies: ·
A cup to the dead already—
   And hurrah for the next that dies!

Cut off from the land that bore us,
   Betrayed by the land we find,
When the brightest have gone before us,
   And the dullest are most behind,—
Stand, stand to your glasses, steady!
   'Tis all we have left to prize:
One cup to the dead already—
   Hurrah for the next that dies!

BARTHOLOMEW DOWLING.

THE OLD CHURCH-YARD OF BONCHURCH

THE church-yard leans to the sea with·its dead—
   It leans to the sea with its dead so long.
   Do they hear, I wonder, the first bird's song,
When the winter's anger is all but fled,—
   The high, sweet voice of the west wind,
   The fall of the warm, soft rain,
   When the second month of the year
   Puts heart in the earth again?

Do they hear, through the glad April weather,
   The green grasses waving above them?
   Do they think there are none left to love them,
They have lain for so long there together?
   Do they hear the note of the cuckoo,
   The cry of gulls on the wing,
   The laughter of winds and waters,
   The feet of the dancing Spring?

Do they feel the old land slipping seaward,
   The old land, with its hills and its graves,
   As they gradually slide to the waves
With the wind blowing on them from leeward?
   Do they know of the change that awaits them,
   The sepulchre vast and strange?
   Do they long for days to go over,
   And bring that miraculous change?

PHILIP BOURKE MARSTON.

HIS FOOTSTEPS

THE wilderness a secret keeps
   Upon whose guess I go:
Eye hath not seen, ear hath not heard;
   And yet I know, I know,

Some day the viewless latch will lift,
   The door of air swing wide
To one lost chamber of the wood
   Where those shy mysteries hide,—

One yet unfound, exceeding depth,
   From which the wood-thrush sings,
Still luring me to darker shades,
   In — in — to colder springs.

There is no wind abroad to-day;
   But hark the pine-tops' war,
That sleep, and in their dreams repeat
   The music of the shore.

What wisdom stirs among the pines?
   What song is that they sing?
Those airs that search the forest's heart,
   What rumor do they bring?

A hushed excitement fills the gloom,
   And in the stillness, clear
The river's tell-tale warning rings:
   « 'Tis near — 'tis near — 'tis near! »

As in the fairy tale, more loud
   The ghostly music plays,
When, toward the enchanted bower, the prince
   Draws closer through the maze.

Nay, nay — I track a fleeter game,
   A wilder than ye know,
To lairs beyond the utmost haunt
   Of thrush or vireo.

This way it passed: the scent lies fresh;
   The ferns still lightly shake.
Ever I follow hard upon,
   But never overtake.

HENRY AUGUSTIN BEERS.

THE INDIAN'S DEATH SONG

THE sun sets in night and the stars shun the day,
 But glory remains when their light fades away.
 Begin, ye tormentors — your threats are in vain,
For the son of Alknomook shall never complain.

Remember the arrows he shot from his bow!
Remember the chiefs whom his hatchet laid low!
Why so slow? do you think I will shrink from the pain?
No! the son of Alknomook shall never complain.

Remember the place where in ambush we lay,
And the scalps that we tore from your nation away.—
Now the flame rises fast, you exult in my pain;
But the son of Alknomook shall never complain.

I go to the land where my father has gone:
His ghost shall rejoice at the fame of his son.
Death comes like a friend, to release me from pain;
And thy son, O Alknomook, has scorned to complain.

ANNE HUNTER.

THE PLACE TO DIE

How little recks it where men die,
 When once the moment's past
 In which the dim and glazing eye
 Has looked on earth its last;
Whether beneath the sculptured urn
 The coffined form shall rest,
Or in its nakedness, return
 Back to its mother's breast.

The soldier falls 'mid corses piled
 Upon the battle-plain,
Where reinless war-steeds gallop wild
 Above the gory slain;
But though his corse be grim to see,
 Hoof-trampled on the sod,
What recks it when the spirit free
 Has soared aloft to God?

The coward's dying eye may close
 Upon his downy bed,

And softest hands his limbs compose,
  Or garments o'er him spread;
But ye who shun the bloody fray
  Where fall the mangled brave,
Go strip his coffin-lid away,
  And see him in his grave!

'Twere sweet indeed to close our eyes
  With those we cherish near,
And wafted upward by their sighs,
  Soar to some calmer sphere;
But whether on the scaffold high,
  Or in the battle's van,
The fittest place where man can die
  Is where he dies for man!

MICHAEL JULAND BARRY.

IF I SHOULD DIE TO-NIGHT

IF I SHOULD die to-night,
  My friends would look upon my quiet face
  Before they laid it in its resting-place,
And deem that death had left it almost fair;
And laying snow-white flowers against my hair,
Would smooth it down with tearful tenderness,
And fold my hands with lingering caress —
  Poor hands, so empty and so cold to-night!

If I should die to-night,
My friends would call to mind, with loving thought,
Some kindly deed the icy hands had wrought;
Some gentle word the frozen lips had said;
Errands on which the willing feet had sped:
The memory of my selfishness and pride,
My hasty words, would all be put aside,
  And so I should be loved and mourned to-night.

If I should die to-night,
Even hearts estranged would turn once more to me,
Recalling other days remorsefully;
The eyes that chill me with averted glance
Would look upon me as of yore, perchance,
And soften in the old familiar way:
For who could war with dumb, unconscious clay?
  So I might rest, forgiven of all, to-night.

O friends, I pray to-night,
Keep not your kisses for my dead, cold brow!
The way is lonely: let me feel them now.
Think gently of me: I am travel-worn;
My faltering feet are pierced with many a thorn.
Forgive, O hearts estranged, forgive, I plead!
When dreamless rest is mine, I shall not need
The tenderness for which I long to-night.

BELLE E. SMITH.

A LITTLE WHILE

BEYOND the smiling and the weeping
        I shall be soon;
    Beyond the waking and the sleeping,
Beyond the sowing and the reaping,
        I shall be soon.
    Love, rest, and home!
        Sweet hope!
    Lord, tarry not, but come.

Beyond the blooming and the fading
        I shall be soon;
Beyond the shining and the shading,
Beyond the hoping and the dreading,
        I shall be soon.
    Love, rest, and home!
        Sweet hope!
    Lord, tarry not, but come.

Beyond the rising and the setting
        I shall be soon;
Beyond the calming and the fretting,
Beyond remembering and forgetting,
        I shall be soon.
    Love, rest, and home!
        Sweet hope!
    Lord, tarry not, but come.

Beyond the gathering and the strowing
        I shall be soon;
Beyond the ebbing and the flowing,
Beyond the coming and the going,
        I shall be soon.

Love, rest, and home!
　　Sweet hope!
Lord, tarry not, but come.

Beyond the parting and the meeting
　　I shall be soon;
Beyond the farewell and the greeting,
Beyond this pulse's fever-beating,
　　I shall be soon.
Love, rest, and home!
　　Sweet hope!
Lord, tarry not, but come.

Beyond the frost-chain and the fever
　　I shall be soon;
Beyond the rock-waste and the river,
Beyond the ever and the never,
　　I shall be soon.
Love, rest, and home!
　　Sweet hope!
Lord, tarry not, but come.

　　　　　　　　　　　　HORATIUS BONAR.

WHEN WE ARE ALL ASLEEP

WHEN He returns, and finds the world so drear,
　　All sleeping, young and old, unfair and fair,
Will he stoop down and whisper in each ear,
　　"Awaken!" or for pity's sake forbear,
Saying, "How shall I meet their frozen stare
Of wonder, and their eyes so full of fear?
　　How shall I comfort them in their despair,
If they cry out, 'Too late! let us sleep here'?"

Perchance he will not wake us up, but when
　　He sees us look so happy in our rest,
Will murmur, "Poor dead women and dead men!
　　Dire was their doom, and weary was their quest,—
Wherefore awake them into life again?
　　Let them sleep on untroubled—it is best."

　　　　　　　　　　　　ROBERT BUCHANAN.

THE MISTLETOE BOUGH

— The happiest of the happy,
When a spring-lock that lay in ambush there
Fastened her down forever.— ROGERS.

THE mistletoe hung in the castle hall,
The holly branch shone on the old oak wall;
And the baron's retainers were blithe and gay,
And keeping their Christmas holiday.
The baron beheld, with a father's pride,
His beautiful child, young Lovell's bride;
While she, with her bright eyes, seemed to be
The star of the goodly company.

« I'm weary of dancing now,» she cried:
« Here tarry a moment — I'll hide — I'll hide!
And, Lovell, be sure thou'rt first to trace
The clue to my secret lurking-place.»
Away she ran — and her friends began
Each tower to search, and each nook to scan;
And young Lovell cried, « Oh! where dost thou hide?
I'm lonely without thee, my own dear bride.»

They sought her that night, and they sought her next
day;
And they sought her in vain, when a week passed away!
In the highest — the lowest — the loneliest spot,
Young Lovell sought wildly — but found her not.
And years flew by, and their grief at last
Was told as a sorrowful tale long past;
And when Lovell appeared, the children cried,
« See! the old man weeps for his fairy bride.»

At length an oak chest, that had long lain hid,
Was found in the castle: they raised the lid;
And a skeleton form lay moldering there
In the bridal wreath of that lady fair!
Oh, sad was her fate! In sportive jest
She hid from her lord in the old oak chest;
It closed with a spring! — and, dreadful doom,
The bride lay clasped in her living tomb!

THOMAS HAYNES BAYLY.

ANDRÉ'S RIDE

WHEN André rode to Pont-du-lac,
　　With all his raiders at his back,
　　Mon Dieu! the tumult in the town!
Scarce clanged the great portcullis down
Ere in the sunshine gleamed his spears,
And up marched all his musketeers,
And far and fast in haste's array
Sped men to fight and priests to pray:
In every street a barricade
Of aught that lay to hand was made;
From every house a man was told,
Nor quittance given to young or old:
Should youth be spared or age be slack
When André rode to Pont-du-lac?

When André rode to Pont-du-lac,
With all his ravening reiver-pack,
The mid lake was a frozen road
Unbending to the cannon's load;
No warmth the sun had as it shone;
The kine were stalled, the birds were gone;
Like wild things seemed the shapes of fur
With which was every street astir,
And over all the huddling crowd
The thick breath hung — a solid cloud; —
Roof, road, and river, all were white;
Men moved benumbed by day — by night
The boldest durst not bivouac,
When André rode to Pont-du-lac.

When André rode to Pont-du-lac,
We scarce could stem his swift attack;
A halt, a cheer, a bugle-call, —
Like wild-cats they were up the wall:
But still as each man won the town,
We tossed him from the ramparts down;
And when at last the stormers quailed,
And back the assailants shrank assailed,
Like wounded wasps that still could sting,
Or tigers that had missed their spring,
They would not fly, but turned at bay
And fought out all the dying day; —

Sweet saints! it was a crimson track
That André left by Pont-du-lac.

When André rode to Pont-du-lac,
Said he, "A troop of girls could sack
This huckster town, that hugs its hoard
But wists not how to wield a sword."
It makes my blood warm now to know
How soon Sir Cockerel ceased to crow,
And how 'twas my sure dagger-point
In André's harness found a joint:
For I, who now am old, was young,
And strong the thews were, now unstrung,
And deadly though our danger then,
I would that day were back again;
Ay, would to God the day were back
When André rode to Pont-du-lac!

A. H. Beesly.

AULD ROBIN GRAY

WHEN the sheep are in the fauld, when the kye's a' at
       hame,
  And a' the weary warld to rest are gane,
The waes o' my heart fa' in showers frae my e'e,
Unkent by my gudeman, wha sleeps sound by me.

Young Jamie lo'ed me weel, and sought me for his bride,
But saving ae crown-piece he had naething else beside;
To mak' the crown a pound my Jamie gaed to sea,
And the crown and the pound—they were baith for me.

He hadna been gane a twelvemonth and a day
When my father brake his arm, and the cow was stown away;
My mither she fell sick—my Jamie was at sea—
And Auld Robin Gray came a-courting me.

My father couldna work, my mother couldna spin;
I toiled day and night, but their bread I couldna win:
Auld Rob maintained them baith, and wi' tears in his e'e,
Said, "Jeanie, for their sakes, will ye no marry me?"

My heart it said na, and I looked for Jamie back:
But hard blew the winds, and his ship was a wrack;

His ship was a wrack— Why didna Jamie dee?
Or why am I spared to cry, Wae is me!

My father urged me sair—my mother didna speak,
But she looket in my face till my heart was like to break;
They gied him my hand—my heart was in the sea—
And so Robin Gray, he was gudeman to me.

I hadna been his wife a week but only four,
When, mournfu' as I sat on the stane at my door,
I saw my Jamie's ghaist—for I couldna think it he
Till he said, "I'm come hame, love, to marry thee."

Oh! sair, sair did we greet, and mickle say of a';
I gi'ed him ae kiss and bade him gang awa'.
I wish that I were dead, but I'm na like to dee,
For though my heart is broken, I'm but young, wae's me!

I gang like a ghaist, and I carena much to spin;
I darena think on Jamie, for that would be a sin:
But I'll do my best a gude wife to be,
For oh! Robin Gray he is kind to me.

LADY ANNE BARNARD.

WERENA MY HEART LICHT

THERE was ance a may and she loved na men;
   She biggit her bonnie bower down i' yon glen:
   But naw she cries Dool! and Well-a-day!
Come down the green gate, and come here away.

When bonnie young Johnnie cam' ower the sea,
He said he saw naething sae lovely as me;
   He hecht me baith rings and manie braw things,
And werena my heart licht I wad dee.

His wee wilfu' tittie she loved na me;
(I was taller and twice as bonnie as she;)
   She raised sic a pother 'twixt him and his mother,
That werena my heart licht I wad dee.

The day it was set for the bridal to be:
The wife took a dwam and lay down to dee;
   She mained and she graned wi' fause dolor and pain,
Till he vowed he never wad see me again.

His kindred socht ane o' higher degree,
Said, Would he wed ane was landless like me?
  Although I was bonnie, I wasna for Johnnie,
And werena my heart licht I wad dee.

They said I had neither coo nor cawf,
Nor dribbles o' drink coming through the draff,
Nor pickles o' meal runnin' frae the mill-e'e,—
And werena my heart licht I wad dee.

His tittie she was baith wylie and slee:
She spied me as I came ower the lea;
  And then she ran in, and made a loud din;—
Believe your ain een an ye trow na me.

His bonnet stood aye fu' round on his brow;
His old ane looked better than many ane's new:
But now he lets 't wear any gait it will hing,
And casts himsel' dowie upon the com-bing.

And now he gaes daundrin' about the dykes,
And a' he dow do is to hound the tykes:
The livelong nicht he ne'er steeks his e'e;
And werena my heart licht I wad dee.

Oh! were we young now as we ance hae been,
We should hae been gallopin' down on yon green,
And linkin' it ower the lily-white lea:
And werena my heart licht I wad dee.

LADY GRIZEL BAILLIE

TO NELL GWYNNE'S LOOKING-GLASS

G LASS antique, 'twixt thee and Nell
    Draw we here a parallel.
      She, like thee, was forced to bear
All reflections, foul or fair;
    Thou art deep and bright within,—
    Depths as bright belonged to Gwynne;
    Thou art very frail as well,
    Frail as flesh is,—so was Nell.

Thou, her glass, art silver-lined,—
She too had a silver mind!

Thine is fresh till this far day,—
Hers till death ne'er wore away.
  Thou dost to thy surface win
  Wandering glances,—so did Gwynne;
  Eyes on thee long love to dwell,—
  So men's eyes would do on Nell.

Lifelike forms in thee are sought,—
Such the forms the actress wrought;
Truth unfailing rests in you,—
Nell, whate'er she was, was true.
  Clear as virtue, dull as sin,
  Thou art oft,—as oft was Gwynne;
  Breathe on thee, and drops will swell,—
  Bright tears dimmed the eyes of Nell.

Thine's a frame to charm the sight,—
Framed was she to give delight.
Waxen forms here truly show
Charles above and Nell below;
  But between them, chin with chin,
  Stuart stands as low as Gwynne,
  Paired, yet parted,—meant to tell
  Charles was opposite to Nell.

Round the glass wherein her face
Smiled so soft, her "arms" we trace;
Thou, her mirror, hast the pair,—
Lion here, and leopard there.
  She had part in these,—akin
  To the lion-heart was Gwynne;
  And the leopard's beauty fell
  With its spots to bounding Nell.

Oft inspected, ne'er seen through,
Thou art firm, if brittle too,—
So her will, on good intent,
Might be broken, never bent.
  What the glass was when therein
  Beamed the face of glad Nell Gwynne,
  Was that face by beauty's spell
  To the honest soul of Nell.

S. LAMAN BLANCHARD.

FROM THE 'ODE TO MALIBRAN'

O MARIA FELICIA! the painter and bard,
    Behind them, in dying, leave undying heirs:
  The night of oblivion their memory spares;
And their great, eager souls, other action debarred,
Against death, against time, having valiantly warred,
    Though struck down in the strife, claim its trophies as
        theirs.

In the iron engraved, one his name leaves enshrined;
With a golden-sweet cadence another's entwined
  Makes forever all those who shall hear it his friends.
Though he died, on the canvas lives Raphael's mind;
  And from death's darkest doom till this world of ours
      ends,
  The mother-clasped infant his glory defends.

As the lamp guards the flame, so the bare marble halls
  Of the Parthenon hold, in their desolate space,
The memory of Phidias enshrined in their walls.
And Praxiteles's child, the young Venus, yet calls
  From the altar, where smiling she still holds her place,
  The centuries conquered, to worship her grace.

Thus, from age after age while new light we receive,
  To rest at God's feet the old glories are gone;
And the accents of genius their echoes still weave
  With the great human voice, till their thoughts are but
      one:
And of thee, dead but yesterday, all thy fame leaves
  But a cross in the dim chapel's darkness — alone.

A cross, and oblivion, silence, and death!
Hark! the wind's softest sob; hark! the ocean's deep breath;
  Hark! the fisher-boy singing his way o'er the plains:
Of thy glory, thy hope, thy young beauty's bright wreath,
  Not a trace, not a sigh, not an echo remains.

                                    ALFRED DE MUSSET.
Translation of Frances Kemble Butler.

THE EARTH AND MAN

A LITTLE·sun, a little rain,
    A soft wind blowing from the west —
And woods and fields are sweet again,
    And warmth within the mountain's breast.

So simple is the earth we tread,
    So quick with love and life her frame:
Ten thousand years have dawned and fled,
    And still her magic is the same.

A little love, a little trust,
    A soft impulse, a sudden dream —
And life as dry as desert dust
    Is fresher than a mountain stream.

So simple is the heart of man,
    So ready for new hope and joy:
Ten thousand years since it began
    Have left it younger than a boy.

STOPFORD A. BROOKE.

THE STRANGE COUNTRY

I HAVE come from a mystical Land of Light
    To a Strange Country;
The land I have left is forgotten quite
    In the land I see.

The round earth rolls beneath my feet,
    And the still stars glow;
The murmuring waters rise and retreat,
    The winds come and go.

Sure as a heart-beat all things seem
    In this Strange Country;
So sure, so still, in a dazzle of dream,
    All things flow free.

'Tis life, all life, be it pleasure or pain,
    In the field and the flood,
In the beating heart, in the burning brain,
    In the flesh and the blood.

Deep as death is the daily strife
    Of this Strange Country:
All things thrill up till they blossom in life,
    And flutter and flee.

Nothing is stranger than the rest,
    From the Pole to the Pole,—
The weed by the way, the eggs in the nest,
    The flesh and the soul.

Look in mine eyes, O man I meet
    In this Strange Country!
Lie in my arms, O maiden sweet,
    With thy mouth kiss me!

Go by, O king, with thy crownèd brow
    And thy sceptred hand —
Thou art a straggler too, I vow,
    From the same Strange Land.

O wondrous faces that upstart
    In this Strange Country!
O souls, O shades, that become a part
    Of my soul and me!

What are ye working so fast and fleet,
    O human-kind?
" We are building cities for those whose feet
    Are coming behind;

"Our stay is short; we must fly again
    From this Strange Country:
But others are growing, women and men,
    Eternally!"

Child, what art thou? and what am *I*?
    But a breaking wave!
Rising and rolling on, we hie
    To the shore of the grave.

I have come from a mystical Land of Light
    To this Strange Country:
This dawn I came; I shall go to-night,
    Ay me! ay me!

I hold my hand to my head, and stand
    'Neath the air's blue arc;

I try to remember the mystical Land,
    But all is dark.

And all around me swim shapes like mine
    In this Strange Country;
They break in the glamour of gleams divine,
    And they moan "Ay me!"

Like waves in the cold moon's silvern breath
    They gather and roll;
Each crest of white is a birth or death,
    Each sound is a soul.

Oh, whose is the eye that gleams so bright
    O'er this Strange Country?
It draws us along with a chain of light.
    As the moon the sea!

                    ROBERT BUCHANAN.

FLOWER OF THE WORLD

WHEREVER men sinned and wept,
    I wandered in my quest;
    At last in a Garden of God
I saw the Flower of the World.

This flower had human eyes;
Its breath was the breath of the mouth:
Sunlight and starlight came,
And the flower drank bliss from both.

Whatever was base and unclean,
Whatever was sad and strange,
Was piled around its roots:
It drew its strength from the same.

Whatever was formless and base
Passed into fineness and form;
Whatever was lifeless and mean
Grew into beautiful bloom.

Then I thought, "O Flower of the World,
Miraculous blossom of things,
Light as a faint wreath of snow
Thou tremblest to fall in the wind;

"O beautiful Flower of the World,
Fall not nor wither away:
He is coming—he cannot be far—
The Lord of the flowers and the stars."

And I cried, "O Spirit divine
That walkest the garden unseen!
Come hither, and bless, ere it dies,
The beautiful Flower of the World."

ROBERT BUCHANAN.

LOVE STILL HATH SOMETHING

LOVE still hath something of the sea
    From whence his mother rose;
  No time his slaves from love can free,
    Nor give their thoughts repose.

They are becalmed in clearest days,
    And in rough weather tossed;
They wither under cold delays,
    Or are in tempests lost.

One while they seem to touch the port;
    Then straight into the main
Some angry wind, in cruel sport,
    The vessel drives again.

At first disdain and pride they fear,
    Which if they chance to 'scape,
Rivals and falsehood soon appear
    In a more dreadful shape.

By such degrees to joy they come,
    And are so long withstood;
So slowly they receive the sum,
    It hardly does them good.

'Tis cruel to prolong a pain;
    And to defer a bliss,
Believe me, gentle Hermione,
    No less inhuman is.

A hundred thousand foes your fears
    Perhaps would not remove;

And if I gazed a thousand years,
  I could no deeper love.

'Tis fitter much for you to guess
  Than for me to explain;
But grant, oh! grant that happiness
  Which only does remain.

SIR CHARLES SEDLEY.

HORIZONS

M<small>Y</small> HEART gives thanks for yonder hill,
  That makes this valley safe and still;
  That shuts from sight my onward way
And sets a limit to my day;
That keeps my thoughts, so tired and weak,
From seeking what they should not seek.
On that fair bound across the west
My eyes find pasturage and rest,
And of its dewy stillness drink,
As do the stars upon its brink;
It shields me from the days to come,
And makes the present hour my home.

Deeper will be my rest to-night
For this near calmness of the height;
Its steadfast boundary will keep
My harbored spirit while I sleep.
Yet somewhere on its wooded sides
To-morrow's onward pathway hides,
And I shall wake at early morn,
To find a world beyond, new-born.

I thank thee, Lord, that thou dost lay
These near horizons on my way.
If I could all my journey see,
There were no charm of mystery,
No veilèd grief, no changes sweet,
No restful sense of tasks complete.
I thank thee for the hills, the night,
For every barrier to my sight;
For every turn that blinds my eyes
To coming pain or glad surprise;

For every bound thou settest nigh,
To make me look more near, more high;
For mysteries too great to know:
For everything thou dost not show.
Upon thy limits rests my heart;
Its safe Horizon, Lord, thou art!

LOUISA BUSHNELL.

THE SECOND PLACE

UNTO my loved ones have I given all:
   The tireless service of my willing hands,
      The strength of swift feet running to their call,
Each pulse of this fond heart whose love commands
The busy brain unto their use; each grace,
   Each gift, the flower and fruit of life. To me
   They give, with gracious hearts and tenderly,
      The second place.

Such joy as my glad service may dispense,
   They spend to make some brighter life more blest;
The grief that comes despite my frail defense,
   They seek to soothe upon a dearer breast.
Love veils his deepest glories from my face;
   I dimly dream how fair the light may be
   Beyond the shade where I hold, longingly,
      The second place.

And yet 'tis sweet to know that though I make
   No soul's supremest bliss, no life shall lie
Ruined and desolated for my sake,
   Nor any heart be broken when I die.
And sweet it is to see my little space
   Grow wider hour by hour; and gratefully
   I thank the tender fate that granteth me
      The second place.

· SUSAN MARR SPALDING. ·

OH THE PLEASANT DAYS OF OLD!

OH THE pleasant days of old, which so often people praise!
　　True, they wanted all the luxuries that grace our modern
　　　　days;
Bare floors were strewed with rushes, the walls let in the cold:
Oh, how they must have shivered in those pleasant days of old!

Oh those ancient lords of old, how magnificent they were!
They threw down and imprisoned kings;— to thwart them who
　　　　might dare?
They ruled their serfs right sternly; they took from Jews their
　　　　gold:
Above both law and equity were those great lords of old!

Oh the gallant knights of old, for their valor so renowned!
With sword and lance and armor strong they scoured the country
　　　　round;
And whenever aught to tempt them they met by wood or wold,
By right of sword they seized the prize,— those gallant knights of
　　　　old!

Oh the gentle dames of old! who, quite free from fear or pain,
Could gaze on joust and tournament, and see their champions slain;
They lived on good beefsteaks and ale, which made them strong
　　　　and bold,—
Oh, more like men than women were those gentle dames of old!

Oh those mighty towers of old! with their turrets, moat, and keep,
Their battlements and bastions, their dungeons dark and deep:
Full many a baron held his court within the castle hold;
And many a captive languished there, in those strong towers of
　　　　old.

Oh the troubadours of old! with the gentle minstrelsie
Of hope and joy, or deep despair, whiche'er their lot might be;
For years they served their ladye-love ere they their passions
　　　　told:
Oh, wondrous patience must have had those troubadours of old!

Oh those blessed times of old, with their chivalry and state!
I love to read their chronicles, which such brave deeds relate;
I love to sing their ancient rhymes, to hear their legends told;—
But Heaven be thanked I live not in those blessed times of old!

　　　　　　　　　　　　　　FRANCES BROWN.

BUSY, CURIOUS, THIRSTY FLY

Busy, curious, thirsty fly,
   Drink with me, and drink as I;
   Freely welcome to my cup,
Couldst thou sip and sip it up.
Make the most of life you may:
Life is short, and wears away.

Both alike are mine and thine,
Hastening quick to their decline;
Thine's a summer, mine no more,
Though repeated to threescore.
Threescore summers, when they're gone,
Will appear as short as one.

VINCENT BOURNE.

MY DEAR AND ONLY LOVE

My dear and only love, I pray
   This noble world of thee
    Be governed by no other sway
    But purest monarchie.
For if confusion have a part,—
   Which virtuous souls abhor,—
And hold a synod in thy heart,
   I'll never love thee more.

Like Alexander I will reign,
   And I will reign alone;
My thoughts shall evermore disdain
   A rival on my throne.
He either fears his fate too much,
   Or his deserts are small,
That puts it not unto the touch,
   To win or lose it all.

But if no faithless action stain
   Thy true and constant word,
I'll make thee famous by my pen,
   And glorious by my sword.
I'll serve thee in such noble ways
   As ne'er were known before;
I'll deck and crown thy head with bays,
   And love thee more and more.

JAMES GRAHAM, Earl of Montrose.

THE WEARING OF THE GREEN

O PADDY dear, and did you hear the news that's going round?
   The shamrock is forbid by law to grow on Irish ground;
      St. Patrick's Day no more we'll keep; his colors can't be seen:
For there's a bloody law again' the wearing of the green.
I met with Napper Tandy, and he took me by the hand,
And he said, "How's poor old Ireland, and how does she stand?"
She's the most distressful country that ever yet was seen:
They are hanging men and women for the wearing of the green.

Oh, if the color we must wear is England's cruel red,
Sure Ireland's sons will ne'er forget the blood that they have shed.
You may take the shamrock from your hat and cast it on the sod,
But 'twill take root and flourish there, though under foot 'tis trod.
When law can stop the blades of grass from growing as they grow,
And when the leaves in summer-time their verdure dare not show,
Then I will change the color I wear in my caubeen;
But till that day, please God, I'll stick to wearing of the green.

But if at last our color should be torn from Ireland's heart,
Her sons with shame and sorrow from the dear old isle will part:
I've heard a whisper of a country that lies beyond the sea,
Where rich and poor stand equal in the light of freedom's day.
O Erin, must we leave you, driven by a tyrant's hand?
Must we ask a mother's blessing from a strange and distant land?
Where the cruel cross of England shall nevermore be seen,
And where, please God, we'll live and die still wearing of the green.

DION BOUCICAULT.

THE BURIAL OF SIR JOHN MOORE

NOT a drum was heard, not a funeral note,
   As his corse to the rampart we hurried;
Not a soldier discharged his farewell shot
   O'er the grave where our hero we buried.

We buried him darkly at dead of night,
   The sod with our bayonets turning,
By the struggling moonbeams' misty light,
   And the lantern dimly burning.

No useless coffin inclosed his breast,
   Nor in sheet nor in shroud we wound him;

ARNOLD WINKELRIED'S MONUMENT.

Photogravure from a photograph.

But he lay like a warrior taking his rest,
 With his martial cloak around him!

Few and short were the prayers we said,
 And we spoke not a word of sorrow;
But we steadfastly gazed on the face of the dead,
 And we bitterly thought of the morrow.

We thought, as we hollowed his narrow bed
 And smoothed down his lonely pillow,
That the foe and the stranger would tread o'er his head,
 And we far away on the billow!

Lightly they'll talk of the spirit that's gone,
 And o'er his cold ashes upbraid him;
But little he'll reck if they let him sleep on
 In the grave where a Briton has laid him.

But half of our heavy task was done,
 When the clock struck the hour for retiring;
And we heard the distant and random gun
 That the foe was sullenly firing.

Slowly and sadly we laid him down,
 From the field of his fame fresh and gory;
We carved not a line, we raised not a stone —
 But we left him alone with his glory.

CHARLES WOLFE.

ARNOLD WINKELRIED

" **M**AKE way for liberty!" he cried;
 Made way for liberty, and died!

In arms the Austrian phalanx stood,
A living wall, a human wood!
A wall, where every conscious stone
Seemed to its kindred thousands grown;
A rampart all assaults to bear,
Till time to dust their frame should wear;
A wood like that enchanted grove
In which with fiends Rinaldo strove,
Where every silent tree possessed
A spirit prisoned in its breast,
Which the first stroke of coming strife
Would startle into hideous life:

So dense, so still, the Austrians stood,
A living wall, a human wood!
Impregnable their front appears,
All horrent with projected spears,
Whose polished points before them shine,
From flank to flank, one brilliant line,
Bright as the breakers' splendors run
Along the billows, to the sun.

Opposed to these, a hovering band
Contended for their native land:
Peasants, whose new-found strength had broke
From manly necks the ignoble yoke,
And forged their fetters into swords,
On equal terms to fight their lords;
And what insurgent rage had gained,
In many a mortal fray maintained:
Marshaled once more at Freedom's call,
They came to conquer or to fall,
Where he who conquered, he who fell,
Was deemed a dead or living Tell!
Such virtue had that patriot breathed,
So to the soil his soul bequeathed,
That wheresoe'er his arrows flew,
Heroes in his own likeness grew,
And warriors sprang from every sod
Which his awakening footstep trod.

And now the work of life and death
Hung on the passing of a breath;
The fire of conflict burnt within,
The battle trembled to begin:
Yet while the Austrians held their ground,
Point for attack was nowhere found;
Where'er the impatient Switzers gazed,
The unbroken line of lances blazed.
That line 'twere suicide to meet,
And perish at their tyrants' feet;—
How could they rest within their graves,
And leave their homes the homes of slaves?
Would they not feel their children tread
With clanging chains above their head?

It must not be: this day, this hour,
Annihilates the oppressor's power;

All Switzerland is in the field:
She will not fly, she cannot yield—
She must not fall; her better fate
Here gives her an immortal date.
Few were the number she could boast;
But every freeman was a host,
And felt as though himself were he
On whose sole arm hung victory.

It did depend on *one*, indeed:
Behold him — Arnold Winkelried!
There sounds not to the trump of fame
The echo of a nobler name.
Unmarked, he stood amid the throng
In rumination deep and long,
Till you might see, with sudden grace,
The very thought come o'er his face;
And by the motion of his form
Anticipate the bursting storm;
And by the uplifting of his brow
Tell where the bolt would strike, and how.

But 'twas no sooner thought than done;
The field was in a moment won;—
"Make way for Liberty!" he cried:
Then ran, with arms extended wide,
As if his dearest friend to clasp;
Ten spears he swept within his grasp.
"Make way for Liberty!" he cried:
Their keen points met from side to side;
He bowed amongst them like a tree,
And thus made way for Liberty.

Swift to the breach his comrades fly;
"Make way for Liberty!" they cry,
And through the Austrian phalanx dart,
As rushed the spears through Arnold's heart:
While, instantaneous as his fall,
Rout, ruin, panic, scattered all;—
An earthquake could not overthrow
A city with a surer blow.

Thus Switzerland again was free;
Thus death made way for Liberty!

                          JAMES MONTGOMERY.

LITTLE BELL

Piped the blackbird on the beechwood spray:
   "Pretty maid, slow wandering this way,
      What's your name?" quoth he —
"What's your name? Oh stop and straight unfold,
Pretty maid with showery curls of gold." —
      "Little Bell," said she.

Little Bell sat down beneath the rocks,
Tossed aside her gleaming golden locks;
      "Bonny bird," quoth she,
"Sing me your best song before I go."
"Here's the very finest song I know,
      Little Bell," said he.

And the blackbird piped: you never heard
Half so gay a song from any bird —
      Full of quips and wiles;
Now so round and rich, now soft and slow,
All for love of that sweet face below,
      Dimpled o'er with smiles.

And the while the bonny bird did pour
His full heart out freely o'er and o'er
      'Neath the morning skies,
In the little childish heart below
All the sweetness seemed to grow and grow,
And shine forth in happy overflow
      From the blue, bright eyes.

Down the dell she tripped, and through the glade
Peeped the squirrel from the hazel shade,
      And from out the tree
Swung, and leaped, and frolicked, void of fear,
While bold blackbird piped that all might hear, —
      "Little Bell," piped he.

Little Bell sat down amid the fern, —
"Squirrel, squirrel, to your task return:
      Bring me nuts," quoth she.
Up, away, the frisky squirrel hies, —
Golden wood-lights glancing in his eyes, —
      And adown the tree,

Great ripe nuts, kissed brown by July sun,
In the little lap dropped one by one —
    Hark, how blackbird pipes to see the fun!
        "Happy Bell," pipes he.

Little Bell looked up and down the glade:
"Squirrel, squirrel, if you're not afraid,
        Come and share with me!"
Down came squirrel eager for his fare,
Down came bonny blackbird, I declare;
Little Bell gave each his honest share —
        Ah, the merry three!

And the while these frolic playmates twain
Piped and frisked from bough to bough again
        'Neath the morning skies,
In the little childish heart below
All the sweetness seemed to grow and grow,
And shine out in happy overflow
        From her blue, bright eyes.

By her snow-white cot at close of day
Knelt sweet Bell, with folded palms to pray:
        Very calm and clear
Rose the praying voice to where, unseen,
In blue heaven, an angel shape serene
        Paused awhile to hear.

"What good child is this," the angel said,
"That with happy heart, beside her bed
        Prays so lovingly?"
Low and soft, oh! very low and soft,
Crooned the blackbird in the orchard croft,
        "Bell, dear Bell!" crooned he.

"Whom God's creatures love," the angel fair
Murmured, "God doth bless with angels' care:
        Child, thy bed shall be
Folded safe from harm; Love, deep and kind,
Shall watch around and leave good gifts behind,
        Little Bell, for thee!"

THOMAS WESTWOOD.

AN EXPERIENCE AND A MORAL

I LENT my love a book one day;
　　She brought it back; I laid it by:
'Twas little either had to say,—
　　She was so strange, and I so shy.

But yet we loved indifferent things,—
　　The sprouting buds, the birds in tune,—
And Time stood still and wreathed his wings
　　With rosy links from June to June.

For her, what task to dare or do?
　　What peril tempt? what hardship bear?
But with her—ah! she never knew
　　My heart, and what was hidden there!

And she with me, so cold and coy,
　　Seemed like a maid bereft of sense;
But in the crowd, all life and joy,
　　And full of blushful impudence.

She married,—well, a woman needs
　　A mate, her life and love to share,—
And little cares sprang up like weeds
　　And played around her elbow-chair.

And years rolled by—but I, content,
　　Trimmed my own lamp, and kept it bright,
Till age's touch my hair besprent
　　With rays and gleams of silver light.

And then it chanced I took the book
　　Which she perused in days gone by;
And as I read, such passion shook
　　My soul,—I needs must curse or cry.

For, here and there, her love was writ,
　　In old, half-faded pencil-signs,
As if she yielded—bit by bit—
　　Her heart in dots and underlines.

Ah, silvered fool, too late you look!
　　I know it; let me here record
This maxim: *Lend no girl a book
　　Unless you read it afterward!*

FREDERICK S. COZZENS.

HOW PERSIMMONS TOOK CARE OB DER BABY

PERSIMMONS was a colored lad
   'Way down in Lou'siany,
And all the teaching that he had
   Was given him by his granny.
But he did his duty ever
   As well as you, it may be;
With faithfulness and pride always,
   He minded missus's baby.
He loved the counsels of the saints,—
   And sometimes those of sinners,
To run off 'possum-hunting and
   Steal "watermilion" dinners.
And fervently at meetin' too,
   On every Sunday night,
He'd with the elders shout and pray
   By the pine-knots' flaring light,
And sing their rudest melodies
   With voice so full and strong
You could almost think he learned them
   From the angels' triumph song.

SONG

"We be nearer to de Lord
   Dan de white folks,—and dey knows it:
See de glory-gate unbarred;
Walk in darkies, past de guard—
   Bet you dollar he won't close it.

"Walk in, darkies, troo de gate:
   Hear de kullered angels holler;
Go 'way, white folks, you're too late,—
We's de winnin' kuller. Wait
   Till de trumpet blow to foller."

He would croon this over softly
   As he lay out in the sun;
But the song he heard most often—
   His granny's favorite one—
Was—"Jawge Washington
   Thomas Jefferson
Persimmons Henry Clay, be
   Quick! shut de do',
   Get up off dat flo',
Come heah and mind de baby."

One night there came a fearful storm,—
   Almost a second flood;
The river rose, a torrent swoln
   Of beaten, yellow mud.
It bit at its embankments,
   And lapped them down in foam,
Till surging through a wide crevasse,
   The waves seethed round their home.
They scaled the high veranda,
   They filled the parlors clear,
Till floating chairs and tables
   Clashed against the chandelier.
'Twas then Persimmons's granny,
   Stout of arm and terror-proof,
By means of axe and lever,
   Pried up the veranda roof;
Bound mattresses upon it
   With stoutest cords of rope,
Lifted out her fainting mistress,
   Saying, " Honey, dar is hope!
" *You*, Jawge Washington
      Thomas Jefferson
Persimmons Henry Clay, be
      Quick on dat raf';
      Don't star' like a calf,
But take good cah ob baby!"

The frothing river lifted them
   Out on its turbid tide,
And for a while they floated on
   Together, side by side;
Till, broken by the current strong,
   The frail raft snapt in two,
And Persimmons saw his granny
   Fast fading from his view.

The deck-hands on a steamboat
   Heard, as they passed in haste,
A child's voice singing in the dark,
   Upon the water's waste,
A song of faith and triumph,
   Of Moses and the Lord;
And throwing out a coil of rope,
   They drew him safe on board.

Full many a stranger city
   Persimmons wandered through,

"A-totin' ob der baby," and
  Singing songs he knew.
At length some City Fathers
  Objected to his plan,
Arresting as a vagrant
  Our valiant little man.
They carried out their purposes,
  Persimmons "'lowed he'd spile 'em,"
So, *sloping* from the station-house,
  He stole baby from the 'sylum.

And on that very afternoon,
  As it was growing dark,
He sang, beside the fountain in
  The crowded city park,
A rude camp-meeting anthem,
  Which he had sung before,
While on his granny's fragile raft
  He drifted far from shore:—

SONG

"Moses smote de water, and
    De sea gabe away;
  De chillen dey passed ober, for
    De sea gabe away.
  O Lord! I feel so glad,
    It am always dark 'fo' day;
  So, honey, don't yer be sad,
    De sea 'll gib away."

A lady dressed in mourning
  Turned with a sudden start,
Gave one glance at the baby,
  Then caught it to her heart;
While a substantial shadow
  That was walking by her side
Seized Persimmons by the shoulder,
  And while she shook him, cried:—
"*You*, Jawge Washington
    Thomas Jefferson
  Persimmons Henry Clay, be
      Quick! splain yerself, chile,—
      Stop dat ar fool smile,—
  Whar you done been wid baby?"

ELIZABETH W. CHAMPNEY.

WHILST THEE I SEEK

WHILST thee I seek, protecting Power,
    Be my vain wishes stilled!
And may this consecrated hour
    With better hopes be filled.

Thy love the power of thought bestowed;
    To thee my thoughts would soar:
Thy mercy o'er my life has flowed;
    That mercy I adore.

In each event of life, how clear
    Thy ruling hand I see!
Each blessing to my soul more dear,
    Because conferred by thee.

In every joy that crowns my days,
    In every pain I bear,
My heart shall find delight in praise,
    Or seek relief in prayer.

When gladness wings my favored hour,
    Thy love my thoughts shall fill;
Resigned, when storms of sorrow lower,
    My soul shall meet thy will.

My lifted eye without a tear
    The gathering storms shall see:
My steadfast heart shall know no fear;
    That heart shall rest on thee.

HELEN M. WILLIAMS.

SHIPS AT SEA

I HAVE ships that went to sea
    More than fifty years ago:
None have yet come home to me,
    But keep sailing to and fro.
I have seen them in my sleep,
Plunging through the shoreless deep,
With tattered sails and battered hulls,
While around them screamed the gulls,
    Flying low, flying low.

I have wondered where they stayed
   From me, sailing round the world;
And I've said, "I'm half afraid
   That their sails will ne'er be furled."
Great the treasures that they hold,—
Silks and plumes, and bars of gold;
While the spices which they bear
Fill with fragrance all the air,
   As they sail, as they sail.

Every sailor in the port
   Knows that I have ships at sea,
Of the waves and winds the sport;
   And the sailors pity me.
Oft they come and with me walk,
Cheering me with hopeful talk,
Till I put my fears aside,
And contented watch the tide
   Rise and fall, rise and fall.

I have waited on the piers,
   Gazing from them down the bay,
Days and nights for many years,
   Till I turned heart-sick away.
But the pilots when they land
Stop and take me by the hand,
Saying, "You will live to see
Your proud vessels come from sea,
   One and all, one and all."

So I never quite despair,
   Nor let hope or courage fail;
And some day when skies are fair,
   Up the bay my ship will sail.
I can buy then all I need,—
Prints to look at, books to read,
Horses, wines, and works of art,
Everything except a heart:
   That is lost, that is lost.

Once when I was pure and young,
   Poorer, too, than I am now,
Ere a cloud was o'er me flung,
   Or a wrinkle creased my brow,
There was one whose heart was mine;
But she's something now divine;—

And though come my ships from sea,
They can bring no heart to me,
Evermore, evermore.

R. B. COFFIN.

A WET SHEET AND A FLOWING SEA

A WET sheet and a flowing sea,
   And a wind that follows fast,
And fills the white and rustling sail,
   And bends the gallant mast;
And bends the gallant mast, my boys,
   While, like the eagle free,
Away the good ship flies and leaves
   Old England on the lee.

"Oh for a soft and gentle wind!"
   I heard a fair one cry; —
But give to me the snorting breeze
   And white waves heaving high;
And white waves heaving high, my boys,
   The good ship tight and free:
The world of waters is our home,
   And merry men are we.

There's tempest in yon hornèd moon,
   And lightning in yon cloud;
And hark the music, mariners, —
   The wind is piping loud!
The wind is piping loud, my boys,
   The lightning flashes free, —
While the hollow oak our palace is,
   Our heritage the sea.

ALLAN CUNNINGHAM.

A LIFE ON THE OCEAN WAVE

A LIFE on the ocean wave,
   A home on the rolling deep;
Where the scattered waters rave,
   And the winds their revels keep!
Like an eagle caged I pine
   On this dull, unchanging shore:

Oh, give me the flashing brine,
  The spray and the tempest's roar!

Once more on the deck I stand,
  Of my own swift-gliding craft:
Set sail! farewell to land!
  The gale follows fair abaft.
We shoot through the sparkling foam,
  Like an ocean-bird set free,—
Like the ocean bird, our home
  We'll find far out on the sea.

The land is no longer in view,
  The clouds have begun to frown;
But with a stout vessel and' crew,
  We'll say, Let the storm come down!
And the song of our hearts shall be,
  While the winds and the waters rave,
A home on the rolling sea!
  A life on the ocean wave!

                        EPES SARGENT.

THE WANDERER

HE KNOWS no home; he only knows
      Hunger and cold and pain.
    The four winds are his bedfellows;
      His sleep is dashed with rain.

'Tis naught to him who fails, who thrives:
  He neither hopes nor fears;
Some dim primeval impulse drives
  His footsteps down the years.

He could not, if he would, forsake
  Lone road and field and tree.
Yet, think! it takes a God to make
  E'en such a waif as he.

And once a maiden, asked for bread,
  Saw, as she gave her dole,
No friendless vagrant, but, instead,
  An indefeasible Soul.

                   WILLIAM CANTON.

HESPERUS SINGS

POOR old pilgrim Misery,
  Beneath the silent moon he sate,
A-listening to the screech-owl's cry
  And the cold wind's goblin prate;
Beside him lay his staff of yew
  With withered willow twined,
His scant gray hair all wet with dew,
  His cheeks with grief ybrined:
And his cry it was ever, Alack!
  Alack, and woe is me!

Anon a wanton imp astray
  His piteous moaning hears,
And from his bosom steals away
  His rosary of tears:
With his plunder fled that urchin elf,
  And hid it in your eyes:
Then tell me back the stolen pelf,
  Give up the lawless prize:
Or your cry shall be ever, Alack!
  Alack, and woe is me!

      THOMAS LOVELL BEDDOES.

THE OATEN PIPE

WHEN the musical piping frogs
  Begin to croak and chant
In the marshes, and in the bogs,
  In many a sweet spring haunt,

I think of the legend hoary
  Which little Dutch folk recite,—
How the nightingale's soul, says the story,
  Enters a frog in its flight.

And so when I hear the weird catch
  Where the frogs alone take part,
I fancy I sometimes snatch
  A strain from the nightingale's heart.

      MARY NEWMARCH PRESCOTT.

OVER THE RIVER

OVER the river they beckon to me,
 Loved ones who've crossed to the farther side;
 The gleam of their snowy robes I see,
  But their voices are lost in the dashing tide.
There's one with ringlets of sunny gold,
 And eyes the reflection of heaven's own blue;
He crossed in the twilight gray and cold,
 And the pale mist hid him from mortal view.
We saw not the angels who met him there,
 The gates of the city we could not see:
Over the river, over the river,
 My brother stands waiting to welcome me.

Over the river the boatman pale
 Carried another, the household pet;
Her brown curls waved in the gentle gale,—
 Darling Minnie! I see her yet.
She crossed on her bosom her dimpled hands.
 And fearlessly entered the phantom bark;
We felt it glide from the silver sands,
 And all our sunshine grew strangely dark.
We know she is safe on the farther side,
 Where all the ransomed and angels be:
Over the river, the mystic river,
 My childhood's idol is waiting for me.

For none return from those quiet shores,
 Who cross with the boatman cold and pale:
We hear the dip of the golden oars,
 And catch a gleam of the snowy sail,
And lo! they have passed from our yearning hearts,
 They cross the stream and are gone for aye.
We may not sunder the veil apart
 That hides from our vision the gates of day;
We only know that their barks no more
 May sail with us o'er life's stormy sea:
Yet somewhere, I know, on the unseen shore,
 They watch, and beckon, and wait for me.

And I sit and think, when the sunset's gold
 Is flushing river and hill and shore,
I shall one day stand by the water cold,
 And list for the sound of the boatman's oar:
I shall watch for a gleam of the flapping sail,
 I shall hear the boat as it gains the strand,

I shall pass from sight with the boatman pale,
  To the better shore of the spirit land;
I shall know the loved who have gone before,
  And joyfully sweet will the meeting be,
When over the river, the peaceful river,
  The angel of death shall carry me!

NANCY WOODBURY PRIEST.

OUR MOTHER

BROKEN and worn. For years we saw her so;
  Dropping from strength, from time detaching slow;
    And scarcely could we know
How earth's dark ebb was heaven's bright overflow.

"She is so old," we said. The cloud and pain
Half hid her, till we sought with loving strain
    Her very self in vain.
Her *very self* was growing young again!

She has come back! The cloud and pain are o'er;
The dear freed feet but touched that other shore
    To turn to us once more
The nearer, like her lord who went before.

Our young, strong, angel mother! From the years
Triumphant life its shining garment clears,
    And all its stain of tears
And weariness forever disappears.

Old — broken — weak? 'Twas but the shattering might
With which a grand soul broke toward the light;
    Rending its bands of night
That it might stand full-statured in God's sight.

The calyx burst that it might loose the flower;
We saw the mist but by the sunbeam's power;
    The dusk that seemed to lower
Was of the morning — not the midnight hour.

And so a birth, not death, we stand beside;
Our own fast-gathering years come glorified;
    And braver we abide
That we have seen heaven's great door flung awide.

ADELINE D. T. WHITNEY.

BEN BOLT

DON'T you remember sweet Alice, Ben Bolt—
    Sweet Alice whose hair was so brown,
    Who wept with delight when you gave her a smile,
      And trembled with fear at your frown?
In the old church-yard in the valley, Ben Bolt,
    In a corner obscure and alone,
They have fitted a slab of the granite so gray,
    And Alice lies under the stone.

Under the hickory-tree, Ben Bolt,
    Which stood at the foot of the hill,
Together we've lain in the noonday shade,
    And listened to Appleton's mill.
The mill-wheel has fallen to pieces, Ben Bolt,
    The rafters have tumbled in,
And a quiet that crawls round the walls as you gaze
    Has followed the olden din.

Do you mind the cabin of logs, Ben Bolt,
    At the edge of the pathless wood,
And the button-ball tree with its motley limbs,
    Which nigh by the doorstep stood?
The cabin to ruin has gone, Ben Bolt;
    The tree you would seek for in vain;
And where once the lords of the forest waved,
    Are grass and the golden grain.

And don't you remember the school, Ben Bolt,
    With the master so cruel and grim,
And the shaded nook in the running brook
    Where the children went to swim?
Grass grows on the master's grave, Ben Bolt,
    The spring of the brook is dry,
And of all the boys who were schoolmates then
    There are only you and I.

There is change in the things I loved, Ben Bolt,
    They have changed from the old to the new;
But I feel in the deeps of my spirit the truth,
    There never was change in you.
Twelvemonths twenty have passed, Ben Bolt,
    Since first we were friends; yet I hail
Your presence a blessing, your friendship a truth,
    Ben Bolt of the salt-sea gale!

THOMAS DUNN ENGLISH.

THE OLD OAKEN BUCKET

How dear to this heart are the scenes of my childhood,
  When fond recollection presents them to view!
The orchard, the meadow, the deep-tangled wildwood,
  And every loved spot which my infancy knew;
The wide-spreading pond, and the mill which stood by it,
  The bridge, and the rock where the cataract fell;
The cot of my father, the dairy-house nigh it,
  And e'en the rude bucket which hung in the well!
The old oaken bucket, the iron-bound bucket,
The moss-covered bucket, which hung in the well.

That moss-covered vessel I hail as a treasure;
  For often, at noon, when returned from the field,
I found it the source of an exquisite pleasure,—
  The purest and sweetest that nature can yield.
How ardent I seized it, with hands that were glowing,
  And quick to the white pebbled bottom it fell;
Then soon, with the emblem of truth overflowing,
  And dripping with coolness, it rose from the well:
The old oaken bucket, the iron-bound bucket,
The moss-covered bucket arose from the well.

How sweet from the green mossy brim to receive it,
  As poised on the curb it inclined to my lips!
Not a full-blushing goblet could tempt me to leave it,
  Though filled with the nectar that Jupiter sips.
And now, far removed from the loved situation,
  The tear of regret will intrusively swell,
As fancy reverts to my father's plantation,
  And sighs for the bucket which hangs in the well;
The old oaken bucket, the iron-bound bucket,
The moss-covered bucket, which hangs in the well.

SAMUEL WOODWORTH.

THE BRAVE OLD OAK

A song to the oak, the brave old oak,
  Who hath ruled in the greenwood long;
Here's health and renown to his broad green crown,
  And his fifty arms so strong.
There's fear in his frown when the sun goes down,
  And the fire in the west fades out;

And he showeth his might on a wild midnight,
    When the storms through his branches shout.

Then here's to the oak, the brave old oak,
    Who stands in his pride alone;
And still flourish he, a hale green tree,
    When a hundred years are gone!

In the days of old, when the spring with cold
    Had brightened his branches gray,
Through the grass at his feet crept maidens sweet,
    To gather the dew of May.   .
And on that day to the rebeck gay
    They frolicked with lovesome swains:
They are gone, they are dead, in the church-yard laid,
    But the tree it still remains.

Then here's to the oak, etc.

He saw the rare times when the Christmas chimes
    Was a merry sound to hear,
When the squire's wide hall and the cottage small
    Were filled with good English cheer.
Now gold hath the sway we all obey,
    And a ruthless king is he;
But he never shall send our ancient friend
    To be tossed on the stormy sea.

Then here's to the oak, etc.

HENRY FOTHERGILL CHORLEY.

WOODMAN, SPARE THAT TREE!

WOODMAN, spare that tree!
    Touch not a single bough!
In youth it sheltered me,
    And I'll protect it now.
'Twas my forefather's hand
    That placed it near his cot;
There, woodman, let it stand,
    Thy axe shall harm it not!

That old familiar tree,
    Whose glory and renown
Are spread o'er land and sea —
    And wouldst thou hew it down?

Woodman, forbear thy stroke!
　Cut not its earth-bound ties;
Oh, spare that agèd oak,
　Now towering to the skies!

When but an idle boy,
　I sought its grateful shade;
In all their gushing joy
　Here too my sisters played.
My mother kissed me here;
　My father pressed my hand,—
Forgive this foolish tear,
　But let that old oak stand!

My heart-strings round thee cling,
　Close as thy bark, old friend!
Here shall the wild bird sing,
　And still thy branches bend.
Old tree! the storm still brave!
　And, woodman, leave the spot:
While I've a hand to save,
　Thy axe shall harm it not!

　　　　　　　　GEORGE P. MORRIS.

THE OLD ARM-CHAIR

I LOVE it, I love it; and who shall dare
　To chide me for loving that old arm-chair?
　I've treasured it long as a sainted prize;
I've bedewed it with tears, and embalmed it with sighs.
'Tis bound by a thousand bands to my heart:
Not a tie will break, not a link will start.
Would ye learn the spell?—a mother sat there;
And a sacred thing is that old arm-chair.

In childhood's hour I lingered near
The hallowèd seat with listening ear;
And gentle words that mother would give
To fit me to die, and teach me to live.
She told me shame would never betide,
With truth for my creed and God for my guide;
She taught me to lisp my earliest prayer,
As I knelt beside that old arm-chair.

I sat and watched her many a day,
When her eye grew dim, and her locks grew gray;
And I almost worshiped her when she smiled,
And turned from her Bible to bless her child.
Years rolled on; but the last one sped:
My idol was shattered, my earth-star fled;
I learnt how much the heart can bear,
When I saw her die in that old arm-chair.

'Tis past, 'tis past; but I gaze on it now
With quivering breath and throbbing brow:
'Twas there she nursed me; 'twas there she died:
And Memory flows with lava tide.
Say it is folly, and deem me weak,
While the scalding drops start down my cheek:
But I love it, I love it; and cannot tear
My soul from a mother's old arm-chair.

ELIZA COOK.

SONG OF STEAM

HARNESS me down with your iron bands,
    Be sure of your curb and rein,
    For I scorn the strength of your puny hands
        As the tempest scorns a chain.
How I laughed, as I lay concealed from sight
    For many a countless hour,
At the childish boast of human might,
    And the pride of human power!

When I saw an army upon the land,
    A navy upon the seas,
Creeping along, a snail-like band,
    Or waiting the wayward breeze;
When I marked the peasant faintly reel,
    With the toil that he daily bore,
As he feebly turned the tardy wheel,
    Or tugged at the weary oar;

When I measured the panting courser's speed,
    The flight of the carrier dove,
As they bore the law a king decreed,
    Or the lines of impatient love;—

I could but think how the world would feel,
    As these were outstripped afar,
When I should be bound to the rushing keel,
    Or chained to the flying car!

Ha! ha! ha! they found me at last;
    They invited me forth at length:
And I rushed to my throne with a thunder-blast,
    And laughed in my iron strength:
Oh! then ye saw a wondrous change
    On the earth and ocean wide,
Where now my fiery armies range,
    Nor wait for wind or tide.

Hurrah! hurrah! the waters o'er,
    The mountain's steep decline;
Time, space, have yielded to my power,
    The world — the world is mine!
The rivers the sun hath earliest blest,
    Or those where his beams decline,
The giant streams of the queenly West,
    Or the Orient floods divine.

The Ocean pales wherever I sweep,
    To hear my strength rejoice;
And monsters of the briny deep
    Cower, trembling, at my voice.
I carry the wealth of the lord of earth,
    The thoughts of his godlike mind;
The wind lags after my going forth,
    The lightning is left behind.

In the darksome depths of the fathomless mine,
    My tireless arm doth play,
Where the rocks ne'er saw the sun's decline,
    Or the dawn of the glorious day;
I bring earth's glittering jewels up
    From the hidden caves below,
And I make the fountain's granite cup
    With a crystal gush o'erflow.

I blow the bellows, I forge the steel,
    In all the shops of trade;
I hammer the ore, and turn the wheel
    Where my arms of strength are made;

I manage the furnace, the mill, the mint,
  I carry, I spin, I weave;
And all my doings I put in print
  On every Saturday eve.

I've no muscles to weary, no brains to decay,
  No bones to be "laid on the shelf";
And soon I intend you may "go and play,"
  While I manage the world myself.
But harness me down with your iron bands;
  Be sure of your curb and rein;
For I scorn the strength of your puny hands,
  As the tempest scorns a chain.

                    GEORGE W. CUTTER.

TUBAL CAIN

OLD Tubal Cain was a man of might,
    In the days when earth was young;
By the fierce red light of his furnace bright,
    The strokes of his hammer rung;
And he lifted high his brawny hand
  On the iron glowing clear,
Till the sparks rushed out in scarlet showers,
  As he fashioned the sword and spear.
And he sang, "Hurrah for my handiwork!
  Hurrah for the spear and the sword!
Hurrah for the hand that shall wield them well,
  For he shall be king and lord!"

To Tubal Cain came many a one,
  As he wrought by his roaring fire,
And each one prayed for a strong steel blade
  As the crown of his desire;
And he made them weapons sharp and strong,
  Till they shouted loud for glee,
And gave him gifts of pearl and gold,
  And spoils of the forest free.
And they said, "Hurrah for Tubal Cain,
  Who hath given us strength anew!
Hurrah for the smith, hurrah for the fire,
  And hurrah for the metal true!"

But a sudden change came o'er his heart
　　Ere the setting of the sun,
And Tubal Cain was filled with pain
　　For the evil he had done:
He saw that men with rage and hate
　　Made war upon their kind,
That the land was red with the blood they shed
　　In their lust for carnage blind.
And he said, "Alas that ever I made,
　　Or that skill of mine should plan,
The spear and the sword for men whose joy
　　Is to slay their fellow-man!"

And for many a day old Tubal Cain
　　Sat brooding o'er his woe;
And his hand forbore to smite the ore,
　　And his furnace smoldered low.
But he rose at last with a cheerful face,
　　And a bright courageous eye,
And bared his strong right arm for work,
　　While the quick flames mounted high;
And he sang, "Hurrah for my handiwork!"
　　And the red sparks lit the air:
"Not alone for the blade was the bright steel
　　　made,"—
　　And he fashioned the first plowshare.

And men, taught wisdom from the past,
　　In friendship joined their hands,
Hung the sword in the hall, the spear on the wall,
　　And plowed the willing lands;
And sung, "Hurrah for Tubal Cain!
　　Our stanch good friend is he;
And for the plowshare and the plow
　　To him our praise shall be.
But while oppression lifts its head,
　　Or a tyrant would be lord,
Though we may thank him for the plow,
　　We'll not forget the sword!"

CHARLES MACKAY.

DIFFERENCES

THE king can drink the best of wine —
    So can I;
And has enough when he would dine —
    So have I;
And cannot order rain or shine —
    Nor can I.
Then where's the difference — let me see —
Betwixt my lord the king and me?

Do trusty friends surround his throne
    Night and day?
Or make his interest their own?
    No, not they.
Mine love me for myself alone —
    Blessed be they!
And that's the difference which I see
Betwixt my lord the king and me.

Do knaves around me lie in wait
    To deceive?
Or fawn and flatter when they hate,
    And would grieve?
Or cruel pomps oppress my state
    By my leave?
No, Heaven be thanked! And here you see
More difference 'twixt the king and me.

He has his fools, with jests and quips,
    When he'd play;
He has his armies and his ships —
    Great are they;
But not a child to kiss his lips —
    Well-a-day!
And that's a difference sad to see
Betwixt my lord the king and me.

I wear the cap and he the crown —
    What of that?
I sleep on straw and he on down —
    What of that?
And he's the king and I'm the clown —
    What of that?
If happy I, and wretched he,
Perhaps the king would change with me.

CHARLES MACKAY.

STONEWALL JACKSON'S WAY

COME, stack arms, men! Pile on the rails,
 Stir up the camp-fire bright;
No growling if the canteen fails,
 We'll make a roaring night.
Here Shenandoah brawls along,
There burly Blue Ridge echoes strong,
To swell the brigade's rousing song
 Of "Stonewall Jackson's way."

We see him now—the queer slouched hat
 Cocked o'er his eye askew;
The shrewd, dry smile; the speech so pat,
 So calm, so blunt, so true.
The "Blue-Light Elder" knows 'em well:
Says he, "That's Banks—he's fond of shell;
Lord save his soul! we'll give him—" Well!
 That's "Stonewall Jackson's way."

Silence! ground arms! kneel all! caps off!
 Old Blue Light's goin' to pray.
Strangle the fool that dares to scoff!
 Attention! it's his way.
Appealing from his native sod,
In forma pauperis to God:—
"Lay bare thine arm; stretch forth thy rod!
 Amen!" That's "Stonewall Jackson's way."

He's in the saddle now. Fall in!
 Steady! the whole brigade!
Hill's at the ford, cut off; we'll win
 His way out, ball and blade!
What matter if our shoes are worn?
What matter if our feet are torn?
"Quick step! we're with him before morn!"
 That's "Stonewall Jackson's way."

The sun's bright lances rout the mists
 Of morning, and, by George!
Here's Longstreet, struggling in the lists,
 Hemmed in an ugly gorge;
Pope and his Dutchman, whipped before.
"Bay'nets and grape!" hear Stonewall roar;
"Charge, Stuart! Pay off Ashby's score!"
 In "Stonewall Jackson's way."

Ah, maidens, wait and watch and yearn
    For news of Stonewall's band!
Ah, widow, read with eyes that burn,
    That ring upon thy hand!
Ah, wife, sew on, pray on, hope on! ·
Thy life shall not be all forlorn:
The foe had better ne'er been born
    That gets in "Stonewall's way."

John Williamson Palmer.

THE CAUSE OF THE SOUTH

THE fallen cause still waits,—
    Its bard has not come yet;
His song through one of to-morrow's gates
    Shall shine, but never set.

But when he comes, he'll sweep
    A harp with tears all stringed;
And the very notes he strikes will weep
    As they come from his hand, woe-winged.

Ah! grand shall be his strain,   .
    And his songs shall fill all climes;
And the Rebels shall rise and march again
    Down the lines of his glorious rhymes.

And through his verse shall gleam
    The swords that flashed in vain;
And the men who wore the gray shall seem
    To be marshaling again.

But hush! between his words
    Peer faces sad and pale,
And you hear the sound of broken chords
    Beat through the poet's wail.

Through his verse the orphans cry —
    The terrible undertone!
And the father's curse and the mother's sigh,
    And the desolate young wife's moan. . . .

I sing, with a voice too low
    To be heard beyond to-day,
In minor keys of my people's woe;
    And my songs will pass away.

To-morrow hears them not,—
  To-morrow belongs to fame:
My songs, like the birds', will be forgot,
  And forgotten shall be my name.

And yet, who knows! betimes
  The grandest songs depart,
While the gentle, humble, and low-toned rhymes
  Will echo from heart to heart.

ABRAM J. RYAN.

THE AULD STUARTS BACK AGAIN

THE auld Stuarts back again,
  The auld Stuarts back again;
    Let howlet Whig do what they can,
  The Stuarts will be back again.
Wha cares for a' their creeshy duds,
And a' Kilmarnock sowen suds?
We'll wauk their hides and file their fuds,
  And bring the Stuarts back again.

There's Ayr and Irvine, wi' the rest,
And a' the cronies i' the west,
Lord! sic a scawed and scabbit nest!
  How they'll set up their crack again!
But wad they come, or dare they come,
Afore the bagpipe and the drum,
We'll either gar them a' sing dumb,
  Or "Auld Stuarts back again."

Give ear unto my loyal sang,
A' ye that ken the right frae wrang,
And a' that look and think it lang,
  For auld Stuarts back again.
Were ye wi' me to chase the rae,
Out owre the hills and far away,
And saw the lords were there that day,
  To bring the Stuarts back again.

There ye might see the noble Mar,
Wi' Athol, Huntly, and Traquair,
Seaforth, Kilsyth, and Auldubair,
  And mony mae, whatreck, again.

Then what are a' their westland crews?
We'll gar the tailors tack again:
Can they forestand the tartan trews,
And auld Stuarts back again?

Anonymous Jacobite Song, 1714.

THE HEATH-COCK

THE heath-cock crawed o'er muir an' dale;
Red rase the sun o'er distant vale;
Our Northern clans, wi' distant yell,
　　Around their chiefs were gathering.

"O Duncan, are ye ready yet,
M'Donald, are ye ready yet,
O Frazer, are ye ready yet,
　　To join the clans in the morning?"

Nae mair we'll chase the fleet, fleet roe
O'er dowie glen or mountain brow,
But rush like tempest on the foe,
　　Wi' sword an' targe this morning.

"O Duncan," etc.

The Prince has come to claim his ain,
A stem o' Stuart's glorious name;
What Highlander his sword wad hain
　　For Charlie's cause this morning?

"O Duncan," etc.

On yonder hills our clans appear,
The sun back frae their spears shines clear;
The Southron trumps fall on my ear;—
　　'Twill be an awfu' morning.

"O Duncan," etc.

The contest lasted sair an' lang;
The pipers blew, the echoes rang;
The cannon roared the clans amang,
　　Culloden's awfu' morning.

Duncan now nae mair seems keen;
He's lost his dirk an' tartan sheen;
His bannet's stained that ance was clean;—
Foul fa' that awfu' morning.

But Scotland lang shall rue the day
She saw her flag sae fiercely flee;
Culloden hills were hills o' wae,—
　　It was an awfu' morning.

　　　Duncan now, etc.

Fair Flora's gane her love to seek;
The midnight dew fa's on her cheek;—
What Scottish heart that will not weep
　　For Charlie's fate that morning?

　　　Duncan now nae mair seems keen;
　　　He's lost his dirk an' tartan sheen;
　　　His bannet's stained that ance was clean;—
　　　Foul fa' that awfu' morning.

WILLIAM NICHOLSON.

WHAT'S A' THE STEER, KIMMER?

HE

WHAT'S a' the steer, kimmer?
　　What's a' the steer?

SHE

Charlie he is landed,
　　An', faith, he'll soon be here.
The win' was at his back, carle,
　　The win' was at his back;
I carena, sin' he's come, carle,
　　We were na worth a plack.

HE

I'm right glad to hear 't, kimmer,
　　I'm right glad to hear 't;
I ha'e a gude braid claymore,
　　And for his sake I'll wear 't.

TOGETHER

Sin' Charlie he is landed,
　　We ha'e nae mair to fear;
Sin' Charlie he is come, kimmer,
　　We'll ha'e a jub'lee year.

ROBERT ALLAN.

WAE'S ME FOR PRINCE CHARLIE!

A WEE bird came to our ha' door;
    He warbled sweet and clearly;
And aye the o'ercome o' his sang
    Was "Wae's me for Prince Charlie!"
Oh, when I heard the bonny, bonny bird,
    The tears came drapping rarely;
I took my bonnet aff my head,
    For weel I lo'ed Prince Charlie.

Quoth I: "My bird, my bonny, bonny bird,
    Is that a tale ye borrow?
Or is 't some words ye've learned by rote,
    Or a lilt o' dool and sorrow?"
"Oh no, no, no!" the wee bird sang:
    "I've flown sin' morning early;
But sic a day o' wind and rain!—
    Oh, wae's me for Prince Charlie!

"On hills that are by right his ain
    He roams a lonely stranger;
On ilka hand he's pressed by want,
    On ilka side by danger.
Yestreen I met him in the glen,—
    My heart near bursted fairly;
For sadly changed indeed was he —
    Oh, wae's me for Prince Charlie!

"Dark night came on; the tempest howled
    Out owre the hills and valleys:
And where was 't that your prince lay down,
    Whase hame should be a palace?
He rowed him in a Highland plaid,
    Which covered him but sparely,
And slept beneath a bush o' broom —
    Oh, wae's me for Prince Charlie!"

But now the bird saw some redcoats,
    And he shook his wings wi' anger:
"Oh, this is no a land for me —
    I'll tarry here nae langer."
Awhile he hovered on the wing,
    Ere he departed fairly;
But weel I mind the farewell strain —
    'Twas "Wae's me for Prince Charlie!"

WILLIAM GLEN.

THE WEAVING OF THE TARTAN

I SAW an old dame weaving,
    Weaving, weaving,
I saw an old dame weaving
    A web of tartan fine.
"Sing high," she said, "sing low," she said,
    "Wild torrent to the sea,
That saw my exiled bairnies torn
    In sorrow far frae me.
And warp well the long threads,
The bright threads, the strong threads,
    Woof well the cross threads,
    To make the colors shine."

She wove in red for every deed
Of valor done for Scotia's need;
She wove in green, the laurel's sheen,
In memory of her glorious dead.
    She spake of Alma's steep incline,
    The desert march, the "thin red line";
Of how it fired the blood and stirred the heart
    Where'er a bairn of hers took part.
    "'Tis for the gallant lads," she said,
    "Who wear the kilt and tartan plaid;
'Tis for the winsome lasses too,
Just like my dainty bells of blue:
So weave well the bright threads,
The red threads, the green threads,
Woof well the strong threads
    That bind their hearts to mine."

I saw an old dame sighing,
    Sighing, sighing;
I saw an old dame sighing,
    Beside a lonely glen.
"Sing high," she said, "sing low," she said,
    "Wild tempest to the sea,
The wailing of the pibroch's note,
    That bade farewell to me.
And wae fa' the red deer,
The swift deer, the strong deer,
Wae fa' the cursed deer,
    That take the place o' men."

Where'er a noble deed is wrought,
Where'er the brightest realms of thought,
The artist's skill, the martial thrill,
Be sure to Scotia's land is wed.
She casts the glamour of her name
O'er Britain's throne and statesman's fame;
From distant lands 'neath foreign names,
Some brilliant son his birthright claims.
For ah! she has reared them mid tempests,
   And cradled them in snow,
To give the Scottish arms their strength,
   Their hearts a kindly glow.
So weave well the bright threads,
The red threads, the green threads,
Woof well the strong threads,
   That bind their hearts to thine.

              ALICE C. MACDONELL.

MUCKLE-MOU'D MEG

"OH, WHA hae ye brought us hame now, my brave lord,
   Strappit flaught ower his braid saddle-bow?
Some bauld Border reiver to feast at our board
   An' herry our pantry, I trow.
He's buirdly an' stalwart in lith an' in limb:
   Gin ye were his master in war
The field was a saft eneugh litter for him —
   Ye needna hae brought him sae far;—
Then saddle an' munt again, harness an' dunt again,
An' when ye gae hunt again, strike higher game." —

"Hoot, whist ye, my dame, for he comes o' gude kin,
   An' boasts o' a lang pedigree;
This night he maun share o' our gude cheer within,
   At morning's gray dawn he maun dee.
He's gallant Wat Scott, heir o' proud Harden Ha',
   Wha ettled our lands clear to sweep;
But now he is snug in auld Elibank's paw,
   An' shall swing frae our donjon-keep.
Though saddle an' munt again, harness an' dunt again,
I'll ne'er when I hunt again strike higher game." —

"Is this young Wat Scott? an' wad ye rax his craig,
　　When our daughter is fey for a man?
Gae, gaur the loun marry our muckle-mou'd Meg,
　　Or we'll ne'er get the jaud aff our han'!"—
"'Od, hear our gudewife! she wad fain save your life;—
　　Wat Scott, will ye marry or hang?"
But Meg's muckle mou set young Wat's heart agrue,
　　Wha swore to the woodie he'd gang.
Ne'er saddle nor munt again, harness nor dunt again,
Wat ne'er shall hunt again, ne'er see his hame.

Syne muckle-mou'd Meg pressed in close to his side,
　　An' blinkit fu' sleely and kind;
But aye as Wat glowered on his braw proffered bride,
　　He shook like a leaf in the wind.
"A bride or a gallows; a rope or a wife!"
　　The morning dawned sunny and clear:
Wat boldly strode forward to part wi' his life,
　　Till he saw Meggy shedding a tear;
Then saddle an' munt again, harness an' dunt again,
Fain wad Wat hunt again, fain wad he hame.

Meg's tear touched his bosom—the gibbet frowned high—
　　An' slowly Wat strode to his doom;
He gae a glance round wi' a tear in his eye,—
　　Meg shone like a star through the gloom.
She rushed to his arms; they were wed on the spot,
　　An' lo'ed ither muckle and lang.
Nae bauld border laird had a wife like Wat Scott:
　　'Twas better to marry than hang.
So saddle an' munt again, harness an' dunt again,
Elibank hunt again, Wat's snug at hame.

JAMES BALLANTYNE.

YE GENTLEMEN OF ENGLAND

YE GENTLEMEN of England
　　That live at home at ease,
Ah! little do you think upon
　　The dangers of the seas.
Give ear unto the mariners,
　　And they will plainly show
All the cares and the fears
　　When the stormy winds do blow.

If enemies oppose us
    When England is at war
With any foreign nation,
    We fear not wound or scar:
Our roaring guns shall teach 'em
    Our valor for to know,
Whilst they reel on the keel,
    And the stormy winds do blow.

Then courage, all brave mariners,
    And never be dismayed:
While we have bold adventurers,
    We-ne'er shall want a trade;'
Our merchants will employ us
    To fetch them wealth, we know:
Then be bold — work for gold,
    When the stormy winds do blow.

MARTYN PARKER.

HANDS ALL ROUND

FIRST drink a health, this solemn night,
    A health to England, every guest:
That man's the best cosmopolite
    Who loves his native country best.
May freedom's oak for ever live
    With stronger life from day to day:
That man's the best Conservative
    Who lops the moldered branch away.
    Hands all round!
    God the tyrant's hope confound!
To this great cause of Freedom drink, my friends,
And the great name of England, round and round.

A health to Europe's honest men!
    Heaven guard them from her tyrants' jails!
From wronged Poerio's noisome den,
    From iron limbs and tortured nails!
We curse the crimes of southern kings,
    The Russian whips and Austrian rods:
We likewise have our evil things,—
    Too much we make our ledgers, gods.

Yet hands all round!
God the tyrant's cause confound!
To Europe's better health we drink, my friends,
And the great name of England, round and round!

What health to France, if France be she,
    Whom martial progress only charms?
Yet tell her — better to be free
    Than vanquish all the world in arms.
Her frantic city's flashing heats
    But fire, to blast the hopes of men.
Why change the titles of your streets?
    You fools, you'll want them all again.
        Hands all round!
    God the tyrant's cause confound!
To France, the wiser France, we drink, my friends,
And the great name of England, round and round.

Gigantic daughter of the West,
    We drink to thee across the flood!
We know thee and we love thee best;
    For art thou not of British blood?
Should war's mad blast again be blown,
    Permit not thou the tyrant powers
To fight thy mother here alone,
    But let thy broadsides roar with ours.
        Hands all round!
    God the tyrant's cause confound!
To our great kinsman of the West, my friends,
And the great name of England, round and round.

Oh rise, our strong Atlantic sons,
    When war against our freedom springs!
Oh, speak to Europe through your guns!
    They *can* be understood by kings.
You must not mix our Queen with those
    That wish to keep their people fools:
Our freedom's foemen are her foes;
    She comprehends the race she rules.
        Hands all round!
    God the tyrant's cause confound!
To our great kinsmen in the West, my friends,
And the great cause of Freedom, round and round.

ALFRED TENNYSON.

RECESSIONAL

In the London Times at the end of the Queen's Jubilee, 1897

GOD of our fathers, known of old,
     Lord of our far-flung battle-line,
   Beneath whose awful hand we hold
     Dominion over palm and pine —
Lord God of Hosts, be with us yet,
Lest we forget — lest we forget!

The tumult and the shouting dies;
   The captains and the kings depart:
Still stands thine ancient sacrifice,
   An humble and a contrite heart.
Lord God of Hosts, be with us yet,
Lest we forget — lest we forget!

Far-called, our navies melt away;
   On dune and headland sinks the fire:
Lo, all our pomp of yesterday
   Is one with Nineveh and Tyre!
Judge of the nations, spare us yet,
Lest we forget — lest we forget!

If, drunk with sight of power, we loose
   Wild tongues that have not thee in awe,—
Such boasting as the Gentiles use,
   Or lesser breeds without the Law,—
Lord God of Hosts, be with us yet,
Lest we forget — lest we forget!

For heathen heart that puts her trust
   In reeking tube and iron shard,—
All valiant dust that builds on dust,
   And guarding, calls not thee to guard,—
For frantic boast and foolish word,
Thy mercy on thy people, Lord!
                         Amen.

                    RUDYARD KIPLING.

THE STAR-SPANGLED BANNER

O SAY, can you see by the dawn's early light
　　What so proudly we hailed at the twilight's last gleam-
　　　　ing?—
Whose broad stripes and bright stars through the perilous fight,
　　O'er the ramparts we watched, were so gallantly streaming!
And the rocket's red glare, the bombs bursting in air,
Gave proof through the night that our flag was still there:
O say, does that star-spangled banner yet wave
O'er the land of the free and the home of the brave?

On that shore dimly seen through the mists of the deep,
　　Where the foe's haughty host in dread silence reposes,
What is that which the breeze, o'er the towering steep,
　　As it fitfully blows, now conceals, now discloses?
Now it catches the gleam of the morning's first beam,
Its full glory reflected now shines on the stream:
'Tis the star-spangled banner; oh, long may it wave
O'er the land of the free and the home of the brave!

And where is that band who so vauntingly swore
　　That the havoc of war and the battle's confusion
A home and a country should leave us no more?
　　Their blood has washed out their foul footsteps' pollution.
No refuge could save the hireling and slave
From the terror of flight, or the gloom of the grave;
And the star-spangled banner in triumph doth wave
O'er the land of the free and the home of the brave.

Oh, thus be it ever, when freemen shall stand
　　Between their loved homes and the war's desolation!
Blest with victory and peace, may the heaven-rescued land
　　Praise the power that hath made and preserved us a nation.
Then conquer we must, for our cause it is just;
And this be our motto,—"In God is our trust:"
And the star-spangled banner in triumph shall wave
O'er the land of the free and the home of the brave.

FRANCIS SCOTT KEY.

THE MARSEILLAISE.

Roguet de Lisle singing his famous song before the Mayor of Strasburg.
Photogravure from a painting by Pils.

THE MARSEILLAISE

YE SONS of Freedom, wake to glory!
 Hark! hark! what myriads bid you rise!
Your children, wives, and grandsires hoary,
 Behold their tears and hear their cries!
Shall hateful tyrants, mischiefs breeding,
 With hireling hosts, a ruffian band,
Affright and desolate the land,
While peace and liberty lie bleeding?
 To arms! to arms! ye brave!
 The avenging sword unsheathe;
 March on! march on! all hearts resolved
 On victory or death!

Now, now the dangerous storm is rolling,
 Which treacherous kings confederate raise;
The dogs of war, let loose, are howling,
 And lo! our fields and cities blaze:
And shall we basely view the ruin,
 While lawless force, with guilty stride,
 Spreads desolation far and wide,
With crimes and blood his hands imbruing?
 To arms! to arms! ye brave!
 The avenging sword unsheathe;
 March on! march on! all hearts resolved
 On victory or death!

O Liberty! can man resign thee,
 Once having felt thy generous flame?
Can dungeons, bolts, or bars confine thee?
 Or whips thy noble spirit tame?
Too long the world has wept, bewailing
 That falsehood's dagger tyrants wield;
 But freedom is our sword and shield,
And all their arts are unavailing.
 To arms! to arms! ye brave!
 The avenging sword unsheathe;
 March on! march on! all hearts resolved
 On victory or death!

(Abbreviated.)   ROUGET DE LISLE.

THE DEPARTURE FOR SYRIA

(LE DÉPART 1809, POUR LA SYRIE)

[The music of this song, which was composed by Queen Hortense, mother of Napoleon III., became the national air of the French Empire.]

TO SYRIA young Dunois will go,
    That gallant, handsome knight,
And prays the Virgin to bestow
    Her blessing on the fight.
"O Thou who reign'st in heaven above,"
    He prayed, "grant this to me:
The fairest maiden let me love,
    The bravest warrior be."

He pledges then his knightly word,
    His vow writes on the stone,
And following the count, his lord,
    To battle he has gone.
To keep his oath he ever strove,
    And sang aloud with glee,
"The fairest maid shall have my love,
    And honor mine shall be."

Then said the count, "To thee we owe
    Our victory, I confess;
Glory on me thou didst bestow,—
    I give thee happiness:
My daughter, whom I fondly love,
    I gladly give to thee;
She, who is fair all maids above,
    Should valor's guerdon be."

They kneel at Mary's altar both,—
    The maid and gallant knight,—
And there with happy hearts their troth
    Right solemnly they plight.
It was a sight all souls to move;
    And all cried joyously,
"Give honor to the brave, and love
    Shall beauty's guerdon be."

             M. DE LABORDE.

THE WATCH ON THE RHINE

A VOICE resounds like thunder-peal,
    'Mid dashing waves and clang of steel:—
    "The Rhine, the Rhine, the German Rhine!
Who guards to-day my stream divine?"

Chorus

    Dear Fatherland, no danger thine:
    Firm stand thy sons to watch the Rhine!

They stand, a hundred thousand strong,
Quick to avenge their country's wrong;
With filial love their bosoms swell,
They'll guard the sacred landmark well!

The dead of a heroic race
From heaven look down and meet their gaze;
They swear with dauntless heart, "O Rhine,
Be German as this breast of mine!"

While flows one drop of German blood,
Or sword remains to guard thy flood,
While rifle rests in patriot hand,—
No foe shall tread thy sacred strand!

Our oath resounds, the river flows,
In golden light our banner glows;
Our hearts will guard thy stream divine:
The Rhine, the Rhine, the German Rhine!

                  MAX SCHNECKENBURGER.

A CINQUE PORT

B ELOW the down, the stranded town
    What may betide forlornly waits;
    With memories of smoky skies,
      When Gallic navies crossed the straits,
When waves with fire and blood grew bright,
And cannon thundered through the night.

With swinging stride the rhythmic tide
    Bore to the harbor barque and sloop;

Across the bar the ship of war,
    In castled stern and lanterned poop,
Came up with conquests on her lee,
The stately mistress of the sea.

Where argosies have wooed the breeze,
    The simple sheep are feeding now;
And near and far across the bar
    The plowman whistles at the plow;
Where once the long waves washed the shore,
Larks from their lowly lodgings soar.

Below the down the stranded town
    Hears far away the rollers beat;
About the wall the sea-birds call;
    The salt wind murmurs through the street:
Forlorn, the sea's forsaken bride
Awaits the end that shall betide.

                            JOHN DAVIDSON.
From 'Ballads and Songs.'

APRIL IN IRELAND

SHE hath a woven garland all of the sighing sedge,
    And all her flowers are snowdrops grown in the winter's edge;
    The golden looms of Tir na n'Og wove all the winter through
Her gown of mist and raindrops shot with a cloudy blue.

Sunlight she holds in one hand, and rain she scatters after,
And through the rainy twilight we hear her fitful laughter.
She shakes down on her flowers the snows less white than they,
Then quickens with her kisses the folded "knots o' May."

She seeks the summer-lover that never shall be hers;
Fain for gold leaves of autumn she passes by the furze,
Though buried gold it hideth; she scorns her sedgy crown,
And pressing blindly sunwards she treads her snowdrops down.

Her gifts are all a fardel of wayward smiles and tears,
Yet hope she also holdeth, this daughter of the years—
A hope that blossoms faintly set upon sorrow's edge:
She hath a woven garland all of the sighing sedge.

                            NORA HOPPER.

ADIEU FOR EVERMORE

[Tennyson once quoted to Ruskin this stanza as the most romantic of lyrics; and Ruskin said he knew it well, and that it was among the best things ever done by anybody.

> He turned his charger as he spake,
> Upon the river shore,
> He gave his bridle-reins a shake,
> Said Adieu for evermore,
> My love!
> And adieu for evermore.

Scott used it in 'Rokeby.' Its original is the old Scotch ballad which follows.]

"IT WAS a' for our rightful king,
That we left fair Scotland's strand,
It was a' for our rightful king,
That we e'er saw Irish land,
My dear,
That we e'er saw Irish land.

"Now all is done that man can do,
And all is done in vain,
My love! My native land, adieu!
For I must cross the main,
My dear,
For I must cross the main."

He turned him round and right about,
All on the Irish shore,
He gave his bridle-reins a shake,
With "Adieu for evermore,
My dear!
Adieu for evermore!

"The soldier frae the war returns,
And the marchant frae the main,
But I hae parted wi' my love,
And ne'er to meet again,
My dear,
And ne'er to meet again.

"When the day is gone and night is come,
And a' are boun' to sleep,
I think on them that's far awa
The lee-lang night, and weep,
My dear,
The lee-lang night, and weep."

WILLY REILLY

[The story on which this ballad is founded happened some eighty years ago; and as the lover was a young Catholic farmer, and the lady's family of high Orange principles, it got a party character which, no doubt, contributed to its great popularity.]

"O RISE up, Willy Reilly! and come along with me;
   I mean for to go with you and leave this counterie,—
   To leave my father's dwelling, his houses and free
      land:"
And away goes Willy Reilly and his dear Coolen Bawn.*

They go by hills and mountains, and by yon lonesome plain,
Through shady groves and valleys all dangers to refrain;
But her father followed after with a well-armèd band,
And taken was poor Reilly and his dear Coolen Bawn.

It's home then she was taken, and in her closet bound;
Poor Reilly all in Sligo jail lay on the stony ground,
'Till at the bar of justice before the judge he'd stand,
For nothing but the stealing of his dear Coolen Bawn.

"Now in the cold, cold iron my hands and feet are bound;
I'm handcuffed like a murderer, and tied unto the ground:
But all the toil and slavery I'm willing for to stand,
Still hoping to be succored by my dear Coolen Bawn."

The jailer's son to Reilly goes, and thus to him did say:—
"O get up, Willy Reilly,—you must appear this day;
For great Squire Foillard's anger you never can withstand;—
I'm afeared you'll suffer sorely for your dear Coolen Bawn.

"This is the news, young Reilly, last night that I did hear:
The lady's oath will hang you or else will set you clear."
"If that be so," says Reilly, "her pleasure I will stand;
Still hoping to be succored by my dear Coolen Bawn."

Now Willy's drest from top to toe all in a suit of green;
His hair hangs o'er his shoulders most glorious to be seen;
He's tall and straight and comely as any could be found:
He's fit for Foillard's daughter, was she heiress to a crown.

The judge he said, "This lady being in her tender youth,
If Reilly has deluded her she will declare the truth."

* Cailín bán — fair girl.

Then, like a moving beauty bright, before him she did stand —
"You're welcome there, my heart's delight and dear Coolen
    Bawn."

"O gentlemen," Squire Foillard said, "with pity look on me:
This villain came amongst us to disgrace our family;
And by his base contrivances this villainy was planned.
If I don't get satisfaction I'll quit this Irish land."

The lady with a tear began, and thus replièd she: —
"The fault is none of Reilly's, — the blame lies all on me:
I forced him for to leave his place, and come along with me; —
I loved him out of measure, which wrought our destiny."

Out bespoke the noble Fox, — at the table he stood by, —
"O gentlemen, consider on this extremity!
To hang a man for love is a murder you may see:
So spare the life of Reilly, — let him leave this counterie." —

"Good my lord, he stole from her her diamonds and her rings,
Gold watch and silver buckles, and many precious things,
Which cost me in bright guineas more than five hundred pounds.
I'll have the life of Reilly should I lose ten thousand pounds." —

"Good my lord, I gave them him as tokens of true love;
And when we are a-parting I will them all remove. —
If you have got them, Reilly, pray send them home to me." —
"I will, my loving lady, with many thanks to thee." —

"There is a ring among them I allow yourself to wear,
With thirty locket diamonds well set in silver fair;
And as a true-love token wear it on your right hand,
That you'll think on my poor broken heart when you're in foreign
    lands."

Then out spoke noble Fox, "You may let the prisoner go:
The lady's oath has cleared him, as the jury all may know;
She has released her own true love, she has renewed his name; —
May her honor bright gain high estate, and her offspring rise to
    fame."

An Ulster Ballad.

THERE'S NAE LUCK ABOUT THE HOUSE

AND are ye sure the news is true?
   And are ye sure he's weel?
Is this a time to think o' wark?
   Ye jauds, fling by your wheel!
Is this a time to think o' wark,
   When Colin's at the door?
Rax me my cloak,—I'll to the quay
   And see him come ashore.
For there's nae luck about the house,
   There's nae luck at a',
There's little pleasure in the house
   When our gudeman's awa'.

And gie to me my bigonet,
   My bishop's-satin gown,—
For I maun tell the bailie's wife
   That Colin's come to town;
My Turkey slippers maun gae on,
   My hose o' pearl-blue:
It's a' to pleasure my ain gudeman,
   For he's baith leal and true.

Rise up and mak a clean fireside,
   Put on the muckle pot;
Gie little Kate her Sunday gown,
   And Jock his button coat;
And mak their shoon as black as slaes,
   Their hose as white as snaw:
It's a' to please my ain gudeman,
   For he's been long awa'.

There's twa fat hens upo' the bank,—
   They've fed this month and mair,—
Mak haste and thraw their necks about,
   That Colin weel may fare;
And spread the table neat and clean,
   Gar ilka thing look braw:
For wha can tell how Colin fared
   When he was far awa'?

Sae true his heart, sae smooth his speech,
   His breath like caller air;
His very foot has music in 't
   As he comes up the stair.

And will I see his face again?
　　And will I hear him speak?
I'm downright dizzit wi' the thought—
　　In troth I'm like to greet!

Since Colin's weel, I'm weel content—
　　I hae nae mair to crave; ,
Could I but live to mak him blest,
　　I'm blest aboon the lave:
And will I see his face again?
　　And will I hear him speak?
I'm downright dizzit wi' the thought,
　　In troth I'm like to greet.
For there's nae luck about the house,
　　There's nae luck at a':
There's little pleasure in the house
　　When our gudeman's awa'.

　　　　　　　　　JEAN ADAM.

«IT'S HAME, AND IT'S HAME»

IT'S hame, and it's hame, hame fain wad I be,
　　An' it's hame, hame, hame, to my ain countrie!
　　When the flower is i' the bud, and the leaf is on the tree,
The lark shall sing me hame in my ain countrie.
It's hame, and it's hame, hame fain wad I be,
And it's hame, hame, hame, to my ain countrie!

The green leaf o' loyalty's beginning for to fa';
The bonny white rose it is withering an' a':
But I'll water 't wi' the blude of usurping tyrannie,
An' green it will grow in my ain countrie.
It's hame, and it's hame, hame fain wad I be,
And it's hame, hame, hame, to my ain countrie!

There's naught now frae ruin my country can save,—
But the keys o' kind heaven to open the grave;
That a' the noble martyrs wha died for loyaltie,
May rise again and fight for their ain countrie.
It's hame, and it's hame, hame fain wad I be,
An' it's hame, hame, hame, to my ain countrie!

The great now are gane, a' wha ventured to save,—
The new grass is springing on the tap o' their grave;

But the sun through the mirk blinks blithe in my ee—
"I'll shine on ye yet in yer ain countrie."
It's hame, and it's hame, hame fain wad I be,
An' it's hame, hame, hame, to my ain countrie.

ALLAN CUNNINGHAM.

ITS AIN DRAP O' DEW

CONFIDE ye aye in Providence,
    For Providence is kind;
An' bear ye a' life's changes
    Wi' a calm and tranquil mind.
Though pressed and hemmed on every side,
    Ha'e faith, an' ye'll win through;
        For ilka blade o' grass
            Keeps its ain drap o' dew.

Gin reft frae friends, or crossed in love,
    As whiles nae doubt ye've been,
Grief lies deep-hidden in your heart,
    Or tears flow frae your e'en,
Believe it for the best, and trow
    There's good in store for you;
        For ilka blade o' grass
            Keeps its ain drap o' dew.

In lang, lang days o' simmer,
    When the clear and cloudless sky
Refuses ae wee drap o' rain
    To nature, parched and dry,
The genial night, with balmy breath,
    Gars verdure spring anew,
        An' ilka blade o' grass
            Keeps its ain drap o' dew.

Sae lest 'mid fortune's sunshine
    We should feel ower proud an' hie,
An' in our pride forget to wipe
    The tear frae poortith's e'e,
Some wee dark clouds o' sorrow come,
    We ken na whence or hoo;
        But ilka blade o' grass
            Keeps its ain drap o' dew.

THOMAS AIRD.

MINE OWN WORK

I MADE the cross myself whose weight
　　Was later laid on me:
This thought is torture as I toil
　　Up life's steep Calvary.

To think mine own hands drove the nails!
　　I sung a merry song,
And chose the heaviest wood I had
　　To build it firm and strong.

If I had guessed — if I had dreamed
　　Its weight was made for me,
I should have made a lighter cross
　　To bear up Calvary.

　　　　　ANNE REEVE ALDRICH.

DEPARTURE

NOT as in prison pent,
　　Not as a spirit sent
　　　To baser banishment,
I tarried well content
　　The body's guest.

Whithersoe'er I fly,
Let me not wholly die! —
Yet He who shall deny
Or grant this parting cry
　　Knows which is best.

　　　　　WILLIAM CRANSTON LAWTON.

LIFE

AS A shaft that is sped from a bow unseen to an unseen mark,
　　As a bird that gleams in the firelight, and hurries from dark
　　　to dark,
As the face of the stranger who smiled as we passed in the crowded
　　　street, —
Our life is a glimmer, a flutter, a memory, fading, yet sweet!

　　　　　WILLIAM CRANSTON LAWTON.

THE CLOSING DOORS

EILIDH, Eilidh, Eilidh, heart of me, dear and sweet!
    In dreams I am hearing the whisper, the sound of your com-
        ing feet;
The sound of your coming feet that like the sea-hoofs beat
A music by day and night, Eilidh, on the sands of my heart, my
    sweet!

O sands of my heart, what wind moans low along thy shadowy
    shore?
Is that the deep sea-heart I hear with the dying sob at its core?
Each dim lost wave that lapses is like a closing door:
'Tis closing doors they hear at last who soon shall hear no more,
        Who soon shall hear no more.

Eilidh, Eilidh, Eilidh, come home, come home to the heart o' me!
It is pain I am having ever, Eilidh, a pain that will not be.
Come home, come home, for closing doors are as the waves o' the
    sea,—
Once closed they are closed forever, Eilidh, lost, lost for thee and me,
        Lost, lost, for thee and me.

                                        FIONA MACLEOD.

A RHYME OF DEATH'S INN

A RHYME of good Death's inn!
    My love came to that door;
And she had need of many things,
    The way had been so sore.

My love she lifted up her head,
    "And is there room?" said she:
"There was no room in Bethlehem's inn
    For Christ who died for me."

But said the keeper of the inn,
    "His name is on the door."
My love then straightway entered there:
    She hath come back no more.

                                LIZETTE WOODWORTH REESE.

AFTER THE BALL

THEY sat and combed their beautiful hair,
 Their long bright tresses, one by one,
As they laughed and talked in the chamber there,
 After the revel was done.

Idly they talked of waltz and quadrille,
 Idly they laughed like other girls
Who, over the fire, when all is still,
 Comb out their braids and curls.

Robe of satin and Brussels lace,
 Knots of flowers and ribbons too,
Scattered about in every place,—
 For the revel is through.

And Maud and Madge in robes of white,
 The prettiest night-gowns under the sun,
Stockingless, slipperless, sit in the night,
 For the revel is done;

Sit and comb their beautiful hair,
 Those wonderful waves of brown and gold,
Till the fire is out in the chamber there,
 And the little bare feet are cold.

Then out of the gathering winter chill,
 All out of the bitter St. Agnes weather,
While the fire is out and the house is still,
 Maud and Madge together,—

Maud and Madge in robes of white,
 The prettiest night-gowns under the sun,—
Curtained away from the chilly night,
 After the revel is done,—

Float along in a splendid dream,
 To a golden gittern's tinkling tune,
While a thousand lustres shimmering stream
 In a palace's grand saloon.

Flashing of jewels and flutter of laces,
 Tropical odors sweeter than musk,
Men and women with beautiful faces,
 And eyes of tropical dusk;

And one face shining out like a star,
    One face haunting the dreams of each,
And one voice, sweeter than others are,
    Breaking in silvery speech,—

Telling through lips of bearded bloom
    An old, old story over again,
As down the royal bannered room,
    To the golden gittern's strain,

Two and two they dreamily walk,
    While an unseen spirit walks beside,
And all unheard in the lovers' talk
    He claimeth one for a bride.

O Maud and Madge, dream on together,
    With never a pang of jealous fear!
For ere the bitter St. Agnes weather
    Shall whiten another year,

Robed for the bridal, and robed for the tomb,
    Braided brown hair and golden tress,
There'll be only one of you left for the bloom
    Of the bearded lips to press,—

Only one for the bridal pearls,
    The robe of satin and Brussels lace,—
Only one to blush through her curls
    At the sight of a lover's face.

O beautiful Madge, in your bridal white,
    For you the revel has just begun;
But for her who sleeps in your arms to-night
    The revel of life is done!

But robed and crowned with your saintly bliss,
    Queen of heaven and bride of the sun,
O beautiful Maud, you'll never miss
    The kisses another hath won.

                NORA PERRY.

MY CHILD

I CANNOT make him dead!
His fair sunshiny head
Is ever bounding round my study chair;
Yet when my eyes, now dim
With tears, I turn to him,
The vision vanishes — he is not there!

I walk my parlor floor,
And through the open door
I hear a footfall on the chamber stair:
I'm stepping toward the hall
To give the boy a call;
And then bethink me that — he is not there.

I thread the crowded street:
A satchel'd lad I meet,
With the same beaming eyes and colored hair;
And as he's running by,
Follow him with my eye,
Scarcely believing that — *he* is not there!

I cannot make him dead!
When passing by the bed,
So long watched over with parental care,
My spirit and my eye
Seek him inquiringly,
Before the thought comes that — he is not there!

When at the cool gray break
Of day, from sleep I wake,
With my first breathing of the morning air
My soul goes up, with joy,
To Him who gave my boy:
Then comes the sad thought that — he is not there!

When at the day's calm close,
Before we seek repose,
I'm with his mother, offering up our prayer,
Whate'er I may be saying,
I am in spirit praying
For our boy's spirit, though — he is not there!

He lives! — In all the past
He lives; nor to the last,
Of seeing him again will I despair:

In dreams I see him now;
  And on his angel brow
I see it written — " Thou shalt see me *there!* "

  Yes, we all live to God!
  FATHER! thy chastening rod
So help us, thine afflicted ones, to bear,
  That in the spirit land,
  Meeting at thy right hand,
'Twill be our heaven to find that — he is there!

JOHN PIERPONT.

ARE THE CHILDREN AT HOME?

EACH day when the glow of sunset
    Fades in the western sky,
  And the wee ones, tired of playing,
    Go tripping lightly by,
I steal away from my husband,
    Asleep in his easy-chair,
And watch in the open doorway
    Their faces fresh and fair.

Alone in the dear old homestead
    That once was full of life,
Ringing with girlish laughter,
    Echoing boyish strife,
We two are waiting together;
    And oft, as the shadows come,
With tremulous voice he calls me,
    " It is night! are the children home? "

" Yes, love! " I answer him gently,
    " They're all home long ago; " —
And I sing in my quivering treble
    A song so soft and low,
Till the old man drops to slumber
    With his head upon his hand,
And I tell to myself the number
    At home in the better land.

At home, where never a sorrow
    Shall dim their eyes with tears!

Where the smile of God is on them
   Through all the summer years!
I know — yet my arms are empty,
   That fondly folded seven,
And the mother heart within me
   Is almost starved for heaven.

Sometimes in the dusk of evening
   I only shut my eyes,
And the children are all about me,
   A vision from the skies:
The babes whose dimpled fingers
   Lost the way to my breast,
And the beautiful ones, the angels,
   Passed to the world of the blest.

With never a cloud upon them,
   I see their radiant brows,
My boys that I gave to freedom —
   The red sword sealed their vows!
In a tangled Southern forest,
   Twin brothers bold and brave,
They fell; and the flag they died for,
   Thank God! floats over their grave.

A breath, and the vision is lifted
   Away on the wings of light,
And again we two are together,
   All alone in the night.
They tell me his mind is failing,
   But I smile at idle fears:
He is only back with the children,
   In the dear and peaceful years.

And still, as the summer sunset
   Fades away in the west,
And the wee ones, tired of playing,
   Go trooping home to rest,
My husband calls from his corner,
   " Say, love, have the children come ? "
And I answer, with eyes uplifted,
   " Yes, dear! they are all at home. "

MARGARET E. SANGSTER.

[Reprinted by permission of Houghton, Mifflin & Co., publishers.]

LITTLE BOY

LITTLE boy, whose great round eye
    Hath the tincture of the sky,
      Answer now, and tell me true,
Whence and what and why are you?
And he answered, "Mother's boy."—
      Yes, yes, I know,
      But 'twas not so
      Six years ago.
You are mother's anxious joy.
      Mother's pet,
      But yet—
A trouble came within the eye
That had some tincture of the sky.

I looked again: within that eye
There was a question, not reply.
I only shaded back his hair,
      And kissed him there:
      But from that day
There was more thinking and less play;
      And that round eye,
That had a tincture of the sky,
    Was somewhat shaded in its sheen;
It looked and listened far away,
    As if for what cannot be seen.

Then I turned about and cried,
      But who am I,
Prompting thus the dawning soul?
      I cannot hide
      The want of a reply,
Though traveling nearer to the goal
Where we take no note of time;
    I can only say I AM,—
A phrase, a word, that hath no rhyme,—
The name God called himself, the best
To answer the weak patriarch's quest.

"Why talk nonsense to a child?"
    Asks the mother from the fire,
Listening through both back and ears,
Listening with a mother's fears:
"Already is he something wild,

Says that he can fly down-stair!
I do desire
You questioning men would have a care;—
He is my child, my only one,—
You'll make him try to touch the sun!"

WILLIAM BELL SCOTT.

MO CÁILIN DONN

THE blush is on the flower, and the bloom is on the tree,
And the bonnie, bonnie sweet birds are caroling their glee;
And the dews upon the grass are made diamonds by the sun,
All to deck a path of glory for my own Cáilin Donn!

Oh fair she is! Oh rare she is! Oh dearer still to me,
More welcome than the green leaf to winter-stricken tree!
More welcome than the blossom to the weary, dusty bee,
Is the coming of my true love — my own Cáilin Donn!

O sycamore! O sycamore! wave, wave your banners green!
Let all your pennons flutter, O beech! before my queen!
Ye fleet and honeyed breezes, to kiss her hand ye run;
But my heart has passed before ye to my own Cáilin Donn!

Oh fair she is! Oh rare she is! Oh dearer still to me, etc.

Ring out, ring out, O linden, your merry leafy bells!
Unveil your brilliant torches, O chestnut! to the dells;
Strew, strew the glade with splendor, for morn it cometh on!
Oh, the morn of all delight to me — my own Cáilin Donn!

Oh fair she is! Oh rare she is! Oh dearer still to me, etc.

She is coming, where we parted, where she wanders every day;
There's a gay surprise before her who thinks me far away;
Oh, like hearing bugles triumph when the fight of freedom's won,
Is the joy around your footsteps, my own Cáilin Donn!

Oh fair she is! Oh rare she is! Oh dearer still to me,
More welcome than the green leaf to winter-stricken tree!
More welcome than the blossom to the weary, dusty bee,
Is your coming, O my true love — my own Cáilin Donn!

GEORGE SIGERSON.

UNTO THE LEAST OF THESE LITTLE ONES

From Harper's Magazine. Copyright 1889, by Harper & Brothers

O CHILDREN'S eyes unchildlike! Children's eyes
    That make pure, hallowed age seem young indeed —
    Wan eyes that on drear horrors daily feed;
Learned deep in all that leaves us most unwise!
Poor wells, beneath whose troubled depths Truth lies,
    Drowned, drowned, alas! So does my sad heart bleed
    When I remember you; so does it plead
And strive within my breast — as one who cries
For torture of her first-born — that the day,
    The long, bright day, seems thicker sown for me
        With eyes of children than the heavens at night
With stars on stars. To watch you is to pray
    That you may some day see as children see
        When man, like God, hath said, "Let there be light."

Dear Christ, thou hadst thy childhood ere thy cross;
    These, bearing first their cross, no childhood know,
    But, aged with toil, through countless horrors grow
To age more horrible. Rough locks atoss
Above drink-reddened eyes, like Southern moss
    That drops its tangles to the marsh below;
    No standard dreamed or real by which to show
The piteous completeness of their loss;
No rest, no hope, no Christ: the cross alone
    Borne on their backs by day, their bed by night,
        Their ghastly plaything when they pause to weep,
Their threat of torture do they dare to moan;
    A darkness ever dark across their light,
        A weight that makes a waking of their sleep.

Father, who countest such poor birds as fall,
    Count thou these children fallen from their place;
    Lift and console them of thy pity's grace,
And teach them that to suffer is not all;
Hedge them about with love as with a wall,
    Give them in dreams the knowledge of thy face,
    And wipe away such stains as sin doth trace,
Sending deliverance when brave souls call.
Deliver them, O Lord, deliver them! —
    These children — as thy Son was once a child!
    Make them even purer than before they fell,

Radiant in raiment clean from throat to hem;
  For, Lord, till thou hast cleansed these sin-defiled,
  Of such the kingdom, not of heaven, but hell.

AMÉLIE RIVES.

TIRED MOTHERS

A LITTLE elbow leans upon your knee,—
  Your tired knee that has so much to bear;
A child's dear eyes are looking lovingly
  From underneath a thatch of tangled hair.
Perhaps you do not heed the velvet touch
  Of warm, moist fingers holding yours so tight;
You do not prize this blessing overmuch:
  You almost are too tired to pray, to-night.

But it is blessedness! A year ago
  I did not see it as I do to-day:
We are so dull and thankless, and so slow
  To catch the sunshine till it slips away.
And now it seems surpassing strange to me,
  That while I wore the badge of motherhood,
I did not kiss more oft and tenderly
  The little child that brought me only good.

And if, some night, when you sit down to rest,
  You miss this elbow from your tired knee,
This restless, curly head from off your breast,
  This lisping tongue that chatters constantly;
If from your own the dimpled hands had slipped,
  And ne'er would nestle in your palm again;
If the white feet into their grave had tripped,—
  I could not blame you for your heartache then.

I wonder so that mothers ever fret
  At little children clinging to their gown;
Or that the footprints, when the days are wet,
  Are ever black enough to make them frown.
If I could find a little muddy boot,
  Or cap or jacket, on my chamber floor;
If I could kiss a rosy, restless foot,
  And hear it patter in my home once more;

If I could mend a broken cart to-day,
  To-morrow make a kite to reach the sky,—

There is no woman in God's world could say
    She was more blissfully content than I.
But, ah! the dainty pillow next my own
    Is never rumpled by a shining head;
My singing birdling from its nest has flown:
    The little boy I used to kiss is dead!

MAY RILEY SMITH.

THE BEDOUIN-CHILD

[Among the Bedouins, a father in enumerating his children never counts his
daughters, for a daughter is considered a disgrace.]

ILYÀS the prophet, lingering 'neath the moon,
    Heard from a tent a child's heart-withering wail,
    Mixt with the message of the nightingale,
And entering, found, sunk in mysterious swoon,
A little maiden dreaming there alone.
    She babbled of her father sitting pale
    'Neath wings of Death — 'mid sights of sorrow and bale,
And pleaded for his life in piteous tone.

"Poor child, plead on," the succoring prophet saith,
    While she, with eager lips, like one who tries
    To kiss a dream, stretches her arms and cries
To heaven for help,—"Plead on: such pure love-breath
Reaching the Throne, might stay the wings of Death,
    That in the desert fan thy father's eyes."

The drouth-slain camels lie on every hand;
    Seven sons await the morning vultures' claws;
    'Mid empty water-skins and camel-maws
The father sits, the last of all the band.
He mutters, drowsing o'er the moonlit sand,
    "Sleep fans my brow; Sleep makes us all pashas:
    Or if the wings are Death's, why, Azreel draws
A childless father from an empty land."

"Nay," saith a Voice, "the wind of Azreel's wings
    A child's sweet breath hath stilled; so God decrees;" —
    A camel's bell comes tinkling on the breeze,
Filling the Bedouin's brain with bubble of springs
    And scent of flowers and shadow of wavering trees,
Where, from a tent, a little maiden sings.

THEODORE WATTS-DUNTON.

A BURMESE PARABLE

WITH look of woe and garments rent,
　　She walked as one whose strength is spent,
And in her arms a burden dread
She bore,— an infant cold and dead.
Men stood beside, and women wept,
As through the gathering throng she crept,
And fell at last, with covered face,
Before the Buddha's seat of grace.

With startled gaze each Brahmin priest
Drew near: at once the Master ceased
His golden words; for he could read
The suffering spirit's inmost need,
And give with subtlest skill the cure
Which best that spirit could endure.
He bade her speak. She faltered wild,
"They told me thou couldst heal my child!"

"It may be so, but thou must bring
To me this simple offering,—
Some seeds of mustard which have grown
By homes where death was never known,
Nor tears have fallen beside the grave
Of mother, brother, child, or slave.
Go to the happy and the free,
And of their store bring thou to me."

She rose in haste, and all that day
She went her melancholy way.
No door was shut, for pitying eyes
Her quest beheld in kind surprise;
But every stranger answering said,
"We too have looked upon the dead,—
We too have wept beside the grave
Of mother, brother, child, or slave."

At set of sun alone she stood
Within the vine-entangled wood,
And uttered sadly, "I perceive
That every living heart must grieve.
Brief happiness had made me blind
To common griefs of humankind;
My eyes are open now to see
That all the world has wept with me."

Beneath the branches sweet and wild
She made a cradle for her child,
And watched until she saw afar
The village lamps, star after star,
Gleam, burn, and fade. "Our lives," she said,
"Like lamps of night will soon be fled
Sleep soft, my child, until I come
To share thy rest and find thy home."

FRANCES L. MACE.

LULLABY

L ENNAVAN-MO,
Lennavan-mo,
Who is it swinging you to and fro,
With a long low swing and a sweet low croon,
And the loving words of the mother's rune?

Lennavan-mo,
Lennavan-mo,
Who is it swinging you to and fro?
I'm thinking it is an angel fair,—
The Angel that looks on the gulf from the lowest stair
And swings the green world upward by its leagues of sunshine hair.

Lennavan-mo,
Lennavan-mo,
Who is it swings you and the Angel to and fro?
It is He whose faintest thought is a world afar;
It is He whose wish is a leaping seven-mooned star;
It is He, Lennavan-mo,
To whom you and I and all things flow.

Lennavan-mo,
Lennavan-mo,
It is only a little wee lass you are, Eilidh-mo-chree,
But as this wee blossom has roots in the depths of the sky,
So you are at one with the Lord of Eternity —
Bonnie wee lass that you are,
My morning-star,
Eilidh-mo-chree, Lennavan-mo,
Lennavan-mo.

FIONA MACLEOD.

AN ORDER FOR A PICTURE

O GOOD painter, tell me true,
    Has your hand the cunning to draw
    Shapes of things that you never saw?
Aye? Well, here is an order for you.

Woods and cornfields a little brown,—
    The picture must not be over-bright,—
    Yet all in the golden and gracious light
Of a cloud when the summer sun is down;
    Alway and alway, night and morn,
    Woods upon woods, with fields of corn
        Lying between them, not quite sere,
And not in the full, thick, leafy bloom,
When the wind can hardly find breathing-room
        Under their tassels;—cattle near,
Biting shorter the short green grass,
And a hedge of sumach and sassafras,
With bluebirds twittering all around,—
(Ah, good painter, you can't paint sound!)
    These, and the house where I was born,
Low and little, and black and old,
With children, many as it can hold,
All at the windows open wide,—
Heads and shoulders clear outside,
And fair young faces all ablush,—
    Perhaps you may have seen, some day,
    Roses crowding the selfsame way
Out of a wilding, wayside bush.

Listen closer. When you have done
    With woods and cornfields and grazing herds,
A lady, the loveliest ever the sun
    Looked down upon, you must paint for me:
    Oh, if I only could make you see
The clear blue eyes, the tender smile,
    The sovereign sweetness, the gentle grace,
    The woman's soul, and the angel's face
That are beaming on me all the while,
    I need not speak these foolish words:
Yet one word tells you all I would say,—
    She is my mother; you will agree
That all the rest may be thrown away.

Two little urchins at her knee
. You must paint, sir: one like me,—
    The other with a clearer brow,
    And the light of his adventurous eyes
    Flashing with boldest enterprise:
At ten years old he went to sea,—
    God knoweth if he be living now,—
He sailed in the good ship Commodore;
    Nobody ever crossed her track
    To bring us news, and she never came back.
Ah, it is twenty long years and more
Since that old ship went out of the bay
    With my great-hearted brother on her deck:
    I watched him till he shrank to a speck,
And his face was toward me all the way.
Bright his hair was, a golden brown,
    The time we stood at our mother's knee;
That beauteous head, if it did go down,
    Carried sunshine into the sea!

Out in the fields one summer night
    We were together, half afraid
    Of the corn-leaves' rustling, and of the shade
        Of the high hills, stretching so still and far,—
Loitering till after the low little light
    Of the candle shone through the open door,
And over the haystack's pointed top,
All of a tremble and ready to drop,
    The first half-hour, the great yellow star,
    That we, with staring, ignorant eyes,
Had often and often watched to see
    Propped and held in its place in the skies
By the fork of a tall red mulberry-tree
    Which close in the edge of our flax-field grew,—
Dead at the top,—just one branch full
Of leaves, notched round, and lined with wool,
    From which it tenderly shook the dew
Over our heads, when we came to play
In its hand-breadth of shadow, day after day.
    Afraid to go home, sir: for one of us bore
A nest full of speckled and thin-shelled eggs,—
The other, a bird, held fast by the legs,
Not so big as a straw of wheat:
The berries we gave her she wouldn't eat,

But cried and cried, till we held her bill,
So slim and shining, to keep her still.

At last we stood at our mother's knee.
   Do you think, sir, if you try,
   You can paint the look of a lie?
   If you can, pray have the grace
   To put it solely in the face
Of the urchin that is likest me;
   (I think 'twas solely mine, indeed;
   But that's no matter,— paint it so;)
   The eyes of our mother (take good heed)
Looking not on the nestful of eggs,
Nor the fluttering bird, held so fast by the legs,
But straight through our faces down to our lies,
And oh, with such injured, reproachful surprise!
I felt my heart bleed where that glance went, as though
A sharp blade struck through it.
                You, sir, know
That you on the canvas are to repeat
Things that are fairest, things most sweet,—
Woods and cornfields and mulberry-tree,
The mother, the lads, with their bird, at her knee:
   But oh, that look of reproachful woe!
High as the heavens your name I'll shout,
If you paint me the picture, and leave that out.

                      ALICE CARY.

RACHEL

No DAYS that dawn can match for her
   The days before her house was bare;
Sweet was the whole year with the stir
   Of young feet on the stair.

Once was she wealthy with small cares,
   And small hands clinging to her knees;
Now she is poor, and, weeping, bears
   Her strange new hours of ease.

            LIZETTE WOODWORTH REESE.

THE DEAD MOTHER

As I LAY asleep, as I lay asleep,
Under the grass as I lay so deep,
As I lay asleep in my cotton serk
Under the shade of Our Lady's kirk,
I wakened up in the dead of night,
I wakened up in my death-serk white,
And I heard a cry from far away,
And I knew the voice of my daughter May:—
"Mother, mother, come hither to me!
Mother, mother, come hither and see!
Mother, mother, mother dear,
Another mother is sitting here:
My body is bruised, and in pain I cry;
On the straw in the dark afraid I lie;
I thirst and hunger for drink and meat,
And mother, mother, to sleep were sweet!"
I heard the cry, though my grave was deep,
And awoke from sleep, and awoke from sleep.

I awoke from sleep, I awoke from sleep,
Up I rose from my grave so deep!
The earth was black, but overhead
The stars were yellow, the moon was red;
And I walked along all white and thin,
And lifted the latch and entered in.
I reached the chamber as dark as night,
And though it was dark my face was white.
"Mother, mother, I look on thee!
Mother, mother, you frighten me!
For your cheeks are thin and your hair is gray!"
But I smiled, and kissed her fears away;
I smoothed her hair and I sang a song,
And on my knee I rocked her long:
"O mother, mother, sing low to me —
I am sleepy now, and I cannot see!"
I kissed her, but I could not weep,
And she went to sleep, she went to sleep.

As we lay asleep, as we lay asleep,
My May and I, in our grave so deep,
As we lay asleep in the midnight mirk,
Under the shade of Our Lady's kirk,

I wakened up in the dead of night,
Though May my daughter lay warm and white.
And I heard the cry of a little one,
And I knew 'twas the voice of Hugh my son:—
"Mother, mother, come hither to me!
Mother, mother, come hither and see!
Mother, mother, mother dear,
Another mother is sitting here:
My body is bruised and my heart is sad,
But I speak my mind and call them bad;
I thirst and hunger night and day,
And were I strong I would fly away!"
I heard the cry though my grave was deep,
And awoke from sleep, and awoke from sleep.

I awoke from sleep, I awoke from sleep,
Up I rose from my grave so deep:
The earth was black, but overhead
The stars were yellow, the moon was red;
And I walked along all white and thin,
And lifted the latch and entered in.
"Mother, mother, and art thou here?
I know your face, and I feel no fear;
Raise me, mother, and kiss my cheek,
For oh, I am weary and sore and weak."
I smoothed his hair with a mother's joy,
And he laughed aloud, my own brave boy;
I raised and held him on my breast,
Sang him a song and bade him rest.
"Mother, mother, sing low to me—
I am sleepy now, and I cannot see!"
I kissed him, and I could not weep,
As he went to sleep, as he went to sleep.

As I lay asleep, as I lay asleep,
With my girl and boy in my grave so deep,
As I lay asleep, I awoke in fear,—
Awoke, but awoke not my children dear,—
And heard a cry so low and weak
From a tiny voice that could not speak;
I heard the cry of a little one,
My bairn that could neither talk nor run.—
My little, little one, uncaressed,
Starving for lack of the milk of the breast:

And I rose from sleep and entered in,
And found my little one pinched and thin,
And crooned a song and hushed its moan,
And put its lips to my white breast-bone;
And the red, red moon that lit the place
Went white to look at the little face,
And I kissed, and kissed, and I could not weep,
As it went to sleep, as it went to sleep.

As it lay asleep, as it lay asleep,
I set it down in the darkness deep,
Smoothed its limbs and laid it out,
And drew the curtains round about;
And into the dark, dark room I hied,
Where he lay awake at the woman's side;
And though the chamber was black as night,
He saw my face, for it was so white:
I gazed in his eyes, and he shrieked in pain,
And I knew he never would sleep again;
And back to my grave went silently,
And soon my baby was brought to me:
My son and daughter beside me rest,
My little baby is on my breast;
Our bed is warm and our grave is deep,
But he cannot sleep, he cannot sleep.

ROBERT BUCHANAN.

LITTLE WILLIE

Poor little Willie,
    With his many pretty wiles;
Worlds of wisdom in his looks,
    And quaint, quiet smiles;
Hair of amber, touched with
    Gold of heaven so brave;
All lying darkly hid
    In a workhouse grave.

You remember little Willie:
    Fair and funny fellow! he
Sprang like a lily
    From the dirt of poverty.

Poor little Willie!
　Not a friend was nigh,
When, from the cold world,
　He crouched down to die.

In the day we wandered foodless,
　Little Willie cried for bread;
In the night we wandered homeless,
　Little Willie cried for bed.
Parted at the workhouse door,
　Not a word we said:
Ah, so tired was poor Willie,
　And so sweetly sleep the dead.

'Twas in the dead of winter
　We laid him in the earth;
The world brought in the New Year,
　On a tide of mirth.
But for lost little Willie
　Not a tear we crave:
Cold and hunger cannot wake him
　In his workhouse grave.

We thought him beautiful,
　Felt it hard to part;
We loved him dutiful:
　Down, down, poor heart!
The storms they may beat;
　The winter winds may rave;
Little Willie feels not,
　In his workhouse grave.

No room for little Willie;
　In the world he had no part;
On him stared the Gorgon-eye
　Through which looks no heart.
Come to me, said Heaven;
　And if Heaven will save,
Little matters though the door
　Be a workhouse grave.

                                    GERALD MASSEY.

THE APPARITION

I IN the grayness rose:
   I could not sleep for thinking of one dead.
     Then to the chest I went
Where lie the things of my belovèd spread.

     Quietly these I took:
A little glove, a sheet of music torn,
     Paintings, ill-done perhaps;
Then lifted up a dress that she had worn.

     And now I came to where
Her letters are,—they lie beneath the rest,—
     And read them in the haze:
She spoke of many things, was sore opprest.

     But these things moved me not:
Not when she spoke of being parted quite,
     Of being misunderstood,
Or growing weary of the world's great fight.

     Not even when she wrote
Of our dead child, and the handwriting swerved:
     Not even then I shook;
Not even by such words was I unnerved.

     I thought — She is at peace;
Whither the child has gone, she too has passed,
     And a much-needed rest
Is fallen upon her; she is still at last.

     But when at length I took
From under all those letters one small sheet,
     Folded and writ in haste,
Why did my heart with sudden sharpness beat?

     Alas, it was not sad!
Her saddest words I had read calmly o'er.
     Alas, it had no pain!
Her painful words, all these I knew before.

     A hurried, happy line!
A little jest, too slight for one so dead:
     This did I not endure;
Then with a shuddering heart no more I read.

         STEPHEN PHILLIPS.

THE OTHER ONE

SWEET little maid with winsome eyes
    That laugh all day through the tangled hair;
  Gazing with baby looks so wise
    Over the arm of the oaken chair:
Dearer than you is none to me,
  Dearer than you there can be none;
Since in your laughing face I see
  Eyes that tell of another one.

Here where the firelight softly glows,
  Sheltered and safe and snug and warm,
What to you is the wind that blows,
  Driving the sleet of the winter storm?
Round your head the ruddy light
  Glints on the gold from your tresses spun,
But deep is the drifting snow to-night
  Over the head of the other one.

Hold me close as you sagely stand,
  Watching the dying embers shine;
Then shall I feel another hand
  That nestled once in this hand of mine —
Poor little hand, so cold and chill,
  Shut from the light of stars and sun,
Clasping the withered roses still
  That hide the face of the sleeping one.

Laugh, little maid, while laugh you may!
  Sorrow comes to us all, I know; —
Better perhaps for her to stay
  Under the drifting robe of snow.
Sing while you may your baby songs,
  Sing till your baby days are done;
But oh, the ache of the heart that longs
  Night and day for the other one!

HARRY THURSTON PECK.

IN USUM DELPHINI

How fain were I, O Curly-pate,
 To smooth the wrinkle from thy brow,
The tangled sentence to make straight,
 Nor vex thee with the why and how.
But darker riddles for thee wait:
Who may emend the scroll of fate?

That moldering myth of lust and hate
 For thee how gladly I'd revise,
Nor suffer aught to desecrate
 The gleam of those unsullied eyes:
This page I'd spare thee to translate;
But who man's heart can expurgate?

In vain for boyhood's prince-estate
 Our love betrays the bitter trust.
The Three no tribute will abate
 From king or churl: all mortals must —
Or on the throne or at the gate —
Read life's full lesson soon or late.

      GEORGE M. WHICHER.

THE WOODSIDE WAY

I WANDERED down the woodside way,
 Where branching doors ope with the breeze,
And saw a little child at play
 Among the strong and lovely trees:
 The dead leaves rustled to her knees;
Her hair and eyes were brown as they.

"O little child," I softly said,
 "You come a long, long way to me;
The trees that tower overhead
 Are here in sweet reality,
 But you're the child I used to be,
And all the leaves of May you tread."

      ETHELWYN WETHERALD

THE TWO LOCKS OF HAIR

A YOUTH, light-hearted and content,
I wander through the world;
Here, Arab-like, is pitched my tent,
And straight again is furled.

Yet oft I dream that once a wife
Close in my heart was locked,
And in the sweet repose of life
A blessed child I rocked.

I wake! Away, that dream,—away!
Too long did it remain!   .
So long, that both by night and day
It ever comes again.

The end lies ever in my thought;—
To a grave so cold and deep
The mother beautiful was brought;
Then dropped the child asleep.

But now the dream is wholly o'er;
I bathe mine eyes and see;
And wander through the world once more,
A youth so light and free.

Two locks,—and they are wondrous fair,—
Left me that vision mild:
The brown is from the mother's hair,
The blond is from the child.

And when I see that lock of gold,
Pale grows the evening-red;
And when the dark lock I behold,
I wish that I were dead.

GUSTAV PFIZER.

Longfellow's Translation.

THE BRAMBLE FLOWER

THY fruit full well the schoolboy knows,
   Wild bramble of the brake!
So put thou forth thy small white rose:
   I love it for his sake.
Though woodbines flaunt and roses glow
   O'er all the fragrant bowers,
Thou need'st not be ashamed to show
   Thy satin-threaded flowers.

For dull the eye, the heart is dull,
   That cannot feel how fair,
Amid all beauty beautiful,
   Thy tender blossoms are;
How delicate thy gauzy frill,
   How rich thy branchy stem,
How soft thy voice when woods are still,
   And thou sing'st hymns to them;

While silent showers are falling slow,
   And, 'mid the general hush,
A sweet air lifts the little bough,
   Lone whispering through the bush!
The primrose to the grave is gone;
   The hawthorn flower is dead;
The violet by the mossed gray stone
   Hath laid her weary head:

But thou, wild bramble! back dost bring,
   In all their beauteous power,
The fresh green days of life's fair spring,
   And boyhood's blossomy hour.
Scorned bramble of the brake! once more
   Thou bidd'st me be a boy,
To gad with thee the woodlands o'er,
   In freedom and in joy.

EBENEZER ELLIOT.

BEGONE, DULL CARE

BEGONE, dull care!
   I prithee begone from me:
Begone, dull care!
Thou and I can never agree.

Long while thou hast been tarrying here,
And fain thou wouldst me kill;
But i' faith, dull care,
Thou never shalt have thy will.

Too much care
Will make a young man gray;
Too much care
Will turn an old man to clay:
My wife shall dance, and I will sing,
So merrily pass the day;
For I hold it is the wisest thing
To drive dull care away.

Hence, dull care!
I'll none of thy company;
Hence, dull care!
Thou art no pair for me.
We'll hunt the wild boar through the wold,
So merrily pass the day;
And then at night, o'er a cheerful bowl,
We'll drive dull care away.

Author Unknown.

THERE WAS A JOLLY MILLER

THERE was a jolly miller once lived on the river Dee;   [he;
He danced and sang from morn till night, no lark so blithe as
And this the burden of his song forever used to be:—
"I care for nobody, no not I, if nobody cares for me.

"I live by my mill, God bless her! she's kindred, child, and wife;
I would not change my station for any other in life;
No lawyer, surgeon, or doctor e'er had a groat from me:
I care for nobody, no not I, if nobody cares for me."

When spring begins his merry career, oh, how his heart grows gay:
No summer's drought alarms his fear, nor winter's cold decay;
No foresight mars the miller's joy, who's wont to sing and say,
"Let others toil from year to year, I live from day to day."

Thus, like the miller, bold and free, let us rejoice and sing:
The days of youth are made for glee, and time is on the wing;
This song shall pass from me to thee, along the jovial ring:
Let heart and voice and all agree to say, "Long live the king."

"ISAAC BICKERSTAFF."

VANITAS! VANITATUM VANITAS!

I'VE set my heart upon nothing, you see;
            Hurrah!
And so the world goes well with me:
            Hurrah!
And who has a mind to be fellow of mine,
Why, let him take hold and help me drain
        These moldy lees of wine.

I set my heart at first upon wealth;
            Hurrah!
And bartered away my peace and health:
            But ah!
The slippery change went about like air,—
And when I had clutched me a handful here,
        Away it went there!

I set my heart upon woman next;
            Hurrah!
For her sweet sake was oft perplexed:
            But ah!
The False one looked for a daintier lot,
The Constant one wearied me out and out,
        The Best was not easily got.

I set my heart upon travels grand;
            Hurrah!
And spurned our plain old fatherland:
            But ah!
Naught seemed to be just the thing it should,—
Most comfortless beds and indifferent food!
        My tastes misunderstood!

I set my heart upon sounding fame:
            Hurrah!
And lo! I'm eclipsed by some upstart's name;
            And ah!
When in public life I loomed quite high,
The folks that passed me would look awry;
        Their very worst friend was I.

And then I set my heart upon war:
            Hurrah!
We gained some battles with éclat;
            Hurrah!

We troubled the foe with sword and flame—
And some of our friends fared quite the same:
   I lost a leg for fame.

Now I've set my heart upon nothing, you see;
   Hurrah!
And the whole wide world belongs to me:
   Hurrah!
The feast begins to run low, no doubt;
But at the old cask we'll have one good bout—
   Come, drink the lees all out!

GOETHE.

Translation of John Sullivan Dwight.

DEATH AN EPICUREAN

DEATH loveth not the woeful heart,
   Or the soul that's tired of living.
     Nay, it's up and away
     With the heart that's gay
And the life that's worth the giving.

Seldom he stops where his welcome's sure,
   Where age and want are sighing.
     Nay, it's up and away,
     For he scorns to stay
With the wretch who would be dying.

Ah, it's youth and love and a cloudless sky
   The epicurean's after.
     Nay, it's up and away
     When the world's in May
And life is full of laughter.

JEAN WRIGHT.

SIR JOHN BARLEYCORN

THERE came three men out of the West,
    Their victory to try;
And they have taken a solemn oath
    Poor Barleycorn should die.
They took a plow and plowed him in,
    And harrowed clods on his head;
And then they took a solemn oath
    Poor Barleycorn was dead.
There he lay sleeping in the ground
    Till rain from the sky did fall;
Then Barleycorn sprung up his head,
    And so amazed them all.

There he remained till midsummer,
    And looked both pale and wan;
Then Barleycorn he got a beard,
    And so became a man.
Then they sent men with scythes so sharp,
    To cut him off at knee;
And then poor little Barleycorn
    They served him barbarously:
Then they sent men with pitchforks strong,
    To pierce him through the heart;
And, like a dreadful tragedy,
    They bound him to a cart.

And then they brought him to a barn,
    A prisoner, to endure;
And so they fetched him out again,
    And laid him on the floor:
Then they set men with holly clubs
    To beat the flesh from his bones;
But the miller he served him worse than that,
    For he ground him betwixt two stones.
Oh, Barleycorn is the choicest grain
    That ever was sown on land!
It will do more than any grain
    By the turning of your hand.

It will make a boy into a man,
    And a man into an ass;
It will change your gold into silver,
    And your silver into brass:

It will make the huntsman hunt the fox,
    That never wound his horn;
It will bring the tinker to the stocks,
    That people may him scorn;
It will put sack into a glass,
    And claret in the can;
And it will cause a man to drink
    Till he neither can go nor stan'.

Author Unknown.

SPARKLING AND BRIGHT

SPARKLING and bright in liquid light
    Does the wine our goblets gleam in,
With a hue as red as the rosy bed
    Which a bee would choose to dream in.
Then fill to-night, with hearts as light,
    To loves as gay and fleeting,
As bubbles that swim on the beaker's brim
    And break on the lips while meeting.

Oh! if mirth might arrest the flight
    Of time through life's dominions,
We here awhile would now beguile
    The graybeard of his pinions.
So drink to-night, with hearts as light,
    To loves as gay and fleeting,
As bubbles that swim on the beaker's brim
    And break on the lips while meeting.

But since delight can't tempt the wight,
    Nor fond regret delay him,
Nor Love himself can hold the elf,
    Nor sober Friendship stay him,
We'll drink to-night, with hearts as light,
    To loves as gay and fleeting,
As bubbles that swim on the beaker's brim
    And break on the lips while meeting.

CHARLES FENNO HOFFMAN.

WASSAIL CHORUS

From 'The Coming of Love and Other Poems.' John Lane: London and
New York, 1898.

CHORUS

CHRISTMAS knows a merry, merry place,
    Where he goes with fondest face,
      Brightest eye, brightest hair:
Tell the Mermaid where is that one place —
      Where?

RALEIGH

'Tis by Devon's glorious halls,
    Whence, dear Ben, I come again:
Bright with golden roofs and walls —
    El Dorado's rare domain —
Seem those halls when sunlight launches
Shafts of gold through leafless branches,
When the winter's feathery mantle blanches
    Field and farm and lane.

CHORUS

Christmas knows a merry, merry place,
    Where he goes with fondest face,
      Brightest eye, brightest hair:
Tell the Mermaid where is that one place —
      Where?

DRAYTON

'Tis where Avon's wood-sprites weave
    Through the boughs a lace of rime,
While the bells of Christmas Eve
    Fling for Will the Stratford-chime
O'er the river-flags embossed
Rich with flowery runes of frost —
O'er the meads where snowy tufts are tossed —
    Strains of olden time.

CHORUS

Christmas knows a merry, merry place,
    Where he goes with fondest face,
      Brightest eye, brightest hair:

Tell the Mermaid where is that one place
Where?

"MR. W. H."

'Tis, methinks, on any ground
Where our Shakespeare's feet are set.
There smiles Christmas, holly-crowned
With his blithest coronet.
Friendship's face he loveth well:
'Tis a countenance whose spell
Sheds a balm o'er every mead and dell
Where we used to fret.

CHORUS

Christmas knows a merry, merry place,
Where he goes with fondest face,   .
Brightest eye, brightest hair:
Tell the Mermaid where is that one place —
Where?

HEYWOOD

More than all the pictures, Ben,
Winter weaves by wood or stream,
Christmas loves our London, when
Rise thy clouds of wassail-steam —
Clouds like these, that, curling, take
Forms of faces gone, and wake
Many a lay from lips we loved, and make
London like a dream.

CHORUS

Christmas knows a merry, merry place,
Where he goes with fondest face,
Brightest eye, brightest hair:
Tell the Mermaid where is that one place —
Where?

BEN JONSON

Love's old songs shall never die,
Yet the new shall suffer proof;
Love's old drink of Yule brew I,
Wassail for new love's behoof:
Drink the drink I brew, and sing
Till the berried branches swing,

.   Till our song make all the Mermaid ring —
              Yea, from rush to roof.   .

FINALE

Christmas loves this merry, merry place:—
    Christmas saith with fondest face,
        Brightest eye, brightest hair,
"Ben! the drink tastes rare of sack and mace;
              Rare!"

                          THEODORE WATTS-DUNTON.

MEDIÆVAL LATIN STUDENT SONGS

TIME'S A-FLYING (LAURIGER HORATIUS)

["Two lyrics of distinguished excellence, which still hold their place in the
'Commersbuch,' cannot claim certain antiquity in their present form. . . .
The first starts with an allusion to the Horatian *tempus edax rerum*."]

L AUREL-CROWNED Horatius,
        True, how true thy saying!
    Swift as wind flies over us
        Time, devouring, slaying.
Where are, oh! those goblets full
    Of wine honey-laden,
Strifes and loves and bountiful
    Lips of ruddy maiden?

Grows the young grape tenderly,
    And the maid is growing;
But the thirsty poet, see,
    Years on him are snowing!
What's the use on hoary curls
    Of the bays undying,
If we may not kiss the girls,
    Drink while time's a-flying?

Translation of John Addington Symonds.

GAUDEAMUS IGITUR

["Having alluded to 'Gaudeamus Igitur,' I shall close my translations with
a version of it into English. The dependence of this lyric upon the rhythm
and substance of the poem 'On Contempt for the World' . . . is perhaps
the reason why it is sung by German students after the funeral of a comrade.

The Office for the Dead sounding in their ears, occasions the startling *igitur*
["therefore" — "let us *then*"] with which it opens; and their mind reverts to
solemn phrases in the midst of masculine determination to enjoy the present
while it is yet theirs."]

L ET us live, then, and be glad
 While young life's before us!
  After youthful pastime had,
  After old age hard and sad,
 Earth will slumber o'er us.

Where are they who in this world,
 Ere we kept, were keeping?
  Go ye to the gods above;
  Go to hell; inquire thereof:
 They are not: they're sleeping.

Brief is life, and brevity
 Briefly shall be ended:
  Death comes like a whirlwind strong,
  Bears us with his blast along;
 None shall be defended.

Live this university,
 Men that learning nourish;
  Live each member of the same,
  Long live all that bear its name;
 Let them ever flourish!

Live the commonwealth also,
 And the men that guide it!
  Live our town in strength and health,
  Founders, patrons, by whose wealth
 We are here provided!

Live all girls! A health to you,
 Melting maids and beauteous!
  Live the wives and women too,
  Gentle, loving, tender, true,
 Good, industrious, duteous!

Perish cares that pule and pine!
 Perish envious blamers!
  Die the Devil, thine and mine!
  Die the starch-neck Philistine!
 Scoffers and defamers!

Translation of John Addington Symonds.

A CITIZEN OF COSMOPOLIS

WHAT is the name of your country—where
    Is the land of your love that you leave behind?
And what is the country to which you fare,
    And what is the hope that you have in mind?—
"My land is wherever my rest I find,
My home is wherever I chance to be,
    My way and mine end are by fate assigned—
        Io vengo da Cosmopoli!"*

Is there no woman whose songs ensnare
    Your heart to follow, yet unresigned?
No subtle thread of a golden hair,
    Like Lilith's hair, round your heart entwined?—
"In no fetter of gold is my heart confined,
No siren lures me across the sea,
    I am not to hold, I am not to bind—
        Io vengo da Cosmopoli!"

When flames of the burning cities flare,
    And towers fall down, being undermined,
When drums are beaten and trumpets blare,
    And the neigh of the war-horse is on the wind,—
Under which king?—"Since Fortune is blind
And I am her soldier, I do not see
    Or friend or foe in the ranks aligned:
        Io vengo da Cosmopoli!"

ENVOI

"The world, my lords, has been cruel and kind,—
I have laughed and suffered, but not repined:
    If I live or die matters little to me,
Or whether my grave with a cross be signed—
        Io vengo da Cosmopoli!"

                                        ELIZABETH PULLEN.

*"I come from Cosmopolis."

THE TROOPER TO HIS MARE

OLD girl that has borne me far and fast
    On pawing hoofs that were never loath,
Our gallop to-day may be the last
    For you, or for me, or perhaps for both!
As I tighten your girth do you nothing daunt?
    Do you catch the hint of our forming line?
And now the artillery moves to the front,
    Have you never a qualm, Bay Bess of mine?

It is dainty to see you sidle and start,
    As you move to the battle's cloudy marge,
And to feel the swells of your wakening heart
    When our sonorous bugles sound a charge.
At the scream of the shell and the roar of the drum
    You feign to be frightened with roguish glance;
But up the green slopes where the bullets hum
    Coquettishly, darling, I've known you dance.

Your skin is satin, your nostrils red,
    Your eyes are a bird's, or a loving girl's;
And from delicate fetlock to stately head
    A throbbing vein-cordage around you curls.
O joy of my heart! if you they slay,
    For triumph or rout I little care;
For there isn't in all the wide valley to-day
    Such a dear little bridle-wise, thoroughbred mare!

CHARLES G. HALPINE.

THE BALLAD OF THE BOAT

THE stream was smooth as glass: we said, "Arise and let's away;"
    The Siren sang beside the boat that in the rushes lay;
    And, spread the sail and strong the oar, we gayly took our way.
When shall the sandy bar be crossed? When shall we find the bay?

The broadening flood swells slowly out o'er cattle-dotted plains;
The stream is strong and turbulent, and dark with heavy rains:
The laborer looks up to see our shallop speed away.
When shall the sandy bar be crossed? When shall we find the bay?

Now are the clouds like fiery shrouds; the sun, superbly large,
Slow as an oak to woodman's stroke sinks flaming at their marge.

The waves are bright with mirrored light as jacinths on our way.
When shall, the sandy bar be crossed? When shall we find the bay?

The moon is high up in the sky, and now no more we see
The spreading river's either bank; and surging distantly,
There booms a sullen thunder as of breakers far away:
Now shall the sandy bar be crossed; now shall we find the bay!

The sea-gull shrieks high overhead, and dimly to our sight
The moonlit crests of foaming waves gleam towering through the
           night.
We'll steal upon the mermaid soon, and start her from her lay,
When now the sandy bar is crossed, and we are in the bay.

What rises white and awful as a shroud-infolded ghost?
What roar of rampant tumult bursts in clangor on the coast?
Pull back, pull back! The raging flood sweeps every oar away.
O stream, is this thy bar of sand? O boat, is this the bay?

RICHARD GARNETT.

THE CROSS BY THE WAY

(KROAZ ANN HENT)

SWEET in the greenwood a birdie sings;
    Golden-yellow its two bright wings;
    Red its heartikin, blue its crest:
Oh, but it sings with the sweetest breast!

Early, early it 'lighted down
On the edge of my ingle-stone,
As I prayed my morning prayer,—
"Tell me thy errand, birdie fair."

Then sung it as many sweet things to me
As there are roses on the rose-tree:
"Take a sweetheart, lad, an' you may;
To gladden your heart both night and day."

Past the cross by the way as I went,
Monday, I saw her fair as a saint:
Sunday, I will go to mass,
There on the green I'll see her pass.

Water poured in a beaker clear
Dimmer shows than the eyes of my dear;

Pearls themselves are not more bright
Than her little teeth, pure and white.

Then her hands and her cheek of snow,
Whiter than milk in a black pail, show.
Yes, if you could my sweetheart see,
She would charm the heart from thee.

Had I as many crowns at my beck
As hath the Marquis of Poncalec,
Had I a gold-mine at my door,
Wanting my sweetheart I were poor.

If on my door-sill up should come
Golden flowers for furze and broom,
Till my court were with gold piled high,
Little I'd reck, but she were by.

Doves must have their close warm nest,
Corpses must have the tomb for rest;
Souls to Paradise must depart:
And I, my love, must to thy heart.

Every Monday at dawn of day
I'll on my knees to the cross by the way;
At the new cross by the way I'll bend,
In thy honor, my gentle friend!

Mediæval Breton.

Translation of Tom Taylor.

THE FAIRY QUEEN

COME, follow, follow me —
 You, fairy elves that be,
  Which circle on the green —
Come, follow Mab your queen!
Hand in hand let's dance around;
For this place is fairy ground.

 When mortals are at rest,
 And snoring in their nest, —
  Unheard and unespied,
  Through keyholes we do glide;
Over tables, stools, and shelves,
We trip it with our fairy elves.

And if the house be foul
With platter, dish, or bowl,
Up-stairs we nimbly creep,
And find the sluts asleep:
There we pinch their arms and thighs—
None escapes and none espies.

But if the house be swept,
And from uncleanness kept,
We praise the household maid,
And duly she is paid;
For we use, before we go,
To drop a tester in her shoe.

Upon a mushroom's head
Our table-cloth we spread:
A grain of rye or wheat
Is manchet which we eat;
Pearly drops of dew we drink,
In acorn cups, filled to the brink.

The grasshopper, gnat, and fly,
Serve us for our minstrelsy;
Grace said, we dance awhile,
And so the time beguile;
And if the moon doth hide her head,
The glow-worm lights us home to bed.

On tops of dewy grass
So nimbly do we pass,
The young and tender stalk
Ne'er bends when we do walk;
Yet in the morning may be seen
Where we the night before have been.

Author Unknown.

THE FAIRY QUEEN SLEEPING

WE HAVE been o'er land and sea,
    Seeking lovely dreams for thee,—
    Where is there we have not been
Gathering gifts for our sweet queen?
We are come with sound and sight
Fit for fairy's sleep to-night:

First around thy couch shall sweep
Odors such as roses weep
When the earliest spring rain
Calls them into life again;
Next upon thine ear shall float
Many a low and silver note
Stolen from a dark-eyed maid,
When her lover's serenade,
Rising as the stars grew dim,
Wakened from her thoughts of him;
There shall steal o'er lip and cheek
Gales, but all too light to break
Thy soft rest,— such gales as hide
All day orange-flowers inside,
Or that, through hot noontide, dwell
In the purple hyacinth bell;
And before thy sleeping eyes
Shall come glorious pageantries,—
Palaces of gems and gold
Such as dazzle to behold,
Gardens in which every tree
Seems a world of bloom to be,
Fountains whose clear waters show
The white pearls that lie below.

During slumber's magic reign
Other times shall live again:
First thou shalt be young and free
In thy days of liberty,
Then again be wooed and won
By thy stately Oberon;
Or thou shalt descend to earth,
And see all of mortal birth—
No, that world's too full of care
For e'en dreams to linger there.—
But behold, the sun is set,
And the diamond coronet
Of the young moon is on high
Waiting for our revelry;
And the dew is on the flower,
And the stars proclaim our hour:
Long enough thy rest has been,—
Wake, Titania, wake, our queen!

LETITIA ELIZABETH LANDON.

THE MERRY PRANKS OF ROBIN GOOD-FELLOW

FROM Oberon, in fairy-land,
    The king of ghosts and shadowes there,
Mad Robin, I, at his command,
    Am sent to view the night-sports here.
        What revel rout
        Is kept about
In every corner where I go,
        I will o'ersee,
        And merrie be,
And make good sport with ho, ho, ho!

More swift than lightning can I flye
    About this aëry welkïn soone,
And in a minute's space descrye
    Each thing that's done belowe the moone.
        There's not a hag
        Or ghost shall wag,
Or cry 'Ware goblins! where I go;
        But Robin, I,
        Their feates will spy,
And send them home with ho, ho, ho!

Whene'er such wanderers I meete,
    As from their night-sports they trudge home,
With counterfeiting voice I greete,
    And call on them with me to roame
        Through woods, through lakes,
        Through bogs, through brakes;
Or else unseene, with them I go,
        All in the nicke,
        To play some tricke,
And frolick it with ho, ho, ho!

Sometimes I meete them like a man,
    Sometimes an ox, sometimes a hound;
And to a horse I turn me can,
    To trip and trot about them round;
        But if to ride,
        My backe they stride,
More swift than wind away I goe;
        O'er hedge and lands,
        Through pools and ponds,
I whirry, laughing ho, ho, ho!

When lads and lasses merry be,
  With possets and with junkets fine,
Unseene of all the company,
  I eat their cakes and sip their wine;
    And to make sport
    I fume and snort,
And out the candles do I blow;
    The maids I kiss,—
    They shrieke, Who's this?
I answer naught but ho, ho, ho!

Yet now and then, the maids to please,
  At midnight I card up their wooll,
And when they sleepe and take their ease,
  With wheel to threads their flax I pull.
    I grind at mill
    Their malt up still;
I dress their hemp, I spin their tow:
    If any wake,
    And would me take,
I wend me, laughing ho, ho, ho!

When house or hearth doth sluttish lye,
  I pinch the maidens black and blue;
The bedd-clothes from the bedd pull I,
  And lay them naked all to view.
    'Twixt sleepe and wake
    I do them take,
And on the key-cold floor them throw;
    If out they cry,
    Then forth I fly,
And loudly laugh out, ho, ho, ho!

When any need to borrow aught,
  We lend them what they do require,
And for the use demand we naught,—
  Our owne is all we do desire.
    If to repay
    They do delay,
Abroad amongst them then I go;
    And night by night,
    I them afright,
With pinchings, dreams, and ho, ho, ho!

When lazie queans have naught to do
  But study how to cog and lye,

To make debate and mischief too,
  'Twixt one another secretly,
    I marke their gloze,
    And it disclose
To them whom they have wrongèd so.
    When I have done
    I get me gone,
And leave them scolding, ho, ho, ho!

When men do traps and engines set
  In loopeholes where the vermine creepe,
Who from their foldes and houses get
  Their duckes, and geese, and lambes, and sheepe,
    I spy the gin,
    And enter in,
And seeme a vermine taken so;
    But when they there
    Approach me neare,
I leap out, laughing ho, ho, ho!

By wells and rills, in meadowes greene,
  We nightly dance our heyday guise,
And to our fairye kinge and queene
  We chant our moonlighte minstrelsies.
    When larkes 'gin sing,
    Away we fling;
And babes new-born steale as we go,
    And elfe in bed
    We leave instead,
And wend us, laughing ho, ho, ho!

From hag-bred Merlin's time have I
  Thus nightly reveled to and fro;
And for my prankes, men call me by
  The name of Robin Good-Fellow.
    Friends, ghosts, and sprites
    Who haunt the nightes,
The hags and goblins, do me know;
    And beldames old
    My feates have told —
So *vale, vale!* Ho, ho, ho!

Author Unknown.

THE FAIRY NURSE

SWEET babe! a golden cradle holds thee,
And soft the snow-white fleece infolds thee;
In airy bower I'll watch thy sleeping,
Where branchy trees to the breeze are sweeping.
Shuheen, sho, lulo lo!

When mothers languish broken-hearted,
When young wives are from husbands parted,
Ah! little think the keeners lonely,
They weep some time-worn fairy only.
Shuheen, sho, lulo lo!

Within our magic halls of brightness
Trips many a foot of snowy whiteness,—
Stolen maidens, queens of fairy,
And kings and chiefs a slaugh shee airy.
Shuheen, sho, lulo lo!

Rest thee, babe! I love thee dearly,
And as thy mortal mother nearly;
Ours is the swiftest steed and proudest,
That moves where the tramp of the host is loudest.
Shuheen, sho, lulo lo!

Rest, thee, babe! for soon thy slumbers
Shall flee at the magic Koelshie's numbers;
In airy bower I'll watch thy sleeping,
Where branchy trees to the breeze are sweeping.
Shuheen, sho, lulo lo!

EDWARD WALSH.

SONG OF THE FAIRY PEDDLER

LADY and gentleman fays, come buy!
No peddler has such a rich packet as I.

Who wants a gown,
Of purple fold,
Embroidered down
The seams with gold?
See here! A tulip richly laced
To please a royal fairy's taste!

Who wants a cap
　　Of crimson grand?
By great good hap
　　I've one on hand;
Look, sir! A cock's-comb, flowering red:
'Tis just the thing, sir, for your head!

Who wants a frock
　　Of vestal hue?
Or snowy smock?
　　Fair maid, do you?
O me! a lady's smock so white,—
Your bosom's self is not more bright.

Who wants to sport
　　A slender limb?
I've every sort
　　Of hose for him—
Both scarlet, striped, and yellow ones:
This woodbine makes such pantaloons!

Who wants (hush! hush!)
　　A box of paint?
'Twill give a blush
　　Yet leave no taint:
This rose with natural rouge is filled,
From its own dewy leaves distilled.

Then, lady and gentleman fays, come buy!
You never will meet such a merchant as I!

GEORGE DARLEY.

SONG OF THE FAIRIES

BY THE moon we sport and play;
　　With the night begins our day:
　　As we dance the dew doth fall;
Trip it, little urchins, all,

Lightly as the little bee,
Two by two, and three by three,
And about go we, and about go we.

JOHN LYLY.

THE SERENADE.

Photogravure from a painting by Schweniger.

THE FLOWER OF BEAUTY

SWEET in her green dell the flower of beauty slumbers,
    Lulled by the faint breezes sighing through her hair;
Sleeps she, and hears not the melancholy numbers
    Breathed to my sad lute amid the lonely air.

Down from the high cliffs the rivulet is teeming
    To wind round the willow-banks that lure him from above:
Oh that, in tears from my rocky prison streaming,
    I too could glide to the bower of my love!

Ah, where the woodbines with sleepy arms have wound her,
    Opes she her eyelids at the dream of my lay,
Listening like the dove, while the fountains echo round her
    To her lost mate's call in the forest far away.

Come, then, my bird! for the peace thou ever bearest,
    Still Heaven's messenger of comfort to me;
Come! this fond bosom, my faithfulest, my fairest,
    Bleeds with its death-wound,—but deeper yet for thee.

GEORGE DARLEY.

SERENADE

RISE, lady mistress, rise!
    The night hath tedious been;
No sleep has fallen on my eyes,
    Nor slumber made me sin:
Is she not a saint then, say,
Thought of whom keeps sin away?

Rise, madam, rise, and give me light,
    Whom darkness still will cover,
And ignorance, darker than night,
    Till thou smile on thy lover: ·
All want day till thy beauty rise;
For the gray morn breaks from thine eyes.

NATHANIEL FIELD.

FAITHFUL FRIENDS

WHILST as fickle fortune smiled
    Thou and I were both beguiled.
    Every one that flatters thee
Is no friend in misery.
Words are easy, like the wind:
Faithful friends are hard to find.

Every man will be thy friend
Whilst thou hast wherewith to spend;
But if store of crowns be scant,
No man will supply thy want.
If that one be prodigal,
Bountiful they will him call;
And with such-like flattering,
" Pity but he were a king!"
If he be addict to vice,
Quickly him they will entice;
If to woman he be bent,
They have him at commandment.
But if fortune once do frown,
Then farewell his great renown:
They have fawned on him before,
Use his company no more.

He that is thy friend indeed,
He will help thee in thy need:
If thou sorrow he will weep;
If thou wake he cannot sleep:
Thus of every grief in heart
He with thee doth bear a part.
These are certain signs to know
Faithful friend from flattering foe.

RICHARD BARNFIELD.

THE NIGHTINGALE

AS IT fell upon a day
    In the merry month of May,
    Sitting in a pleasant shade
Which a grove of myrtles made,

Beasts did leap and birds did sing,
Trees did grow and plants did spring;
Everything did banish moan
Save the Nightingale alone.
She, poor bird, as all forlorn,
Leaned her breast up till a thorn,
And there sung the doleful'st ditty,
That to hear it was great pity.
Fie, fie, fie, now would she cry;
Teru, teru, by-and-by:
That to hear her so complain
Scarce I could from tears refrain;
For her griefs so lively shown
Made me think upon mine own.—
Ah, thought I, thou mourn'st in vain;
None takes pity on thy pain:
Senseless trees, they cannot hear thee,
Ruthless beasts, they will not cheer thee;
King Pandion, he is dead,
All thy friends are lapped in lead;
All thy fellow-birds do sing
Careless of thy sorrowing:
Even so, poor bird, like thee
None alive will pity me.

RICHARD BARNFIELD.

CRITIC AND POET

NO MAN had ever heard a nightingale,
    When once a keen-eyed naturalist was stirred
        To study and define — *what is a bird;*
To classify by rote and book, nor fail
To mark its structure, and to note the scale
    Whereon its song might possibly be heard.
    Thus far, no farther;— so he spake the word.
When of a sudden,— hark, the nightingale!
Oh, deeper, higher than he could divine,
    That all-unearthly, untaught strain! He saw
The plain brown warbler, unabashed. "Not mine"
    (He cried) "the error of this fatal flaw.
No bird is this,— it soars beyond my line:
    Were it a bird, 'twould answer to my law."

EMMA LAZARUS.

ELLEN TERRY'S BEATRICE

A WIND of spring, that whirls the feignèd snows
    Of blossom petals in the face, and flees;
    Elusive, made of mirthful mockeries,
Yet tender with the prescience of the rose;
A strain desired, that through the memory goes,
    Too subtle-slender for the voice to seize;
    A flame dissembled, only lit to tease,
Whose touch were half a kiss, if one but knows.—

She shows by Leonato's dove-like daughter
    A falcon by a prince to be possessed,
      Gay-graced with bells that ever chiming are;
In azure of the bright Sicilian water,
    A billow that has rapt into its breast
      The swayed reflection of a dancing star!

                  HELEN GRAY CONE.

A VOLUME OF DANTE

I LIE unread alone; none heedeth me:
    Day after day the cobwebs are unswept
    From my dim covers. I have lain and slept
In dust and darkness for a century.
An old forgotten volume I. Yet see!
    Such mighty words within my heart are kept
    That, reading once, great Ariosto wept
In vain despair so impotent to be.
And once with pensive eyes and drooping head,
    Musing, Vittoria Colonna came,
    And touched my leaves with dreamy finger-tips,
Lifted me up half absently, and read;
    Then kissed the page with sudden tender lips,
    And sighed, and murmured one belòvèd name.

            CAROLINE WILDER FELLOWES.

THE LADY POVERTY

THE Lady Poverty was fair,
    But she has lost her looks of late,
    With change of times and change of air.
Ah, slattern! she neglects her hair,

Her gown, her shoes; she keeps no state,
　　As once when her pure feet were bare.

Or — almost worse, if worse can be —
　　She scolds in parlors, dusts, and trims,
Watches and counts. Oh, is this she
Whom Francis met, whose step was free,
　　Who with Obedience caroled hymns,
In Umbria walked with Chastity?

Where is her ladyhood? Not here,
　　Not among modern kinds of men;
But in the stony fields, where clear
Through the thin trees the skies appear,
　　In delicate spare soil and fen,
And slender landscape and austere.

Author Unknown.

THE MAIDEN AND THE LILY

A LILY in my garden grew,
　　Amid the thyme and clover;
　No fairer lily ever blew,
　　Search all the wide world over.
Its beauty passed into my heart:
　　I knew 'twas very silly,
But I was then a foolish maid,
　　And it — a perfect lily.

One day a learnèd man came by,
　　With years of knowledge laden,
And him I questioned with a sigh,
　　Like any foolish maiden: —
"Wise sir, please tell me wherein lies —
　　I know the question's silly —
The something that my art defies,
　　And makes a perfect lily."

He smiled, then bending plucked the flower,
　　Then tore it, leaf and petal,
And talked to me for full an hour,
　　And thought the point to settle: —
"Therein it lies," at length he cries;
　　And I — I know 'twas silly —
Could only weep and say, "But where —
　　O doctor, where's my lily?"

JOHN FRASER.

THE BLACKBIRD'S SONG

MAGDALEN at Michael's gate
    Tirled at the pin; .
On Joseph's thorn sang the blackbird,
    "Let her in! let her in!"

"Hast thou seen the wounds?" said Michael; .
    "Know'st thou thy sin?"
"It is evening, evening," sang the blackbird,
    "Let her in! let her in!"

"Yes, I have seen the wounds,
    And I know my sin."
"She knows it well, well, well," sang the blackbird:
    "Let her in! let her in!"

"Thou bringest no offerings," said Michael,
    "Naught save sin."
And the blackbird sang, "She is sorry, sorry, sorry,
    Let her in! let her in!"

When he had sung himself to sleep,
    And night did begin,
One came and opened Michael's gate,
    And Magdalen went in.

                        HENRY KINGSLEY.

IN SPRINGTIDE

THIS is the hour, the day,
    The time, the season sweet.
    Quick! listen, laggard feet,
    Brook not delay:
Love flies, youth pauses, Maytide will not last;
Forth, forth while yet 'tis time, before the Spring is past.

The Summer's glories shine
    From all her garden ground,
    With lilies prankt around,
    And roses fine; ·
But the pink blooms or white upon the bursting trees,
Primrose and violet sweet, what charm has June like these?

This is the time of song.
From many a joyous throat,
Mute all the dull year long,
Soars love's clear note:
Summer is dumb, and faint with dust and heat;
This is the mirthful time when every sound is sweet.

Fair day of larger light,
Life's own appointed hour,
Young souls bud forth in white—
The world's a-flower.
Thrill, youthful heart; soar upward, limpid voice:
Blossoming time is come—rejoice, rejoice, rejoice!

LEWIS MORRIS.

A SPRING TROUBLE

ALL the meadow-lands were gay
Once upon a morn of May;
All the tree of life was dight
With the blossoms of delight.

And my whole heart was a-tune
With the songs of long ere noon,—
Dew-bedecked and fresh and free
As the unsunned meadows be.

"Lo!" I said unto my spirit,
"Earth and sky thou dost inherit."
Forth I wandered, void of care,
In the largesse of the air.

By there came a damosel;
At a look I loved her well:
But she passed and would not stay—
And all the rest has gone away.

And now no fields are fair to see,
Nor any bud on any tree;
Nor have I share in earth or sky—
All for a maiden passing by!

WILLIAM MACDONALD.

THE SONG OF SPRING

I'LL away to the garden,
    For winter is over;
The Rose is awake
    To the song of her lover!
I will go and discover
The passionate Nightingale singing above her.

From the boughs green and golden
    That slope to the river,
A nymph gathers lemons
    To give to her lover:
I will go and discover
The shy little Nightingale singing above her.

Near the vineyard, where often
    I've spied out a rover,
Sits a damsel who sings
    To be heard by her lover:
I will go and discover
The bold little Nightingale singing above her.

GIL VICENTE (Portuguese).

APRIL WEATHER

OH HUSH, my heart, and take thine ease,
    For here is April weather!
The daffodils beneath the trees
    Are all a-row together.

The thrush is back with his old note;
    The scarlet tulip blowing;
And white — ay, white as my love's throat —
    The dogwood boughs are growing.

The lilac bush is sweet again;
    Down every wind that passes,
Fly flakes from hedgerow and from lane;
    The bees are in the grasses.

And Grief goes out, and Joy comes in,
    And Care is but a feather;
And every lad his love can win:
    For here is April weather.

LIZETTE WOODWORTH REESE.

ASIAN BIRDS

IN THIS May-month, by grace
    of Heaven, things shoot apace.
The waiting multitude
    of fair boughs in the wood,—
How few days have arrayed
    their beauty in green shade!

What have I seen or heard?
    It was the yellow-bird
Sang in the tree: he flew
    a flame against the blue;
Upward he flashed. Again,
    hark! 'tis his heavenly strain.

Another! Hush! Behold,
    many, like boats of gold,
From waving branch to branch
    their airy bodies launch.
What music is like this,
    where each note is a kiss?

The golden willows lift
    their boughs the sun to sift:
Their silken streamers screen
    the sky with veils of green,
To make a cage of song,
    where feathered lovers throng.

How the delicious notes
    come bubbling from their throats!
Full and sweet, how they are shed
    like round pearls from a thread!
The motions of their flight
    are wishes of delight.

Hearing their song, I trace
    the secret of their grace.
Ah, could I this fair time
    so fashion into rhyme,
The poem that I sing
    would be the voice of spring.

ROBERT BRIDGES.

BEFORE AND AFTER THE FLOWER-BIRTH

Before

FIRST VIOLET

LO HERE! how warm and dark and still it is:
Sister, lean close to me, that we may kiss.
Here we go rising, rising — but to where?

SECOND VIOLET

Indeed I cannot tell, nor do I care:
It is so warm and pleasant here. But hark!
What strangest sound was that above the dark?

FIRST VIOLET

As if our sisters all together sang —
Seemed it not so?

SECOND VIOLET

       More loud than that it rang;
And louder still it rings, and seems more near.
Oh! I am shaken through and through with fear —
Now in some deadly grip I seem confined!
Farewell, my sister! Rise, and follow, and find.

FIRST VIOLET

From how far off those last words seemed to fall!
Gone where she will not answer when I call!
How lost? how gone? Alas! this sound above me —
"Poor little violet, left with none to love thee!"
And now, it seems, I break against that sound!
What bitter pain is this that binds me round,
This pain I press into! Where have I come?

After

A CROCUS

Welcome, dear sisters, to our fairy home!
They call this — Garden, and the time is Spring.
Like you I have felt the pain of flowering:
But oh! the wonder and the deep delight
It was to stand here, in the broad sunlight,
And feel the wind flow round me cool and kind;
To hear the singing of the leaves the wind

Goes hurrying through; to see the mighty trees,
Where every day the blossoming buds increase.
At evening, when the shining sun goes in,
The gentler lights we see, and dews begin,
And all is still beneath the quiet sky,
Save sometimes for the wind's low lullaby.

FIRST TREE

Poor little flowers!

SECOND TREE

What would you prate of now?

FIRST TREE

They have not heard: I will keep still.   Speak low.

FIRST VIOLET

The trees bend to each other lovingly.

CROCUS

Daily they talk of fairer things to be.
Great talk they make about the coming Rose,—
The very fairest flower, they say, that blows,
Such scent she hath; her leaves are red, they say,
And fold her round in some divine, sweet way.

FIRST VIOLET

Would she were come, that for ourselves we might
Have pleasure in this wonder of delight!

CROCUS

Here comes the laughing, dancing, hurrying rain;
How all the trees laugh at the wind's light strain!

FIRST VIOLET

We are so near the earth, the wind goes by
And hurts us not; but if we stood up high,
Like trees, then should we soon be blown away.

SECOND VIOLET

Nay; were it so, we should be strong as they.

CROCUS

I often think how nice to be a tree:
Why, sometimes in their boughs the stars I see.

FIRST VIOLET

Have you seen that?

CROCUS

I have, and so shall you;
But hush! I feel the coming of the dew.

[Night.]

SECOND VIOLET

How bright it is! the trees, how still they are!

CROCUS

I never saw so bright a star,
As that which stands and shines just over us.

FIRST VIOLET [*after a pause*]

My leaves feel strange and very tremulous.

CROCUS AND SECOND VIOLET TOGETHER

And mine, and mine!

FIRST VIOLET

O warm, kind sun, appear!

CROCUS

I would the stars were gone, and day were here!

[Just Before Dawn.]

FIRST VIOLET

Sisters! No answer, sisters? Why so still?

ONE TREE TO ANOTHER

Poor little violet, calling through the chill
Of this new frost which did her sister slay,
In which she must herself, too, pass away!
Nay, pretty violet, be not so dismayed:
Sleep only, on your sisters sweet, is laid.

FIRST VIOLET

No pleasant wind about the garden goes;
Perchance the wind has gone to bring the Rose.

O sisters! surely now your sleep is done.
I would we had not looked upon the sun.
My leaves are stiff with pain, O cruel night!
And through my root some sharp thing seems to bite.
Ah me! what pain, what coming change is this?

[*She dies.*

FIRST TREE

So endeth many a violet's dream of bliss.

PHILIP BOURKE MARSTON.

EVENING SONG

THE birds have hid, the winds are low,
  The brake is awake, the grass aglow:
    The bat is the rover,
    No bee on the clover,
    The day is over,
    And evening come.

The heavy beetle spreads her wings,
The toad has the road, the cricket sings:
    The bat is the rover,
    No bee on the clover,
    The day is over,
    And evening come.

JOHN VANCE CHENEY.

BENEDICITE

ALL Green Things on the earth, bless ye the Lord!"
  So sang the choir while ice-cased branches beat
  The frosty window-panes, and at our feet
The frozen, tortured sod but mocked the word,
  And seemed to cry like some poor soul in pain,
"Lord, suffering and endurance fill my days;
The growing green things will their Maker praise—
  The happy green things, growing in warm rain!"—
"So God lacks praise while all the fields are white!"
  I said; then smiled, remembering southward far,
How pampas grass swayed green in summer light.
  Nay, God hears always from this swinging star,
Decani and Cantoris, South and North,
Each answering other, praises pouring forth.

ANNA CALLENDER BRACKETT.

'TWEEN EARTH AND SKY

SEEDS with wings, between earth and sky
　　　　Fluttering, flying;
　　Seeds of a lily with blood-red core
　　Breathing of myrrh and of giroflore:
Where winds drop them, there must they lie
　　　　Living or dying.

Some to the garden, some to the wall,
　　　　Fluttering, falling;
　　Some to the river, some to earth:
　　Those that reach the right soil get birth;
None of the rest have lived at all.
　　　　Whose voice is calling?—

"Here is soil for winged seeds that near,
　　　　Fluttering, fearing,
　　Where they shall root and bourgeon and spread.
　　Lacking the heart-room the song lies dead:
Half is the song that reaches the ear,
　　　　Half is the hearing."

　　　　　　　　　　AUGUSTA WEBSTER.

SONG OF SUMMER

From 'Summer's Last Will and Testament'

FAIR Summer droops, droop men and beasts therefore;
　　So fair a summer look for never more:
　　All good things vanish less than in a day,—
Peace, plenty, pleasure suddenly decay.
　　Go not yet away, bright soul of the sad year,—
　　The earth is hell when thou leav'st to appear.

What! shall those flowers that decked thy garland erst,
Upon thy grave be wastefully dispersed?
O trees, consume your sap in sorrow's source!
Streams, turn to tears your tributary course!
　　Go not yet hence, bright soul of the sad year,—
　　The earth is hell when thou leav'st to appear.

　　　　　　　　　　THOMAS NASH.

A SUMMER SONG

(THIRTEENTH CENTURY)

SUMMER-HUED
  Is the wood,
Heath and field; debonair
  Now is seen
  White, brown, green,
Blue, red, yellow, everywhere.
  Everything
  You see spring
Joyously, in full delight;
  He whose pains
  Dear love deigns
With her favor to requite—
  Ah, happy wight!

  Whosoe'er
  Knows love's care,
Free from care well may be;
  Year by year
  Brightness clear
Of the May shall he see.
  Blithe and gay
  All the play
Of glad love shall he fulfill;
  Joyous living
  Is in the giving
Of high love to whom she will,
  Rich in joys still.

  He's a churl
  Whom a girl
Lovingly shall embrace,
  Who'll not cry
  "Blest am I"—
Let none such show his face.
  This will cure you
  (I assure you)
Of all sorrows, all alarms;
  What alloy
  In his joy
On whom white and pretty arms
  Bestow their charms?

ULRICH VON LIECHTENSTEIN.

Translation of Edward T. McLaughlin.

THE BATHER

WARM from her waist her girdle she unwound,
And cast it down on the insensate turf;
Then copse and cove and deep-secluded vale
She scrutinized with keen though timid eyes,
And stood with ear intent to catch each stir
Of leaf or twig or bird-wing rustling there.
Her startled heart beat quicker even to hear
The wild bee woo the blossom with a hymn,
Or hidden insect break its lance of sound
Against the obdurate silence. Then she smiled,
At her own fears amused, and knew herself
God's only image by that hidden shore;
Out from its bonds her wondrous hair she loosed,—
Hair glittering like spun glass, and bright as though
Shot full of golden arrows. Down below
Her supple waist the soft and shimmering coils
Rolled in their bright abundance, goldener
Than was the golden wonder Jason sought.

Her fair hands then, like white doves in a net,
A moment fluttered 'mid the shining threads,
As with a dexterous touch she higher laid
The gleaming tresses on her shapely head,
Beyond the reach of rudely amorous waves.
Then from her throat her light robe she unclasped,
And dropped it downward with a blush that rose
The higher as the garment lower fell.

Then cast she off the sandals from her feet,
And paused upon the brink of that blue lake:
A sight too fair for either gods or men;
An Eve untempted in her Paradise.
The waters into which her young eyes looked
Gave back her image with so true a truth,
She blushed to look; but blushing looked again,
As maidens to their mirrors oft return
With bashful boldness, once again to gaze
Upon the crystal page that renders back
Themselves unto themselves, until their eyes
Confess their love for their own loveliness.

Her rounded cheeks, in each of which had grown,
With sudden blossoming, a fresh red rose,

' She hid an instant in her dimpled hands;
Then met her pink palms up above her head,
And whelmed her white shape in the welcoming wave.

Around each lithesome limb the waters twined,
And with their lucent raiment robed her form;
And as her hesitating bosom sunk
To the caresses of bewildered waves,
The foamy pearls from their own foreheads gave
For her fair brow, and showered in her hair
The evanescent diamonds of the deep.

Thus dallying with the circumfluent tide,
Her loveliness half hidden, half revealed,
An Undine with a soul, she plunged and rose,
Whilst the white graces of her rounded arms
She braided with the blue of wandering waves,
And saw the shoulders of the billows yield
Before the even strokes of her small hands,
And laughed to see, and held her crimson mouth
Above the crest of each advancing surge
Like a red blossom pendent o'er a pool;
Till, done with the invigorating play,
Once more she gained the bank, and once again
Saw her twin image in the waters born.

From the translucent wave each beauty grew
To strange perfection. Never statue wrought
By cunning art to fullness of all grace,
And kissed to life by love, could fairer seem
Than she who stood upon that grassy slope
So fresh, so human, so immaculate!

Out from the dusky cloisters of the wood
The nun-like winds stole with a saintly step,
And dried the bright drops from her panting form,
As she with hurried hands once more let down
The golden drapery of her glorious hair,
That fell about her like some royal cloak
Dropped from the sunset's rare and radiant loom.

                              MARY ASHLEY TOWNSEND.

THE HAYMAKERS' SONG

HERE'S to him that grows it,
    Drink, lads, drink!
  That lays it in and mows it,
    Clink, jugs, clink!
To him that mows and makes it,
That scatters it and shakes it,
That turns and teds and rakes it,
    Clink, jugs, clink!

Now here's to him that stacks it,
    Drink, lads, drink!
That thrashes and that tacks it,
    Clink, jugs, clink!
That cuts it out for eating,
When March-dropped lambs are bleating,
And the slate-blue clouds are sleeting,
    Drink, lads, drink!

And here's to thane and yeoman,
    Drink, lads, drink!
To horseman and to bowman,
    Clink, jugs, clink!
To lofty and to low man,
Who bears a grudge to no man,
But flinches from no foeman,
    Drink, lads, drink!

ALFRED AUSTIN.

SEPTEMBER

BIRDS that were gray in the green are black in the yellow.
Here where the green remains, rocks one little fellow.

Quaker in gray, do you know that the green is going?
More than that — do you know that the yellow is showing?

Singer of songs, do you know that your youth is flying?
That age will soon at the lock of your life be prying?

Lover of life, do you know that the brown is going?
More than that — do you know that the gray is showing?

S. FRANCES HARRISON ("Seranus").

INDIAN SUMMER

LINGER, O day!
    Let not thy purple haze
    Fade utterly away.
The Indian summer lays
Her tender touch upon the emerald hills.
    Exquisite thrills
Of delicate gladness fill the blue-veined air.
    More restful even than rest,
The passionate sweetness that is everywhere.
    Soft splendors in the west
Touch with the charm of coming changefulness
    The yielding hills.
    Oh linger, day!
    Let not the dear
Delicious languor of thy dreamfulness
    Vanish away!
    Serene and clear,
The brooding stillness of the delicate air,
Dreamier than the dreamiest depths of sleep,
    Falls softly everywhere.
    Still let me keep
One little hour longer tryst with thee,
    O day of days!
    Lean down on me,
In tender beauty of thy amethyst haze.
    Upon the vine,
Rich clinging clusters of the ripening grape
    Hang silent in the sun,
    But in each one
Beats with full throb the quickening purple wine,
Whose pulse shall round the perfect fruit to shape.

    Too dreamy even to dream,
I hear the murmuring bee and gliding stream;
The singing silence of the afternoon,
Lulling my yielding senses till they swoon
    Into still deeper rest:
    While soul released from sense,
    Passionate and intense,
With quick exultant quiver in its wings,
Prophetic longing for diviner things,
    Escapes the unthinking breast;

Pierces rejoicing through the shining mist,
But shrinks before the keen, cold ether, kissed
By burning stars; delirious foretaste
Of joys the soul — too eager in its haste
To grasp ere won by the diviner right
Of birth through death — is far too weak to bear.
   Bathed in earth's lesser light,
Slipping down slowly through the shining air,
Once more it steals into the dreaming breast,
Praying again to be its patient guest.

   And as my senses wake,
The beautiful glad soul again to take,
   The twilight falls.
 A lonely wood-thrush calls
   The day away.
  "Where hast thou been to-day,
O soul of mine?" I wondering question her.
She will not answer while the light winds stir
And rustle near to hear what she may say.

  Thou needst not linger, day!
   My soul and I
Would hold high converse of diviner things.
   Unfold thy wings;
Wrap softly round thyself thy delicate haze,
And gliding down the slowly darkening ways,
   Vanish away!

ALICE WELLINGTON ROLLINS.

INDIAN SUMMER

THESE are the days when birds come back,—
 A very few, a bird or two,—
  To take a backward look.

These are the days when skies put on
The old, old sophistries of June,—
 A blue-and-gold mistake.

Oh! fraud that almost cheats the bee,
Almost thy plausibility
 Induces my belief;

Till ranks of seeds their witness bear,
And softly through the altered air
    Hurries a timid leaf!

Oh, sacrament of summer days!
Oh, last communion in the haze!
    Permit a child to join—

Thy sacred emblems to partake,
Thy consecrated bread to break,
    Taste thine immortal wine.

EMILY DICKINSON.

NOVEMBER IN THE SOUTH

THIS livelong day I listen to the fall
    Of hickory-nuts and acorns to the ground,
The croak of rain-crows and the blue-jay's call,
    The woodman's axe that hews with muffled sound.

And like a spendthrift in a threadbare coat
    That still retains a dash of crimson hue,
An old woodpecker chatters forth a note
    About the better summer days he knew.

Across the road a ruined cabin stands,
    With ragweeds and with thistles at its door,
While withered cypress-vines hang tattered strands
    About its falling roof and rotting floor.

In yonder forest nook no sound is heard,
    Save when the walnuts patter on the earth,
Or when by winds the hectic leaves are stirred
    To dance like witches in their maniac mirth.

Down in the orchard hang the golden pears,
    Half honeycombed by yellowhammer beaks ;
Near by, a dwarfed and twisted apple bears
    Its fruit, brown-red as Amazonian cheeks.

The lonesome landscape seems as if it yearned
    Like our own aching hearts, when first we knew
The one love of our life was not returned,
    Or first we found an old-time friend untrue.

At last the night comes, and the broad white moon
    Is welcomed by the owl with frenzied glee;
The fat opossum, like a satyr, soon
    Blinks at its light from yon persimmon-tree.

The raccoon starts to hear long-dreaded sounds
    Amid his scattered spoils of ripened corn,
The cry of negroes and the yelp of hounds,
    The wild rude pealing of a hunter's horn.

At last a gray mist covers all the land
    Until we seem to wander in a cloud,
Far, far away upon some elfin strand
    Where sorrow drapes us in a mildewed shroud.

No voice is heard in field or forest nigh
    To break the desolation of the spell,
Save one sad mocking-bird in boughs near by,
    Who sings like Tasso in his madman's cell;

While one magnolia blossom, ghostly white,
    Like high-born Leonora, lingering there,
Haughty and splendid in the lonesome night,
    Is pale with passion in her dumb despair.

WALTER MALONE.

THE NIGHT BEFORE CHRISTMAS

'TWAS the night before Christmas, when all through the
    Not a creature was stirring, not even a mouse: [house
    The stockings were hung by the chimney with care,
In hopes that St. Nicholas soon would be there;
The children were nestled all snug in their beds,
While visions of sugar-plums danced through their heads;
And mamma in her kerchief, and I in my cap,
Had just settled our brains for a long winter's nap,—
When out on the lawn there arose such a clatter,
I sprang from my bed to see what was the matter.
Away to the window I flew like a flash,
Tore open the shutters and threw up the sash.
The moon, on the breast of the new-fallen snow,
Gave a lustre of midday to objects below;

When what to my wondering eyes should appear
But a miniature sleigh, and eight tiny reindeer,
With a little old driver, so lively and quick
I knew in a moment it must be St. Nick.
More rapid than eagles his coursers they came,
And he whistled, and shouted, and called them by name:
"Now, Dasher! now, Dancer! now, Prancer! now, Vixen!
On, Comet! on, Cupid! on, Dunder and Blitzen!—
To the top of the porch, to the top of the wall!
Now dash away, dash away, dash away all!"
As dry leaves that before the wild hurricane fly,
When they meet with an obstacle, mount to the sky,
So up to the house-top the coursers they flew,
With the sleigh full of toys, and St. Nicholas too.
And then in a twinkling I heard on the roof
The prancing and pawing of each little hoof.
As I drew in my head, and was turning around,
Down the chimney St. Nicholas came with a bound.
He was dressed all in fur from his head to his foot,
And his clothes were all tarnished with ashes and soot;
A bundle of toys he had flung on his back,
And he looked like a peddler just opening his pack.
His eyes how they twinkled! his dimples how merry!
His cheeks were like roses, his nose like a cherry;
His droll little mouth was drawn up like a bow,
And the beard on his chin was as white as the snow.
The stump of a pipe he held tight in his teeth,
And the smoke, it encircled his head like a wreath.
He had a broad face, and a little round belly
That shook, when he laughed, like a bowlful of jelly.
He was chubby and plump,—a right jolly old elf,—
And I laughed when I saw him, in spite of myself.
A wink of his eye, and a twist of his head,
Soon gave me to know I had nothing to dread.
He spake not a word, but went straight to his work,
And filled all the stockings; then turned with a jerk,
And laying his finger aside of his nose,
And giving a nod, up the chimney he rose.
He sprang to his sleigh, to his team gave a whistle,
And away they all flew like the down of a thistle;
But I heard him exclaim, ere he drove out of sight,
"Happy Christmas to all, and to all a good-night!"

CLEMENT CLARKE MOORE.

THE FROST

THE Frost looked forth, one still, clear night,
    And he said, "Now I shall be out of sight;
So through the valley and over the height
        In silence I'll take my way.
I will not go like that blustering train,
The wind and the snow, the hail and the rain,
Who make so much bustle and noise in vain,
        But I'll be as busy as they!"

Then he went to the mountain, and powdered its crest;
He climbed up the trees, and their boughs he dressed
With diamonds and pearls; and over the breast
        Of the quivering lake he spread
A coat of mail, that it need not fear
The downward point of many a spear
That he hung on its margin, far and near,
        Where a rock could reach its head.

He went to the windows of those who slept,
And over the pane like a fairy crept:
Wherever he breathed, wherever he stepped,
        By the light of the moon were seen
Most beautiful things.   There were flowers and trees,
There were bevies of birds and swarms of bees,
There were cities, thrones, temples, and towers, and these
        All pictured in silver sheen!

But he did one thing that was hardly fair:
He peeped in the cupboard, and finding there
That all had forgotten for him to prepare,—
        "Now, just to set them a-thinking,
I'll bite this basket of fruit," said he;
"This costly pitcher I'll burst in three;
And the glass of water they've left for me
        Shall 'tchick!' to tell them I'm drinking."

                    HANNAH FRANCES GOULD.

THE ROOT'S DREAM

FROM the dark earth cool and fragrant,
  A gnarled unlovely root
Sent forth in the rippling sunshine
  A slender gold-green shoot.

The shoot in the languid breezes
  Was soon by a pale bloom bent;
A sense of its frail white beauty
  The sun to the black root sent.

The root was thrilled by a vision,
  A vision of peace supreme;—
The fragile star of a blossom
  Was the black root's dainty dream.

R. K. MUNKITTRICK.

WILD HONEY

WHERE hints of racy sap and gum
  Out of the old dark forest come;

Where birds their beaks like hammers wield,
And pith is pierced, and bark is peeled;

Where the green walnut's outer rind
Gives precious bitterness to the wind;—

There lurks the sweet creative power,
As lurks the honey in the flower.

In winter's bud that bursts in spring,
In nut of autumn's ripening,

In acrid bulb beneath the mold,
Sleeps the elixir, strong and old,

That Rosicrucians sought in vain,—
Life that renews itself again!

What bottled perfume is so good
As fragrance of split tulip-wood?

What fabled drink of god or Muse
Was rich as purple mulberry-juice?

And what school-polished gem of thought
Is like the rune from Nature caught?

He is a poet strong and true
Who loves wild thyme and honey-dew;

And like a brown bee works and sings
With morning freshness on his wings,

And a gold burden on his thighs,—
The pollen-dust of centuries!

MAURICE THOMPSON.

THE WAKING OF THE LARK

O BONNIE bird that in the brake, exultant, does prepare thee—
As poets do whose thoughts are true—for wings that will
upbear thee,
Oh, tell me, tell me, bonnie bird,
Canst thou not pipe of hope deferred?
Or canst thou sing of naught but spring among the golden meadows?

Methinks a bard (and thou art one) should suit his song to sorrow;
And tell of pain, as well as gain, that waits us on the morrow:
But thou art not a prophet, thou,
If naught but joy can touch thee now;
If, in thy heart, thou hast no vow that speaks of Nature's anguish.

Oh, I have held my sorrows dear, and felt, though poor and slighted,
The songs we love are those we hear when love is unrequited.
But thou art still the slave of dawn,
And canst not sing till night be gone,
Till o'er the pathway of the fawn the sunbeams shine and quiver.

Thou art the minion of the sun that rises in his splendor,
And canst not spare for Dian fair the songs that should attend her:
The moon, so sad and silver pale,
Is mistress of the nightingale;
And thou wilt sing on hill and dale no ditties in the darkness.

For queen and king thou wilt not spare one note of thine outpouring;
And thou'rt as free as breezes be on Nature's velvet flooring:
The daisy, with its hood undone,
The grass, the sunlight, and the sun—
These are the joys, thou holy one, that pay thee for thy singing.

Oh, hush! Oh, hush! how wild a gush of rapture in the distance —
A roll of rhymes, a toll of chimes, a cry for love's assistance;
    A sound that wells from happy throats,
    A flood of song where beauty floats,
And where our thoughts, like golden boats, do seem to cross a river.

This is the advent of the lark, — the priest in gray apparel, —
Who doth prepare to trill in air his sinless summer carol;
    This is the prelude to the lay
    The birds did sing in Cæsar's day,
And will again, for aye and aye, in praise of God's creation.

O dainty thing, on wonder's wing, by life and love elated,
Oh, sing aloud from cloud to cloud, till day be consecrated;
    Till from the gateways of the morn,
    The sun, with all his light unshorn,
His robes of darkness round him torn, doth scale the lofty heavens!

ERIC MACKAY.

TO THE LARK

(T'R EHEDYDD)

SENTINEL of the morning light!
    Reveler of the spring!
  How sweetly, nobly wild thy flight,
    Thy boundless journeying:
Far from thy brethren of the woods, alone,
A hermit chorister before God's throne!

  Oh! wilt thou climb yon heavens for me,
    Yon rampart's starry height,
  Thou interlude of melody
    'Twixt darkness and the light,
And seek with heaven's first dawn upon thy crest,
My lady-love, the moonbeam of the west?

  No woodland caroler art thou;
    Far from the archer's eye,
  Thy course is o'er the mountain's brow,
    Thy music in the sky:
Then fearless float thy path of cloud along,
Thou earthly denizen of angel song.

DAFYDD AP GWILYM.
(Welsh, Fourteenth Century.)

MEADOW-LARKS

SWEET, sweet, sweet! Oh happy that I am!
    (Listen to the meadow-larks, across the fields that sing!)
  Sweet, sweet, sweet! O subtle breath of balm,
    O winds that blow, O buds that grow, O rapture of the
      spring!

Sweet, sweet, sweet! O skies, serene and blue,
  That shut the velvet pastures in, that fold the mountain's
    crest!
Sweet, sweet, sweet! What of the clouds ye knew?
  The vessels ride a golden tide, upon a sea at rest.

Sweet, sweet, sweet! Who prates of care and pain?
  Who says that life is sorrowful? O life so glad, so fleet!
Ah! he who lives the noblest life finds life the noblest gain,
  The tears of pain a tender rain to make its waters sweet.

Sweet, sweet, sweet! O happy world that is!
  Dear heart, I hear across the fields my mateling pipe and call.
Sweet, sweet, sweet! O world so full of bliss,—
  For life is love, the world is love, and love is over all!

                    INA D. COOLBRITH.

MORNING SONG

THE lark now leaves his watery nest,
    And climbing shakes his dewy wings:
  He takes this window for the east;
    And to implore your light, he sings.
Awake, awake! the morn will never rise,
Till she can dress her beauty at your eyes.

The merchant bows unto the seaman's star,
    The plowman from the sun his season takes,
But still the lover wonders what they are
    Who look for day before his mistress wakes.
Awake, awake, break through your veils of lawn,
Then draw your curtains, and begin the dawn.

              SIR WILLIAM DAVENANT.

THE O'LINCON FAMILY

A FLOCK of merry singing-birds was sporting in the grove;
   Some were warbling cheerily, and some were making love:
   There were Bobolincon, Wadolincon, Winterseeble, Conquedle,—
A livelier set was never led by tabor, pipe, or fiddle,—
Crying, "Phew, shew, Wadolincon, see, see, Bobolincon,
Down among the tickletops, hiding in the buttercups!
I know the saucy chap, I see his shining cap
Bobbing in the clover there,—see, see, see!"

Up flies Bobolincon, perching on an apple-tree,
Startled by his rival's song, quickened by his raillery;
Soon he spies the rogue afloat, curvetting in the air,
And merrily he turns about, and warns him to beware!
"'Tis you that would a-wooing go, down among the rushes O!
But wait a week, till flowers are cheery,—wait a week, and ere you
      marry,
Be sure of a house wherein to tarry!
Wadolink, Whiskodink, Tom Denny, wait, wait, wait!"

Every one's a funny fellow; every one's a little mellow:
Follow, follow, follow, follow, o'er the hill and in the hollow!
Merrily, merrily, there they hie; now they rise and now they fly;
They cross and turn, and in and out, and down in the middle, and
      wheel about,—
With a "Phew, shew, Wadolincon! listen to me, Bobolincon!—
Happy's the wooing that's speedily doing, that's speedily doing,
That's merry and over with the bloom of the clover!
Bobolincon, Wadolincon, Winterseeble, follow, follow me!"

Oh what a happy life they lead, over the hill and in the mead!
Now they gambol o'er the clearing—off again, and then appearing;
How they sing, and how they play! see, they fly away, away!
Poised aloft on quivering wing, now they soar, and now they sing:—
"We must all be merry and moving; we must all be happy and
      loving;
For when the midsummer has come, and the grain has ripened its
      ear,
The haymakers scatter our young, and we mourn for the rest of the
      year.
Then, Bobolincon, Wadolincon, Winterseeble, haste, haste away!"

WILSON FLAGG.

TO THE WOOD-ROBIN

THE wooing air is jubilant with song,
                And blossoms swell
        As leaps thy liquid melody along
                The dusky dell,
Where Silence, late supreme, foregoes her wonted spell.

        Ah, whence, in sylvan solitudes remote,
                Hast learned the lore
        That breeds delight in every echoing note
                The woodlands o'er;
As when, through slanting sun, descends the quickening
                shower?

        Thy hermitage is peopled with the dreams
                That gladden sleep;
        Here Fancy dallies with delirious themes
                Mid shadows deep,
· Till eyes unused to tears, with wild emotions weep.

        We rise, alas, to find our visions fled!
                But thine remain.
        Night weaves of golden harmonies the thread,
                And fills thy brain
With joys that overflow in Love's awakening strain.

        Yet thou, from mortal influence apart,
                Seek'st naught of praise;
        The empty plaudits of the emptier heart
                Taint not thy lays:
Thy Maker's smile alone thy tuneful bosom sways.

        Teach me, thou warbling eremite, to sing
                Thy rhapsody;
        Nor borne on vain ambition's vaunting wing,
                But led of thee,
To rise from earthly dreams to hymn Eternity.

                                    JOHN B. TABB.

THE THRUSH'S SONG

(FROM THE GAELIC)

DEAR, dear, dear,
　　In the rocky glen,
　　Far away, far away, far away,
　　　The haunts of men:
There shall we dwell in love
With the lark and the dove,
Cuckoo and corn-rail;
Feast on the bearded snail,
　　Worm and gilded fly;
　Drink of the crystal rill
Winding adown the hill
　　　Never to dry.　·
With glee, with glee, with glee,
　Cheer up, cheer up, cheer up here;
Nothing to harm us, then sing merrily,
　Sing to the loved one whose nest is near.
　　　　Qui, qui, queen, quip,
　　　　Tiurru, tiurru, chipiwi;
　　　　Too-tee, too-tee, chin-choo,
　　　　Chirri, chirri, chooee,
　　　　Quin, qui, qui!

　　　　　　　　W. MACGILLIVRAY.

THE SONG OF THE THRUSH

I WAS on the margin of a plain,
　　Under a wide-spreading tree,
　Hearing the song
Of the wild birds;
Listening to the language
Of the thrush cock,
Who from the wood of the valley
Composed a verse;
From the wood of the steep
He sang exquisitely.
Speckled was his breast
Amongst the green leaves,
As upon branches
Of a thousand blossoms

On the bank of a brook,
All heard
With the dawn the song,
Like a silver bell;
Performing a sacrifice
Until the hour of forenoon;
Upon the green altar
Ministering Bardism.
From the branches of the hazel
Of green broad leaves
He sings an ode
To God the Creator:
With a carol of love
From the green glade
To all in the hollow
Of the glen who love him;
Balm of the heart
To those who love.
I had from his beak
The voice of inspiration,
A song of metres
That gratified me;
Glad was I made
By his minstrelsy.
Then respectfully
Uttered I an address
From the stream of the valley
To the bird:
I requested urgently
His undertaking a message
To the fair one
Where dwells my affection.
Gone is the bard of the leaves
From the small twigs
To the second Lunet,
The sun of the maidens!
To the streams of the plain
St. Mary prosper him,
To bring to me,
Under the green woods
The hue of the snow of one night,
Without delay.

RHYS GOCH AP RHICCART (Welsh).

THE SERVICE OF SONG

SOME keep the Sabbath going to church:
    I keep it staying at home,
With a bobolink for a chorister
    And an orchard for a dome.

Some keep the Sabbath in surplice:
    I just wear my wings;
And instead of tolling the bell for church,
    Our little sexton sings.

God preaches, a noted clergyman,
    And the sermon is never long;
So instead of getting to heaven at last,
    I'm going all along!

EMILY DICKINSON.

EARLY SPRING

O TREES, all a-throb and a-quiver
    With the stirring pulse of the ·spring,
    Your tops so misty against the blue,
With the buds where the green not yet looks through,
I know the beauty the days will bring,
But your cloudy tops are a wonderful thing!

Like the first faint streak of the dawning,
    Which tells that the day is nigh;
Like the first dear kiss of the maiden,
    So absolute, though so shy;
Like the joy divine of the mother
    Before her child she sees —
So faint, so dear, and so blessed
    Are your misty tops, O trees!

I can feel the delicate pulses
    That stir in each restless fold
Of leaflets and bunches of blossoms —
    The life that never grows old:
Yet wait, ah wait, though they woo you —
    The sun, the rain-drops, the breeze;
Break not too soon into verdure,
    O misty, beautiful trees!

ANNA CALLENDER BRACKETT.

TO A DAISY

Ah! I'm feared thou's come too sooin,
    Little daisy!
  Pray whativer wor ta doin'?
    Are ta crazy?
Winter winds are blowin' yet:
Tha'll be starved, mi little pet!

Did a gleam o' sunshine warm thee,
    An' deceive thee?
Niver let appearance charm thee:
    Yes, believe me,
Smiles tha'lt find are oft but snares
Laid to catch thee unawares.

An' yet, I think it looks a shame
    To talk such stuff;
I've lost heart, an' thou'lt do t' same,
    Ay, sooin enough!
An', if thou'rt happy as tha art,
Trustin' must be t' wisest part.

Come! I'll pile some bits o' stoan
   · Round thi dwellin';
They may cheer thee when I've goan,—
    Theer's no tellin':
An' when spring's mild day draws near,
I'll release thee, niver fear!

An' if then thi pretty face
    Greets me smilin',
I may come an' sit by th' place,
    Time beguilin';
Glad to think I'd paar to be
Of some use, if but to thee!

                      John Hartley.

BACCHUS

Listen to the tawny thief,
    Hid behind the waxen leaf,
      Growling at his fairy host,—
Bidding her with angry boast

Fill his cup with wine distilled
From the dew the dawn has spilled:
Stored away in golden casks
Is the precious draught he asks.

Who — who makes this mimic din
In this mimic meadow inn,
Sings in such a drowsy note,
Wears a golden-belted coat;
Loiters in the dainty room
Of this tavern of perfume;
Dares to linger at the cup
Till the yellow sun is up?

Bacchus 'tis, come back again
To the busy haunts of men;
Garlanded and gayly dressed,
Bands of gold about his breast;
Straying from his paradise,
Having pinions angel-wise,—
'Tis the honey-bee, who goes
Reveling within a rose!

FRANK DEMPSTER SHERMAN.

SPRING

From 'Summer's Last Will and Testament'

SPRING, the sweet Spring, is the year's pleasant king:
    Then blooms each thing, then maids dance in a ring;
    Cold doth not sting, the pretty birds do sing —
        Cuckoo, jug, jug, pu we, to witta woo.

The palm and may make country-houses gay;
Lambs frisk and play, the shepherds pipe all day;
And we hear aye birds tune this merry lay —
    Cuckoo, jug, jug, pu we, to witta woo.

The fields breathe sweet, the daisies kiss our feet;
Young lovers meet, old wives a-sunning sit;
In every street these tunes our ears do greet —
    Cuckoo, jug, jug, pu we, to witta woo.
        Spring, the sweet Spring.

THOMAS NASH.

THE APPLE-TREE

From 'Poems' by Julia C. R. Dorr. Copyright 1874, 1885, 1892, by Charles Scribner's Sons

GRACEFUL and lithe and tall,
　It stands by the garden wall,
　　In the flush of its pink-white bloom
　　Elate with its own perfume,
Tossing its young bright head
　In the first glad joy of May,
While its singing leaves sing back
　To the bird on the dancing spray.
"I'm alive! I'm abloom!" it cries
To the winds and the laughing skies.
Ho! for the gay young apple-tree
　That stands by the garden wall!

Sturdy and broad and tall,
Over the garden wall
It spreads its branches wide—
A bower on either side.
For the bending boughs hang low;
　And with shouts and gay turmoil
The children gather like bees
　To garner the golden spoil;
While the smiling mother sings,
"Rejoice for the gift it brings!
Ho! for the laden apple-tree
　That stands by our garden wall!"

The strong swift years fly past,
Each swifter than the last;
And the tree by the garden wall
Sees joy and grief befall.
Still from the spreading boughs
　Some golden apples swing;
But the children come no more
　For the autumn harvesting.
The tangled grass lies deep
Where the long path used to creep;
Yet ho! for the brave old apple-tree
　That leans over the crumbling wall!

New generations pass,
Like shadows on the grass.

What is there that remains
For all their toil and pains?
A little hollow place
    Where once a hearthstone lay;
An empty, silent space
    Whence life hath gone away;
Tall brambles where the lilacs grew,
Some fennel, and a clump of rue,
And this one gnarled old apple-tree
    Where once was the garden wall!

                                    JULIA C. R. DORR.

THE HOUSE OF THE TREES

OPE your doors and take me in,
    Spirit of the wood;
        Wash me clean of dust and din,
        Clothe me in your mood.

Take me from the noisy light
    To the sunless peace,
Where at midday standeth Night,
    Signing Toil's release.

All your dusky twilight stores
    To my senses give;
Take me in and lock the doors,
    Show me how to live.

Lift your leafy roof for me,
    Part your yielding walls;
Let me wander lingeringly
    Through your scented halls.

Ope your doors and take me in,
    Spirit of the wood;
Take me — make me next of kin
    To your leafy brood.

                            ETHELWYN WETHERALD.

IN GREEN OLD GARDENS

IN GREEN old gardens hidden away
  From sight of revel and sound of strife,
    Where the bird may sing out his soul ere he dies,
Nor fears for the night, so he lives his day;
Where the high red walls, which are growing gray
  With their lichen and moss embroideries,
    Seem sadly and sternly to shut out Life,
Because it is often as sad as they;

Where even the bee has time to glide
  (Gathering gayly his honeyed store)
    Right to the heart of the old-world flowers,—
China-asters and purple stocks,
Dahlias and tall red hollyhocks,
    Laburnums raining their golden showers,
  Columbines prim of the folded core,
And lupins, and larkspurs, and « London pride »;

Where the heron is waiting amongst the reeds,
  Grown tame in the silence that reigns around,
    Broken only, now and then,
By shy woodpecker or noisy jay,
By the far-off watch-dog's muffled bay;
    But where never the purposeless laughter of men,
  Or the seething city's murmurous sound,
Will float up under the river-weeds; —

Here may I live what life I please,
  Married and buried out of sight,—
    Married to pleasure, and buried to pain,—
Hidden away amongst scenes like these,
Under the fans of the chestnut-trees;
    Living my child-life over again,
  With the further hope of a fuller delight,
Blithe as the birds and. wise as the bees.

In green old gardens hidden away
  From sight of revel and sound of strife,—
    Here have I leisure to breathe and move,
And to do my work in a nobler way;
To sing my songs, and to say my say;

To dream my dreams, and to love my love;
To hold my faith, and to live my life,
Making the most of its shadowy day.

«Violet Fane» (Lady Currie).

A BENEDICTINE GARDEN

THROUGH all the wind-blown aisles of May
    Faint bells of perfume swing and fall.
    Within this apple-petaled wall
(A gray east flecked with rosy day)
The pink Laburnum lays her cheek
    In married, matchless, lovely bliss,
Against her golden mate, to seek
        His airy kiss.

Tulips, in faded splendor drest,
    Brood o'er their beds, a slumbrous gloom;
    Dame Peony, red and ripe with bloom,
Swells the silk housing of her breast;
The Lilac, drunk to ecstasy,
    Breaks her full flagons on the air,
And drenches home the reeling bee
        Who found her fair.

O cowlèd legion of the Cross,
    What solemn pleasantry is thine,
    Vowing to seek the life divine
Through abnegation and through loss!
Men but make monuments of sin
    Who walk the earth's ambitious round;
Thou hast the richer realm within
        This garden ground.

No woman's voice hath sweeter note
    Than chanting of this plumèd choir;
    No jewel ever wore the fire
Hung on the dewdrop's quivering throat.
A ruddier pomp and pageantry
    Than world's delight o'erfleets thy sod;
And choosing this, thou hast in fee
        The peace of God.

ALICE BROWN.

THE BLACKBERRY FARM

NATURE gives with freèst hands
    Richest gifts to poorest lands.
    When the lord has sown his last,
And his field's to desert passed,
She begins to claim her own,
And instead of harvest flown —
Sunburnt sheaves and golden ears —
Sends her hardier pioneers:
Barbarous brambles, outlawed seeds;
The first families of weeds
Fearing neither sun nor wind,
With the flowers of their kind
(Outcasts of the garden-bound),
Colonize the expended ground,
Using (none her right gainsay)
Confiscations of decay:
Thus she clothes the barren place,
Old disgrace, with newer grace.

Title-deeds, which cover lands
Ruled and reaped by buried hands,
She — disowning owners old,
Scorning their "to have and hold" —
Takes herself: the moldering fence
Hides with her munificence;
O'er the crumbled gate-post twines
Her proprietary vines;
On the doorstep of the house
Writes in moss "Anonymous,"
And, that beast and bird may see,
"This is Public Property;"
To the bramble makes the sun
Bearer of profusion;
Blossom-odors breathe in June ·
Promise of her later boon,
And in August's brazen heat
Grows the prophecy complete;—
Lo, her largess glistens bright,
Blackness diamonded with light!

Then, behold, she welcomes all
To her annual festival:

"Mine the fruit, but yours as well,"
Speaks the Mother Miracle;
"Rich and poor are welcome; come,
Make to-day millennium
In my garden of the sun:
Black and white to me are one.
This my freehold use content,—
Here no landlord rides for rent;
I proclaim my jubilee,
In my Black Republic, free.
Come," she beckons; "enter, through
Gates of gossamer, doors of dew
(Lit with summer's tropic fire),
My Liberia of the brier."

JOHN JAMES PIATT.

FROM A POEM ON THOREAU

IF I COULD find that little poem,
  With the daintiest sort of proem,
  Which the poet squirrel made
On a leaf that would not fade,
And slyly hid, one darksome night,
By the wicked glow-worm's light!
It was all about Thoreau—
How the squirrels loved him so;
Since, whenever he went walking,
He would stop to hear them talking,—
Often smiling when they chattered,
Or their brown nuts downward pattered:

Nay, could I but find that bird
Who told me once that she had heard
Robins, wrens, and others tell
How he knew their language well,
And how he turned, a thousand times,
Birdic into English rhymes!

H. A. BLOOD.

THE SOUTH

NIGHT; and beneath star-blazoned summer skies
   Behold the spirit of the musky South,—
A creole, with still-burning, languid eyes,
   Voluptuous limbs and incense-breathing mouth:
     Swathed in spun gauze is she,
From fibres of her own anana tree.

Within these sumptuous woods she lies at ease,
   By rich night-breezes, dewy cool, caressed:
'Twixt cypresses and slim palmetto-trees,
   Like to the golden oriole's hanging nest,
     Her airy hammock swings,
And through the dark her mocking-bird yet sings.

How beautiful she is! A tulip-wreath
   Twines round her shadowy, free-floating hair:
Young, weary, passionate, and sad as death,
   Dark visions haunt for her the vacant air,
     While movelessly she lies
With lithe, lax, folded hands and heavy eyes.

Full well knows she how wide and fair extend
   Her groves bright-flowered, her tangled everglades,
Majestic streams that indolently wend
   Through lush savanna or dense forest shades,
     Where the brown buzzard flies
To broad bayous 'neath hazy-golden skies.

Hers is the savage splendor of the swamp,
   With pomp of scarlet and of purple bloom;
Where blow warm, furtive breezes faint and damp,
   Strange insects whir, and stalking bitterns boom—
     Where from stale waters dead
Oft looms the great-jawed alligator's head.

Her wealth, her beauty, and the blight on these,
   Of all she is aware: luxuriant woods,
Fresh, living, sunlit, in her dream she sees;
   And ever midst those verdant solitudes
     The soldier's wooden cross,
O'ergrown by creeping tendrils and rank moss.

Was hers a dream of empire? was it sin?
   And is it well that all was borne in vain?

She knows no more than one who slow doth win,
  After fierce fever, conscious life again,
      Too tired, too weak, too sad,
By the new light to be or stirred or glad.

From rich sea-islands fringing her green shore,
  From broad plantations where swart freemen bend
Bronzed backs in willing labor, from her store
  Of golden fruit, from stream, from town, ascend
      Life-currents of pure health:
Her aims shall be subserved with boundless wealth.

Yet now how listless and how still she lies,
  Like some half-savage, dusky Indian queen,
Rocked in her hammock 'neath her native skies,
  With the pathetic, passive, broken mien
      Of one who, sorely proved,
Great-souled, hath suffered much and much hath loved!

But look! along the wide-branched dewy glade
  Glimmers the dawn: the light palmetto-trees
And cypresses reissue from the shade,
  And *she* hath wakened. Through clear air she sees
      The pledge, the brightening ray,
And leaps from dreams to hail the coming day.

EMMA LAZARUS.

RESPITE

SING, lark, far up the sky!
    Sing, throstle, for love's sake!
Sing, sing, as if no heart might ever break!

  Softly, O summer sigh
  Of winds, let patter down
The blossom-rain, as if no storms had blown!

  Smile, flowers, along the way,—
  Your dainty presence stirs
Such blessed thoughts, ye little comforters.

  O earth, for one kind day
  Let me be glad again,—
Forgetting grief that is, and that has been.

INA D. COOLBRITH.

When the world is burning,
Fired within, yet turning
Round with face unscathed;
Ere fierce flames, uprushing,
O'er all lands leap, crushing,
Till earth fall fire-swathed;—
Up amidst the meadows,
Gently through the shadows,
Gentle flames will glide,
Small and blue and golden,
Though by bard beholden
When in calm dreams folden,—
Calm his dreams will bide.

Where the dance is sweeping,
Through the greensward peeping,
Shall the soft lights start;
Laughing maids, unstaying,
Deeming it trick-playing,
High their robes upswaying,
O'er the lights shall dart;
And the woodland haunter
Shall not cease to saunter,
When far down some glade
Of the great world's burning,
One soft flame upturning
Seems, to his discerning,
Crocus in the shade.

EBENEZER JONES.

THE TRYST OF THE NIGHT

Out of the uttermost ridge of dusk, where the dark and the day are mingled,
The voice of the Night rose cold and calm—it called through the shadow-swept air;
Through all the valleys and lone hillsides it pierced, it thrilled, it tingled—
It summoned me forth to the wild sea-shore, to meet with its mystery there.

Out of the deep ineffable blue, with palpitant swift repeating
 Of gleam and glitter and opaline glow, that broke in ripples of
  light —
In burning glory it came and went, — I heard, I saw it beating,
 Pulse by pulse, from star to star, — the passionate heart of Night!

Out of the thud of the rustling sea — the panting, yearning, throbbing
 Waves that stole on the startled shore, with coo and mutter of
  spray —
The wail of the Night came fitful-faint, — I heard her stifled sobbing;
 The cold salt drops fell slowly, slowly, gray into gulfs of gray.

There through the darkness the great world reeled, and the great
  tides roared, assembling —
 Murmuring hidden things that are past, and secret things that
  shall be;
There at the limits of life we met, and touched with a rapturous
  trembling —
 One with each other, I and the Night, and the skies, and the stars,
  and sea.

MARY C. GILLINGTON BYRON.

THE GOLDEN SUNSET

THE golden sea its mirror spreads
 Beneath the golden skies,
And but a narrow strip between
 Our earth and shadow lies.

The cloud-like cliffs, the cliff-like clouds,
 Dissolved in glory float,
And midway of the radiant floods
 Hangs silently the boat.

The sea is but another sky,
 The sky a sea as well;
And which is earth, and which the heavens,
 The eye can scarcely tell.

So when for me life's latest hour
 Soft passes to its end,
May glory born of earth and heaven
 The earth and heaven blend;

Flooded with light the spirit float,
  With silent rapture glow,
Till where earth ends and heaven begins,
  The soul can scarcely know.

THE FLIGHT OF THE CROWS

THE autumn afternoon is dying o'er
  The quiet western valley where I lie
Beneath the maples on the river shore,
  Where tinted leaves, blue waters, and fair sky
Environ all; and far above some birds are flying by

To seek their evening haven in the breast
  And calm embrace of silence, while they sing
Te Deums to the night, invoking rest
  For busy chirping voice and tired wing —
And in the hush of sleeping trees their sleeping-cradles swing.

In forest arms the night will soonest creep,
  Where sombre pines a lullaby intone,
Where Nature's children curl themselves to sleep,
  And all is still at last, save where alone
A band of black, belated crows arrive from lands unknown.

Strange sojourn has been theirs since waking day;
  Strange sights and cities in their wanderings blend
With fields of yellow maize, and leagues away
  With rivers where their sweeping waters wend
Past velvet banks to rocky shores, in cañons bold to end.

O'er what vast lakes that stretch superbly dead,
  Till lashed to life by storm-clouds, have they flown?
In what wild lands, in laggard flight have led
  Their aerial career unseen, unknown,
Till now with twilight come their cries in lonely monotone?

The flapping of their pinions in the air
  Dies in the hush of distance, while they light
Within the fir tops, weirdly black and bare,
  That stand with giant strength and peerless height,
To shelter fairy, bird, and beast throughout the closing night.

Strange black and princely pirates of the skies,
　　Would that your wind-tossed travels I could know!
Would that my soul could see, and seeing, rise
　　To unrestricted life where ebb and flow
Of Nature's pulse would constitute a wider life below!

Could I but live just here in Freedom's arms,
　　A kingly life without a sovereign's care!
Vain dreams! Day hides with closing wings her charms,
　　And all is cradled in repose, save where
Yon band of black, belated crows still frets the evening air.

　　　　E. PAULINE JOHNSON ("Tekahionwake").

THE NORTHERN LIGHTS

HELL'S gates swing open wide!
　　Hell's furious chiefs forth ride!
　　　The deep doth redden
With flags of armies marching through the night,
As kings shall lead their legions to the fight
　　　At Armageddon.

　　Peers and princes mark I,
　　Captains and chiliarchi;
Thou burning angel of the Pit, Abaddon!
　Charioteers from Hades, land of gloom,
　　Gigantic thrones, and heathen troopers, whom
The thunder of the far-off fight doth madden.

　　Lo! Night's barbaric khans,
　　Lo! the waste Gulf's wild clans,
Gallop across the skies with fiery bridles!
　Lo! flaming sultanas, infernal czars,
　　In deep-ranked squadrons gird the glowing cars
Of Lucifer and Ammon, towering idols.

　　See yonder red platoons!
　　See! see the swift dragoons,
Whirling aloft their sabres to the zenith!
　See the tall regiments whose spears incline,
　　Beyond the circle of that steadfast sign
Which to the streams of ocean never leaneth.*

　　Whose yonder dragon-crest?
　　Whose that red-shielded breast?

* Iliad, xviii. 489.

Chieftain Satanas! Emperor of the Furnace!
　　What bright centurions, what blazing earls,
　　In mail of hell's hot ores and burnished pearls,
Alarm the kingdoms with their gleaming harness?

　　　All shades and spectral hosts,
　　　All forms and gloomy ghosts,
All frowning phantoms from the Gulf's dim gorges,
　　Follow the kings in wavering multitude;
　　While savage giants of the night's old brood
In pagan mirth toss high their crackling torches.

　　　Monarchs, on guarded thrones,
　　　Ruling earth's southern zones,
Mark ye the wrathful archers of Gehenna;
　　How gleam, affrighted lords of Europe's crowns,
　　Their blood-red arrows o'er your bastioned towns,
Moscow, and purple Rome, and cannon-girt Vienna?
　　Go bid your prophets watch the troubled skies!
" Why through the vault cleave those infernal glances?
　　Why, ye pale wizards, do those portents rise,
Rockets and fiery shafts and lurid lances?"

　　　Still o'er the silent Pole
　　　Numberless armies roll,
Columns all plumed and cohorts of artillery;
　　Still girdled nobles cross the snowy fields
　　In flashing chariots, and their crimson shields
Kindle afar thy icy peaks, Cordillera!

　　　On, lords of dark despair!
　　　Prince of the powers of air,
Bear your broad banners through the constellations!
　　Wave, all ye Stygian hordes,
　　Through the black sky your swords;
Startle with warlike signs the watching nations.
　　March, ye mailed multitudes, across the deep;
　　Far shine the battlements on Heaven's steep.
Dare ye again, fierce thrones and scarlet powers,
Assail with hell's wild host those crystal towers?
　　Tempt ye again the angels' shining blades,
Ithuriel's spear, and Michael's circling truncheon,—
　　The seraph-cavalier, whose winged brigades
Drove you in dreadful rout down to the night's vast dungeon?

GUY HUMPHREY MCMASTER.

THE TORNADO

WHOSE eye has marked his gendering? On his
        throne
  He dwells apart in roofless caves of air,
Born of the stagnant, blown of the glassy heat
  O'er the still mere Sargasso. When the world
Has fallen voluptuous, and the isles are grown
  So bold they cry, God sees not!—as a rare
Sun-flashing iceberg towers on high, and fleet
  As air-ships rise, by upward currents whirled,
Even so the bane of lustful islanders
Wings him aloft. And scarce a pinion stirs.

There gathering hues, he stoopeth down again—
  Down from the vault. Locks of the gold-tipped cloud
Fly o'er his head; his eyes, St. Elmo flames;
  His mouth, a surf on a red coral reef.
Embroidered is his cloak of dark-blue stain
  With lightning jags. Upon his pathway crowd
Dull Shudder, wan-faced Quaking, Ghastly-Dreams.
  And after these, in order near their chief,
Start, Tremor, Faint-Heart, Panic, and Affray,
Horror with blanching eyes, and limp Dismay,

Unroll a gray-green carpet him before
  Swathed in thick foam: thereon adventuring, bark
Need never hope to live; that yeasty pile
  Bears her no longer; to the mast-head plunged
She writhes and groans, careens, and is no more.
  Now, prickt by fear, the man-devourer shark,
Gale-breasting gull, and whale that dreams no guile
  Till the sharp steel quite to the life has lunged,
Before his pitiless, onward-hurling form
Hurry toward land for shelter from the storm.

In vain. Tornado and his pursuivants,
  Whirlwind of giant bulk, and Water-Spout,—
The grewsome, tortuous devil-fish of rain,—
  O'ertake them on the shoals and leave them dead.
Doomsday has come. Now men in speechless trance
  Glower unmoved upon the hideous rout,
Or shrieking, fly to holes, or yet complain
  One moment to that lordly face of dread

Before he quits the mountain of his wave,
And strews for all impartially their grave.

And as in court-yard corners on the wind
　　Sweep the loose straws, houses and stately trees
Whirl in a vortex. His unswerving tread
　　Winnows the island as a thresher's floor.
His eyes are fixed; he looks not once behind,
　　But at his back fall silence and the breeze.
Scarce is he come, the lovely wraith is sped.
　　Ashamed, the lightning shuts its purple door.
And heaven still knows the robes of gold and dun,
While placid Ruin gently greets the sun.

　　　　　　　　　　　　　　CHARLES DE KAY.

THE RIVER CHARLES

BESIDE thee, O my river, where I wait
　　Through vista long of years, and drink my fill
　　Of beauty and of light, a steady rill
Of never-failing good, whate'er my state,—

How speechless seem these lips, my soul how dull,
　　Never to say, nor half to say, how dear
The washing of thy ripples, nor the full
　　And silent flow which speaks not to the ear!

Thou hast been unto me a gracious nurse,
　　Telling me many a tale in listening hours
　　Of those who praised thee with their ripening powers,—
Our elder poets, nourished at thy source.

O happy Cambridge meadows! where now rest
　　Forever the proud memories of their lives;
O happy Cambridge air! forever blest
　　With deathless song the bee of time still hives;—

And farther on, where many a wild flower blooms
　　Through a fair Sunday up and down thy banks,
　　Beautiful with thy blossoms, ranks on ranks,
What vanished eyes have sought thy dewy rooms!

I too have known thee, rushing, bright with foam,
　　Or sleeping idly, even as thou dost now,

Reflecting every wall and tower and dome,
    And every vessel, clear from stern to prow,

Or in the moonlight, when the night is pale,
    And the great city is still, and only thou
    Givest me sign of life, and on thy brow
A beauty evanescent, flitting, frail!

O river! ever drifting toward the sea,
    How common is thy fate! thus purposeless
To drift away, nor think what 'tis to be,
    And sink in the vast wave of nothingness.

But ever to love's life a second life
    Is given, and his narrow river of days
    Shall flow through other lives, and sleep in bays
Of quiet thought and calm the heart at strife.

Fortunate river! that through the poet's thought
    Hast run and washed life's burden from his sight;
O happy river! thou his song hast brought,
    And thou shalt live in poetry and light.

ANNIE FIELDS.

ORARA

A TRIBUTARY OF THE CLARENCE RIVER

THE strong sob of the chafing stream,
    That seaward fights its way
Down crags of glitter, dells of gleam,
    Is in the hills to-day.

But far and faint a gray-winged form
    Hangs where the wild lights wane —
The phantoms of a bygone storm,
    A ghost of wind and rain.

The soft white feet of afternoon
    Are on the shining meads;
The breeze is as a pleasant tune
    Amongst the happy reeds.

The fierce, disastrous, flying fire,
    That made the great caves ring,
And scarred the slope, and broke the spire,
    Is a forgotten thing.

The air is full of mellow sounds;
   The wet hill-heads are bright;
And down the fall of fragrant grounds
   The deep ways flame with light.

A rose-red space of stream I see,
   Past banks of tender fern;
A radiant brook, unknown to me,
   Beyond its upper turn.

The singing silver life I hear,
   Whose home is in the green
Far-folded woods of fountains clear,
   Where I have never been.

Ah, brook above the upper bend,
   I often long to stand
Where you in soft, cool shades descend
   From the untrodden land;

But I may linger long, and look,
   Till night is over all—
My eyes will never see the brook,
   Or strange, sweet waterfall.

The world is round me with its heat,
   And toil, and cares that tire:
I cannot with my feeble feet
   Climb after my desire.

HENRY CLARENCE KENDALL.

TO SENECA LAKE

ON THY fair bosom, silver lake,
   The wild swan spreads his snowy sail,
And round his breast the ripples break,
   As down he bears before the gale.

On thy fair bosom, waveless stream,
   The dipping paddle echoes far,
And flashes in the moonlight gleam,
   And bright reflects the polar star.

The waves along thy pebbly shore,
   As blows the north-wind, heave their foam,

And curl around the dashing oar,
    As late the boatman hies him home.

How sweet, at set of sun, to view
    Thy golden mirror spreading wide,
And see the mist of mantling blue
    Float round the distant mountain's side.

At midnight hour, as shines the moon,
    A sheet of silver spreads below,
And swift she cuts, at highest noon,
    Light clouds like wreaths of purest snow.

On thy fair bosom, silver lake,
    Oh, I could ever sweep the oar,
When early birds at morning wake,
    And evening tells us toil is o'er!

JAMES GATES PERCIVAL.

SEA WITCHERY

YON headland, with the twinkling-footed sea
    Beyond it, conjures shapes and stories fair
    Of young Greek days: the lithe immortal air
Carries the sound of Siren-song to me;
Soon shall I mark Ulysses daringly
    Swing round the cape, the sea-wind in his hair;
    And look! the Argonauts go sailing there
A golden quest, shouting their godlike glee.

The vision is compact of blue and gold,
    Of sky and water, and the drift of foam,
        And thrill of brine-washed breezes from the west:
        Wide space is in it, and the unexpressed
Great heart of Nature, and the magic old
    Of legend, and the white ships coming home.

RICHARD BURTON.

WITH A NANTUCKET SHELL

I SEND a shell from the ocean beach;
　But listen thou well, for my shell hath speech.
　　　Hold to thine ear,
　　　And plain thou'lt hear
　　　Tales of ships
　　　That were lost in the rips,
　　　Or that sunk on the shoals
　　　Where the bell-buoy tolls,
And ever and ever its iron tongue rolls
In a ceaseless lament for the poor lost souls.

　　　And a song of the sea
　　　Has my shell for thee:
　　　The melody in it
　　　Was hummed at Wauwinet,
　　　And caught at Coatue
　　　By the gull that flew
Outside to the ships with its perishing crew.
　　　But the white wings wave
　　　Where none may save,
And there's never a stone to mark a grave.

　　　See, its sad heart bleeds
　　　For the sailor's needs;
　　　But it bleeds again
　　　For more mortal pain,
　　　More sorrow and woe,
　　　Than is theirs who go
With shuddering eyes and whitening lips
Down in the sea in their shattered ships.

　　　Thou fearest the sea?
　　　And a tyrant is he,—
A tyrant as cruel as tyrant may be;
　　　But though winds fierce blow,
　　　And the rocks lie low,
　　　And the coast be lee,
　　　This I say to thee:
Of Christian souls more have been wrecked on shore
　　　Than ever were lost at sea!

CHARLES HENRY WEBB.

SONGS OF THE SEA

INTRODUCTORY — THE OLD TAVERN

IN THE North End of Boston, long ago,—
    Although 'tis yet within my memory,—
There were of gabled houses many a row,
    With overhanging stories two or three,
And many with half-doors over whose end,
    Leaning upon her elbows, the good-wife
At eventide conversed with many a friend
    Of all the little chances of their life;
Small ripples in the stream which ran full slow
In the North End of Boston, long ago.

And 'mid these houses was a Hostelrie
Frequented by the people of the sea,
Known as the Boy and Barrel, from its sign —
A jolly urchin on a cask of wine,
Bearing the words which puzzled every eye,
Orbus in Tactu Mainet, Heaven knows why.
Even there a bit of Latin made a show,
In the North End of Boston, long ago.

And many a sailor, when his cruise was o'er,
Bore straight for it soon as he touched the shore:
In many a stormy night upon the sea
He'd thought upon the Boy — and of the spree
He'd have when there, and let all trouble go,
In the North End of Boston, long ago.

There, like their vessels in a friendly port,
    Met many mariners of every kind,
Spinning strange yarns of many a varied sort,
    Well sheltered from the ocean and the wind:
In a long, low, dark room they lounged at ease.
    Strange men there were from many a distant land,
And there above the high old chimney-piece
    Were curiosities from many a strand,
Which often made strange tales and memories flow
In the North End of Boston, long ago.

And there I often sat to hear those tales,
    From men who'd passed through storm and fight and
        fire,

Of mighty icebergs and stupendous whales,
    Of shipwrecked crews and of adventures dire;
Until the thought came to me on a time,   ·
    While I was listening to that merry throng,
That I would write their stories out in rhyme,
    And weave into it many a sailor's song,
That men might something of the legends know
Of the North End of Boston, long ago.

First it was said that Captain Kidd in truth
    Had reveled in that tavern with his crew,
And there it was he lost the Golden Tooth
    Which brought him treasure; and the gossips knew
Moll Pitcher dwelt there in the days of yore,
And Peter Rugg had stopped before the door;
Tom Walker there did with the Devil go
In the North End of Boston, long ago.

Nor had I long to wait; for at the word
    Some one observed that he had seen in Spain
A captain hung — which Abner Chapin heard,
    And said, "I too upon the Spanish Main
Met with a man well known unto us all,
Who nearly hung a captain-general."
He told the tale, and I did rhyme it so,
In the North End of Boston, long ago.

El Capitan-General

THERE was a captain-general who ruled in Vera Cruz,
    And what we used to hear of him was always evil news:
    He was a pirate on the sea — a robber on the shore,
The Señor Don Alonzo Estabán San Salvador.

There was a Yankee skipper who round about did roam;
His name was Stephen Folger, and Nantucket was his home:
And having gone to Vera Cruz, he had been skinned full sore
By the Señor Don Alonzo Estabán San Salvador.

But having got away alive, though all his cash was gone,
He said, "If there is vengeance, I will surely try it on!
And I do wish I may be damned if I don't clear the score
With Señor Don Alonzo Estabán San Salvador!"

He shipped a crew of seventy men — well-armèd men were they,
And sixty of them in the hold he darkly stowed away;

And sailing back to Vera Cruz, was sighted from the shore
By the Señor Don Alonzo Estabán San Salvador.

With twenty-five soldados he came on board so pleased,
And said, "*Maldito* Yankee — again your ship is seized.
How many sailors have you got?" Said Folger, "Ten — no more,"
To the Captain Don Alonzo Estabán San Salvador.

"But come into my cabin and take a glass of wine.
I do suppose, as usual, I'll have to pay a fine:
I have got some old Madeira, and we'll talk the matter o'er —
My Captain Don Alonzo Estabán San Salvador."

And as over that Madeira the captain-general boozed,
It seemed to him as if his head was getting quite confused;
For it happened that some morphine had traveled from "the
  store"
To the glass of Don Alonzo Estabán San Salvador.

"What is it makes the vessel roll? What sounds are these I
  hear?
It seems as if the rising waves were beating on my ear!" —
"Oh, it is the breaking of the surf — just that and nothing more,
My Captain Don Alonzo Estabán San Salvador!"

The governor was in a sleep which muddled all his brains;
The seventy men had got his gang and put them all in chains:
And when he woke the following day he could not see the shore,
For he was out on the blue water — the Don San Salvador.

"Now do you see that yard-arm — and understand the thing?"
Said Captain Folger. "For all from that yard-arm you shall
  swing,
Or forty thousand dollars you must pay me from your store,
My Captain Don Alonzo Estabán San Salvador."

The Capitano took a pen — the order he did sign —
"O Señor Yankee! but you charge amazing high for wine!"
But 'twas not till the draft was paid they let him go ashore,
El Señor Don Alonzo Estabán San Salvador.

The greatest sharp some day will find another sharper wit;
It always makes the Devil laugh to see a biter bit;
It takes two Spaniards any day to come a Yankee o'er —
Even two like Don Alonzo Estabán San Salvador.

DAVY JONES

Down in the sea among sand and stones,
There lives the old fellow called Davy Jones.

When storms come up he sighs and groans,
And that is the singing of Davy Jones.*

His chest is full of dead men's bones,
And that is the locker of Davy Jones.

Davy is Welsh you may hear by his tones,
For a regular Welsher is Davy Jones.

Whenever a fish gets drowned, he moans
So tender-hearted is Davy Jones.

Thousands of ships the old man owns,
But none go a-sailing for Davy Jones.

ONE, TWO, THREE

I saw three witches as the wind blew cold
    In a red light to the lee;
Bold they were and over-bold
    As they sailed over the sea,
Calling for One, Two, Three!
Calling for One, Two, Three!
    And I think I can hear
    It a-ringing in my ear,
A-howling for their One, Two, Three!

And clouds came over the sky,
    And the wind it blew hard and free,
And the waves grew bold and over-bold
    As we sailed over the sea—
Howling for One, Two, Three!
Howling for their One, Two, Three!
    Oh I think I can hear
    It a-ringing in my ear,
A-howling for their One, Two, Three!

And the storm came roaring on,
    Such a storm as I never did see,
And the storm it was bold and over-bold,
    And as bad as a storm could be—

A-roaring for its One, Two, Three!
A-howling for its One, Two, Three!
Oh I think I can hear
It a-howling in my ear,
A-growling for its One, Two, Three!

And a wave came over the deck,
As big as a wave could be,
And it took away the captain and the mate and a man:
It had got the One, Two, Three!
And it went with the One, Two, Three!
Oh I think I can hear
·It a-rolling in my ear,
As it went with the One, Two, Three.

THE BEAUTIFUL WITCH

A PRETTY witch was bathing
By the beach one summer day:
There came a boat with pirates
Who carried her away.

The ship had a breeze behind her,
Over the waves went she!
" O signor capitano,
O captain of the sea!
I'll give you a hundred ducats
If you will set me free!"

" I will not take a hundred,—
You're worth much more, you know;
I'll sell you to the Sultan
For a thousand golden sequins:
You put yourself far too low."

" You will not take a hundred?
Very well then, let them be!
But I have a constant lover,
Who, as you may discover,
Will never abandon me."

On the deck, before the rover,
The witch began to sing —
" Oh come to me, my lover!"
And the wind as it stole over
Began to howl and ring.

Louder and ever louder
   Became the tempest's roar.
The captain in a passion
   Thus at the lady swore:—
" I believe that your windy lover
   Is the Devil and nothing more!"

Wilder and ever wilder
   The tempest raged and rang.
" There are rocks ahead, and the wind dead aft —
Thank you, my love!" the lady laughed
   As unto the wind she sang.

" Oh, go with your cursed lover
   To *inferno* to sing for me!"
So cried the angry captain,
And threw the lady over
   To sink in the stormy sea.

But changing into a sea-gull,
   Over the waves she flew.
" O captain, captain bold," sang she,
" 'Tis true you've missed the gallows-tree,
But now you'll drown in the foaming sea:
   O captain, forever adieu!"

Time For Us to Go

WITH sails let fall and sheeted home, and clear of the ground
          were we,
   We passed the bank, stood round the light, and sailed away
        to sea;
The wind was fair and the coast was clear, and the brig was noways
      slow,
For she was built in Baltimore, and 'twas time for us to go.
          Time for us to go,
          Time for us to go,
For she was built in Baltimore, and 'twas time for us to go.

A quick run to the west we had, and when we made the Bight,
We kept the offing all day long, and crossed the bar at night.
Six hundred niggers in the hold, and seventy we did stow;
And when we'd clapped the hatches on, 'twas time for us to go.

We hadn't been three days at sea before we saw a sail:
So we clapped on every inch she'd stand, although it blew a gale,

And we walked along full fourteen knots; for the barkie she did
    know,
As well as ever a soul on board, 'twas time for us to go.

We carried away the royal yards, and the stun's'l boom was gone.
Says the skipper, "They may go or stand, I'm darned if I don't
    crook on.
So the weather braces we'll round in, and the trys'l set also,
And we'll keep the brig three p'ints away, for it's time for us to go."

Oh, yard-arm under she did plunge in the trough of the deep seas,
And her masts they thrashed about like whips as she bowled before
    the breeze,
And every yard did buckle up like to a bending bow;
But her spars were tough as whalebone, and 'twas time for us to go.

We dropped the cruiser in the night, and our cargo landed we,
And ashore we went, with our pockets full of dollars, on the spree.
And when the liquor it is out, and the locker it is low,
Then to sea again, in the ebony trade, 'twill be time for us to go:
          Time for us to go,
          Time for us to go,
Then to sea again, in the ebony trade, 'twill be time for us to go.

The Lover to the Sailor

Now tell me this, my sailor boy,
    As sure as you love your wine,—
Oh, did you ever see a ship
    As trim as that girl of mine?

And you who've been in many a gale,
    And stood on many a deck,
Oh, did you ever see a sail
    As white as my true love's neck?

And you who have been where the red rose blows
    In many a Southern place,
Oh, did you ever see a rose
    Like those in my sweetheart's face?

Here's a cheer for the women with jet-black curls,
    Of Spain or of Portugal!
And seven for the Yankee and English girls,
    The prettiest of them all!

CHARLES GODFREY LELAND.

THE ROCK AND THE SEA

THE ROCK

I AM the Rock, presumptuous Sea!
　I am set to encounter thee.
　Angry and loud, or gentle and still,
I am set here to limit thy power, and I will—
　　I am the Rock!

I am the Rock. From age to age
I scorn thy fury and dare thy rage.
Scarred by frost and worn by time,
Brown with weed and green with slime,
Thou mayst drench and defile me and spit in my face,
But while I am here thou keep'st thy place!
　　I am the Rock!

I am the Rock, beguiling Sea!
I know thou art fair as fair can be,
With golden glitter and silver sheen,
And bosom of blue and garments of green.
Thou mayst pat my cheek with baby hands,
And lap my feet in diamond sands,
And play before me as children play;
But plead as thou wilt, I bar the way!
　　I am the Rock!

I am the Rock. Black midnight falls;
The terrible breakers rise like walls;
With curling lips and gleaming teeth
They plunge and tear at my bones beneath.
Year upon year they grind and beat
In storms of thunder and storms of sleet—
Grind and beat and wrestle and tear,
But the rock they beat on is always there!
　　I am the Rock!

THE SEA

I am the Sea. I hold the land
As one holds an apple in his hand.
Hold it fast with sleepless eyes,
Watching the continents sink and rise.
Out of my bosom the mountains grow,
Back to its depths they crumble slow:

The earth is a helpless child to me —
   I am the Sea! .

I am the Sea. When I draw back
Blossom and verdure follow my track,
And the land I leave grows proud and fair,
For the wonderful race of man is there;
And the winds of heaven wail and cry
While the nations rise and reign and die —
Living and dying in folly and pain,
While the laws of the universe thunder in vain.
What is the folly of man to me?
   I am the Sea!

I am the Sea. The earth I sway;
Granite to me is potter's clay;
Under the touch of my careless waves
It rises in turrets and sinks in caves;
The iron cliffs that edge the land
I grind to pebbles and sift to sand,
And beach-grass bloweth and children play
In what were the rocks of yesterday;
It is but a moment of sport to me —
   I am the Sea!

I am the Sea. In my bosom deep
Wealth and Wonder and Beauty sleep;
Wealth and Wonder and Beauty rise
In changing splendor of sunset skies,
And comfort the earth with rains and snows
Till waves the harvest and laughs the rose.
Flower and forest and child of breath
With me have life — without me, death.
What if the ships go down in me? —
   I am the Sea!

      CHARLOTTE PERKINS STETSON.

THE HUNGRY SEA

THE fierce wind drove o'er hedgerow and lea,
 It bowed the grasses, it broke the tree, —
  It shivered the topmost branch of the tree!
And it buried my love in the deep, deep sea,

In the dark lone grave of the hungry sea,—
　　. Woe is me!

The bonnie white daisy closed her e'e,
And bent to the blast that swept the lea.
Blossom and grass bowed low on the lea,
But white sails dipped and sank in the sea;
They dipped and sank in the pitiless sea!
　　Woe is me!

'Neath the mother's breast in the leafy tree
Nestled and crept her birdies wee,
Nor heeded the blast, though weak and wee.
But no mother can save on the stormy sea;
Deaf to her cry is the merciless sea!
　　Woe is me!

Oh, well for the fishers of Galilee,
When they left their nets by that inland sea,
To follow Him who walked on the sea;
At whose word the pitiless waves did flee —
The hungry, insatiate waves did flee,
　　And left them free!

Golden the light on flower and tree
In the land where my sailor waits for me,—
The country of heaven that has no sea —
No ruthless, moaning, terrible sea;
There is the haven where I would be.

　　　　　　　FRANCES FREELING BRODERIP.
　　　　　　　(Daughter of Thomas Hood.)

DRIFT

A SHIP went sailing from the shore,
　　And vanished in the gleaming west,
Where purple clouds a lining bore
　　Of gold and amethyst.

Poised in the air, a sea-gull flashed
　　His white wings in the sun's last ray;
A moment hung, then downward dashed
　　To revel in the spray.

The fishers drew their long nets in
    With careful eye and steady hand,
Till.olive back and silvery fin
    Strewed all the tawny sand.

Again I trod the shore: again
   . The sea-gull circled high in air;
Again the sturdy fishermen
    Drew in their nets with care.

The sunset's gold and amethyst
    Shone fairly, as I paced the shore,
But back from out the gleaming west
    The ship came — nevermore!

       *   *   *

A flood of sunlight through a rift
    Between two mounds of yellow sand;
Three sea-gulls on a bit of drift
    Slow surging inward toward the land;

An old dumb-beacon all awry,
    With drabbled seaweed round its feet;
A star-like sail against the sky,
    Where sapphire heaven and ocean meet; —

This, with the waters swirling o'er
    A shifting stretch of land and shell,
Will make, for him who loves the shore,
    A picture that may please him well.

       *   *   *

O cool, green waves that ebb and flow,
    Reflecting calm blue skies above,
How gently now ye come and go,
    Since ye have drowned my love!

       *   *   *

The breakers come and the breakers go
    Along the silvery sand,
With a changing line of feathery snow
    Between the water and land.

Seaweeds gleam in the sunset light,
    On the ledges of wave-worn stone;
Orange and crimson, purple and white,
    In regular windrows strown.

The waves grow calm in the dusk of eve,
    When the wind goes down with the sun;
So fade the smiles of those who deceive,
    When the coveted heart is won.

GEORGE ARNOLD.

LONDON

ATHWART the sky a lowly sigh
    From west to east the sweet wind carried:
The sun stood still on Primrose Hill;
    His light in all the city tarried:
The clouds on viewless columns bloomed
Like smoldering lilies unconsumed.

"O sweetheart, see! how shadowy,
    Of some occult magician's rearing,
Or swung in space of heaven's grace
    Dissolving, dimly reappearing,
Afloat upon ethereal tides
St. Paul's above the city rides!"

A rumor broke through the thin smoke
    Enwreathing abbey, tower, and palace,
The parks, the squares, the thoroughfares,
    The million-peopled lanes and alleys,
An ever-muttering prisoned storm,—
The heart of London beating warm.

JOHN DAVIDSON.

IN THE DOCKS

WHERE the bales thunder till the day is done,
    And the wild sounds with wilder odors cope;
    Where over crouching sail and coiling rope,
Lascar and Moor along the gangway run;
Where stifled Thames spreads in the pallid sun
    A hive of anarchy from slope to slope;—
    Flag of my birth, my liberty, my hope,
I see thee at the masthead, joyous one!
O thou good guest! So oft as, young and warm,

To the home-wind thy hoisted colors bound,
Away, away from this too thoughtful ground,
  Sated with human trespass and despair,
Thee only, from the desert, from the storm,
  A sick mind follows into Eden air.

LOUISE IMOGEN GUINEY.

THE MOUNTAINEER

OH, AT the eagle's height
    To lie i' the sweet of the sun,
  While veil after veil takes flight,
    And God and the world are one.

Oh, the night on the steep!
  All that his eyes saw dim
Grows light in the dusky deep,
  And God is alone with him.

"A. E." (GEORGE WM. RUSSELL.)

THE SETTLER

HIS echoing axe the settler swung
    Amid the sea-like solitude,
  And rushing, thundering, down were flung
    The Titans of the wood;
Loud shrieked the eagle, as he dashed
From out his mossy nest, which crashed
    With its supporting bough,
And the first sunlight, leaping, flashed
    On the wolf's haunt below. . . .

His roof adorned a pleasant spot;
  Mid the black logs green glowed the grain,
And herbs and plants the woods knew not
    Throve in the sun and rain.
The smoke-wreath curling o'er the dell,
The low, the bleat, the tinkling bell,—
    All made a landscape strange,
Which was the living chronicle
    Of deeds that wrought the change.

The violet sprung at spring's first tinge,
   The rose of summer spread its glow,
The maize hung out its autumn fringe,
   Rude winter brought his snow;
And still the lone one labored there,
His shout and whistle broke the air,
   As cheerily he plied
His garden-spade, or drove his share
   Along the hillock's side.

He marked the fire-storm's blazing flood
   Roar crackling on its path,
And scorching earth, and melting wood,
   Beneath its greedy wrath;
He marked the rapid whirlwind shoot,
Trampling the pine-tree with its foot,
   And darkening thick the day
With streaming bough and severed root,
   Hurled whizzing on its way.

His gaunt hound yelled, his rifle flashed,
   The grim bear hushed his savage growl;
In blood and foam the panther gnashed
   His fangs with dying howl;
The fleet deer ceased its flying bound,
   And with its moaning cry
The beaver sank beneath the wound
   Its pond-built Venice by.

Humble the lot, yet his the race,
   When Liberty sent forth her cry,
Who thronged in conflict's deadliest place,
   To fight — to bleed — to die!
Who cumbered Bunker's height of red,
By hope through weary years were led,
   And witnessed Yorktown's sun
Blaze on a nation's banner spread,
   A nation's freedom won.

ALFRED B. STREET.

THE WINTER PINE

Dost think the heart of winter hard?
　　Her soul without its love?
Attune thine ear to yonder pine
　　Musing the summer song.

New England's heart is wintry cold?
　　Her soul without a love?
Unstop thy stranger ear; and hear
　　Her summer song of pines.

CHARLES WELLINGTON STONE.

THE VIRGINIANS OF THE VALLEY

The knightliest of the knightly race
　　That since the days of old
Have kept the lamp of chivalry
　　Alight in hearts of gold;
The kindliest of the kindly band
　　That, rarely hating ease,
Yet rode with Spotswood round the land,
　　And Raleigh round the seas;

Who climbed the blue Virginian hills
　　Against embattled foes,
And planted there, in valleys fair,
　　The lily and the rose;
Whose fragrance lives in many lands,
　　Whose beauty stars the earth,
And lights the hearths of happy homes
　　With loveliness and worth.

We thought they slept!—the sons who kept
　　The names of noble sires,
And slumbered while the darkness crept
　　Around their vigil fires;
But aye the "Golden Horseshoe" knights
　　Their Old Dominion keep,
Whose foes have found enchanted ground,
　　But not a knight asleep.

FRANCIS ORRERY TICKNOR.

MY MARYLAND

THE despot's heel is on thy shore,
   Maryland!
His torch is at thy temple door.
   Maryland!
Avenge the patriotic gore
That flecked the streets of Baltimore,
And be the battle queen of yore,
   Maryland, My Maryland!

Hark to thy wandering son's appeal,
   Maryland!
My mother State, to thee I kneel,
   Maryland!
For life and death, for woe and weal,
Thy peerless chivalry reveal,
And gird thy beauteous limbs with steel,
   Maryland, My Maryland!

Thou wilt not cower in the dust,
   Maryland!
Thy beaming sword shall never rust,
   Maryland!
Remember Carroll's sacred trust,
Remember Howard's warlike thrust,
And all thy slumberers with the just,
   Maryland, My Maryland!

Come, 'tis the red dawn of the day,
   Maryland!
Come with thy panoplied array,
   Maryland!
With Ringgold's spirit for the fray,
With Watson's blood at Monterey,
With fearless Lowe and dashing May,
   Maryland, My Maryland!

Dear mother, burst the tyrant's chain,
   Maryland!
Virginia should not call in vain,
   Maryland!
She meets her sisters on the plain:
"Sic semper!" 'tis the proud refrain

That baffles minions back amain,
Maryland, My Maryland!

Come, for thy shield is bright and strong,
Maryland!
Come, for thy dalliance does thee wrong,
Maryland!
Come to thine own heroic throng,
That stalks with liberty along,
And give a new key to thy song,
Maryland, My Maryland!

I see the blush upon thy cheek,
Maryland!
But thou wast ever bravely meek,
Maryland!
But lo! there surges forth a shriek
From hill to hill, from creek to creek;
Potomac calls to Chesapeake,
Maryland, My Maryland!

Thou wilt not yield the Vandal toll,
Maryland!
Thou wilt not crook to his control,
Maryland!
Better the fire upon thee roll,
Better the shot, the blade, the bowl,
Than crucifixion of the soul,
Maryland, My Maryland!

I hear the distant thunder hum,
Maryland!
The Old Line's bugle, fife, and drum,
Maryland!
She is not dead, nor deaf, nor dumb —
Huzza! she spurns the Northern scum;
She breathes, she burns — she'll come! she'll come!
Maryland, My Maryland!

JAMES R. RANDALL.

THE GREAT BELL ROLAND*

SUGGESTED BY THE PRESIDENT'S FIRST CALL FOR VOLUNTEERS

TOLL, Roland, toll!
　　In old St. Bavon's tower,
　　　At midnight hour,
　　The great Bell Roland spoke!
All souls that slept in Ghent awoke!
　What meant the thunder-stroke?
　Why trembled wife and maid?
　Why caught each man his blade?

　　Why echoed every street
　　With tramp of thronging feet,
　All flying to the city's wall?
　　It was the warning call
That Freedom stood in peril of a foe!
　And even timid hearts grew bold
　　Whenever Roland tolled,
　And every hand a sword could hold!
　　　So acted men
　　　Like patriots then—
　　Three hundred years ago!

　　　Toll, Roland, toll!
　　Bell never yet was hung,
　　Between whose lips there swung
　　　So grand a tongue!
　　If men be patriots still,
　　　At thy first sound
　　　True hearts will bound,
　　Great souls will thrill!
　　Then toll and strike the test
　　　Through each man's breast,
　Till loyal hearts shall stand confest,—
　And may God's wrath smite all the rest!

　　　Toll, Roland, toll!
　Not now in old St. Bavon's tower—
　　Not now at midnight hour—
Not now from River Scheldt to Zuyder Zee,—
　　But here, this side the sea!
　　Toll here, in broad, bright day!

---

*The famous bell Roland, of Ghent, was an object of great affection to
the people because it rang to arm them when liberty was in danger.

For not by night awaits
A noble foe without the gates,
But perjured friends within betray,
   And do the deed at noon!
      Toll, Roland, toll!
   Thy sound is not too soon!
To arms! Ring out the Leader's call!
Re-echo it from East to West
   Till every hero's breast
Shall swell beneath a soldier's crest!
      Toll, Roland, toll!
Till cottager from cottage wall
Snatch pouch and powder-horn and gun!
The sire bequeathed them to the son
When only half their work was done!
      Toll, Roland, toll!
   Till swords from scabbards leap!
      Toll, Roland, toll!
What tears can widows weep
Less bitter than when brave men fall!
      Toll, Roland, toll!
   In shadowed hut and hall
   Shall lie the soldier's pall,
And hearts shall break while graves are filled!
   Amen! So God hath willed!
And may his grace anoint us all!

      Toll, Roland, toll!
   The Dragon on thy tower
   Stands sentry to this hour,
And Freedom so stands safe in Ghent!
   And merrier bells now ring,
And in the land's serene content
   Men shout "God save the King!"
Until the skies are rent!
      So let it be!
   A kingly king is he
Who keeps his people free!
      Toll, Roland, toll!
Ring out across the sea!
No longer They but We
Have now such need of thee!
      Toll, Roland, toll!
Nor ever may thy throat
Keep dumb its warning note

Till Freedom's perils be outbraved!
    Toll, Roland, toll!
Till Freedom's flag, wherever waved,
Shall shadow not a man enslaved!
    Toll, Roland, toll!
From Northern lake to Southern strand,
    Toll, Roland, toll!
Till friend and foe, at thy command,
Once more shall clasp each other's hand,
And shout, one-voiced, "God save the land!"
And love the land that God hath saved!
    Toll, Roland, toll!

THEODORE TILTON.

THE DRAFT RIOT

IN THE UNIVERSITY TOWER: NEW YORK, JULY 1863

IS IT the wind, the many-tongued, the weird,
    That cries in sharp distress about the eaves?
Is it the wind whose gathering shout is heard
    With voice of peoples myriad like the leaves?
Is it the wind? Fly to the casement, quick,
And when the roar comes thick,
      Fling wide the sash,
      Await the crash!

Nothing. Some various solitary cries,—
    Some sauntering woman's short hard laugh,
Or honester, a dog's bark,—these arise
    From lamplit street up to this free flagstaff:
Nothing remains of that low threatening sound;
The wind raves not the eaves around.
      Clasp casement to,—
      You heard not true.

Hark there again! a roar that holds a shriek!
    But not without—no, from below it comes:
What pulses up from solid earth to wreak
    A vengeful word on towers and lofty domes?
What angry booming doth the trembling ear,
Glued to the stone wall, hear—
      So deep, no air
      Its weight can bear?

Grieve! 'tis the voice of ignorance and vice,—
 The rage of slaves who fancy they are free:
Men who would keep men slaves at any price,
 Too blind their own black manacles to see.
Grieve! 'tis that grisly spectre with a torch,
Riot — that bloodies every porch,
   Hurls justice down
   And burns the town.

CHARLES DE KAY.

CIVIL WAR

"RIFLEMAN, shoot me a fancy shot
 Straight at the heart of yon prowling vidette;
Ring me a ball in the glittering spot
 That shines on his breast like an amulet!"

"Ah, captain! here goes for a fine-drawn bead:
 There's music around when my barrel's in tune!"
Crack! went the rifle, the messenger sped,
 And dead from his horse fell the ringing dragoon.

"Now, rifleman, steal through the bushes, and snatch
 From your victim some trinket to handsel first blood,—
A button, a loop, or that luminous patch
 That gleams in the moon like a diamond stud!"

"O captain! I staggered, and sunk on my track,
 When I gazed on the face of that fallen vidette!
For he looked so like you, as he lay on his back,
 That my heart rose upon me, and masters me yet.

"But I snatched off the trinket,—this locket of gold;
 An inch from the centre my lead broke its way,
Scarce grazing the picture, so fair to behold,
 Of a beautiful lady in bridal array."

"Ha! rifleman, fling me the locket!—'tis she,
 My brother's young bride—and the fallen dragoon
Was her husband— Hush, soldier, 'twas Heaven's decree;—
 We must bury him there, by the light of the moon!

"But hark! the far bugles their warnings unite!
 War is a virtue, weakness a sin:
There's a lurking and loping around us to-night;—
 Load again, rifleman, keep your hand in!"

CHARLES DAWSON SHANLY.

AT THE BREACH

ALL over for me,
    The struggle, and possible glory!
  All swept past,
In the rush of my own brigade.
  Will charges instead,
And fills up my place in the story;
  Well,—'tis well,
By the merry old games we played.

There's a fellow asleep, the lout! in the shade of the hillock yonder;
  What a dog it must be, to drowse in the midst of a time like this!
Why, the horses might neigh contempt at him;—what is he like, I
    wonder?
  If the smoke would but clear away, I have strength in me yet to
    hiss.

  Will, comrade and friend,
We parted in hurry of battle;
  All I heard
Was your sonorous "Up, my men!"
  Soon conquering pæans
Shall cover the cannonade's rattle;
  Then, home bells,—
Will you think of me sometimes, then?

How that rascal enjoys his snooze! Would he wake to the touch of
    powder?
  A reveillè of broken bones, or a prick of the sword, might do.
Hi, man! the general wants you;—if I could but for once call louder!
  There is something infectious here, for my eyelids are drooping
    too.

  Will, can you recall
The time we were lost on the Bright Down?
  Coming home late in the day,
  As Susie was kneeling to pray,
Little blue eyes and white night-gown,
Saying, "Our Father, who art—
Art what?" so she stayed with a start.
"In Heaven," your mother said softly.
  And Susie sighed, "So far away!"
'Tis nearer, Will, now to us all.

'Tis strange how that fellow sleeps! stranger still that his sleep
    should haunt me;—
If I could but command his face, to make sure of the lesser ill!
I will crawl to his side and see, for what should there be to daunt
    me?
What there? what there? O Father in Heaven, not Will!

      Will, dead Will!
    Lying here, I could not feel you!
      Will, brave Will!
    Oh, alas for the noble end!
      Will, dear Will!
    Since no love nor remorse could heal you,
      Will, good Will!
    Let me die on your breast, old friend!

              SARAH WILLIAMS.

MUSIC IN CAMP

TWO armies covered hill and plain,
    Where Rappahannock's waters
Ran deeply crimsoned with the stain
    Of battle's recent slaughters.

The summer clouds lay pitched like tents
    In meads of heavenly azure;
And each dread gun of the elements
    Slept in its hid embrasure.

The breeze so softly blew, it made
    No forest leaf to quiver,
And the smoke of the random cannonade
    Rolled slowly from the river.

And now, where circling hills looked down
    With cannon grimly planted,
O'er listless camp and silent town
    The golden sunset slanted:

When on the fervid air there came
    A strain—now rich, now tender;
The music seemed itself aflame
    With day's departing splendor.

A Federal band, which, eve and morn,
    Played measures brave and nimble.

Had just struck up, with flute and horn
   And lively clash of cymbal.

Down flocked the soldiers to the banks,
   Till, margined by its pebbles,
One wooded shore was blue with " Yanks,"
   And one was gray with " Rebels."

Then all was still, and then the band,
   With movement light and tricksy,
Made stream and forest, hill and strand,
   Reverberate with 'Dixie.'

The conscious stream with burnished glow
   Slipped proudly o'er its pebbles,
But thrilled throughout its deepest flow
   With yelling of the Rebels.

Again a pause, and then again
   The trumpets pealed sonorous,
And 'Yankee Doodle' was the strain
   To which the shore gave chorus.

The laughing ripple shoreward flew,
   To kiss the shining pebbles;
Loud shrieked the swarming Boys in Blue
   Defiance to the Rebels.

And yet once more the bugles sang
   Above the stormy riot;
No shout upon the evening rang,—
   There reigned a holy quiet.

The sad, slow stream its noiseless flood
   Poured o'er the glistening pebbles;
And silent now the Yankees stood,
   And silent stood the Rebels.

No unresponsive soul had heard
   That plaintive note's appealing,
So deeply 'Home, Sweet Home' had stirred
   The hidden founts of feeling.

Or Blue or Gray, the soldier sees,
   As by the wand of fairy,
The cottage 'neath the live-oak trees,
   The cabin by the prairie.

Or cold or warm, his native skies
  Bend in their beauty o'er him;
Seen through the tear-mist in his eyes,
  His loved ones stand before him.

As fades the iris after rain
  In April's tearful weather,
The vision vanished, as the strain
  And daylight died together.

But memory, waked by music's art,
  Expressed in simplest numbers,
Subdued the sternest Yankee's heart,
  Made light the Rebel's slumbers.

And fair the form of Music shines,—
  That bright, celestial creature,
Who still, 'mid war's embattled lines,
  Gave this one touch of Nature.

JOHN RANDOLPH THOMPSON.

THE BIVOUAC OF THE DEAD

THE muffled drum's sad roll has beat
  The soldier's last tattoo;
  No more on life's parade shall meet
  That brave and fallen few.
On fame's eternal camping-ground
  Their silent tents are spread,
And Glory guards with solemn round
  The bivouac of the dead.

No rumor of the foe's advance
  Now swells upon the wind;
No troubled thought at midnight haunts
  Of loved ones left behind;
No vision of the morrow's strife
  The warrior's dream alarms;
No braying horn or screaming fife
  At dawn shall call to arms.

Their shivered swords are red with rust,
  Their plumèd heads are bowed;
Their haughty banner trailed in dust
  Is now their martial shroud.

And plenteous funeral tears have washed
  The red stains from each brow;
And the proud forms, by battle gashed,
  Are free from anguish now.

The neighing troop, the flashing blade,
  The bugle's stirring blast,
The charge, the dreadful cannonade,
  The din and shout, are past;
Nor war's wild note nor glory's peal
  Shall thrill with fierce delight
Those breasts that nevermore may feel
  The rapture of the fight.

Like the fierce northern hurricane
  That sweeps his great plateau,
Flushed with the triumph yet to gain,
  Came down the serried foe.
Who heard the thunder of the fray
  Break o'er the field beneath,
Knew well the watchword of that day
  Was "Victory or death."

                              THEODORE O'HARA.

THE KEARSARGE

IN THE gloomy ocean bed
    Dwelt a formless thing, and said,
  In the dim and countless æons long ago,
    "I will build a stronghold high,
    Ocean's power to defy,
And the pride of haughty man to lay low."

    Crept the minutes for the sad,
    Sped the cycles of the glad,
But the march of time was neither less nor more;
    While the formless atom died,
    Myriad millions by its side,
And above them slowly lifted Roncador.

    Roncador of Caribee,
    Coral dragon of the sea,
Ever sleeping with his teeth below the wave;

Woe to him who breaks the sleep!
Woe to them who sail the deep!
Woe to ship and man that fear a shipman's grave!

Hither many a galleon old,
Heavy-keeled with guilty gold,
Fled before the hardy rover smiting sore;
But the sleeper silent lay
Till the preyer and his prey
Brought their plunder and their bones to Roncador.

Be content, O conqueror!
Now our bravest ship of war,
War and tempest who had often braved before,
All her storied prowess past,
Strikes her glorious flag at last
To the formless thing that builded Roncador.

JAMES JEFFREY ROCHE.

MONTEREY

WE WERE not many — we who stood
    Before the iron shot that day;
    Yet many a gallant spirit would
Give half his years if he but could
    Have been with us at Monterey.

Now here, now there, the shot is hailed
    In deadly drifts of fiery spray;
Yet not a single soldier quailed
When wounded comrades round them wailed
    Their dying shouts at Monterey.

And on, still on, our column kept
    Through walls of flame its withering way:
Where fell the dead the living stept,
Still charging on the guns which swept
    The slippery streets at Monterey.

The foe himself recoiled aghast,
    When, striking where he strongest lay,
We swooped his flanking batteries past,
And braving full their murderous blast,
    Stormed home the towers of Monterey.

Our banners on our turrets wave,
  And there the evening bugles play,
Where orange boughs above their grave
Keep green the memory of the brave
  Who fought and fell at Monterey.

We are not many — we who pressed
  Beside the brave who fell that day;
But who of us has not confessed
He'd rather share their warrior rest
  Than not have been at Monterey?

CHARLES FENNO HOFFMAN.

THE MIDNIGHT REVIEW

AT DEAD of night the drummer
    From out his grave awakes,
  And with his drum parading,
    His wonted round he takes.

His arms all bare and fleshless
  In eddying circles flew,
And beat the roll with vigor,
  The larum and tattoo.

Oh, strange and loud resounded
  That drum amidst the gloom.
The warriors that slumbered
  Awakened in their tomb;

And they who sleep congealing
  'Mid northern ice and snow,
And they who lie in Italy
  Where scorching summers glow,

And they whom the Nile's slime covers,
  And Araby's glowing sand,
From out their graves arising
  All take their arms in hand.

The trumpeter at midnight
  Quits, too, his grave to blow
His blast so shrill and piercing,
  And rideth to and fro.

There, coming on spectral chargers,
  The ghastly dead behold!
The blood-stained ancient squadrons
  With weapons manifold!

The grinning skulls so ghastly
  Beneath their helmets peer;
In their bony hands uplifted
  Their gleaming swords appear.

At midnight's ghostly hour
  The chieftain quits his grave;
Advances, slowly riding,
  Amid his chosen brave.

No plume his helm adorneth,
  His garb no regal pride,
And small is the polished sabre
  That's girded to his side.

The moon shines bright, illuming
  The plain with silver rays;
That chief with the plumeless helmet
  His warrior host surveys.

The ranks, their arms presenting,
  Then shoulder arms anew,
And pass with music's clangor
  Before him in review.

The generals and marshals
  Round in a circle stand;
The chieftain whispers softly
  To one at his right hand.

From rank to rank resounding
  It fleeth o'er the plain:
"La France,"—this is their watchword;
  The password, "St. Hélène!"

Thus at the midnight hour,
  In the Elysian plain,
The dead and mighty Cæsar
  Reviews his warrior train.

JOSEPH CHRISTIAN ZEDLITZ.

THE PRIVATE OF THE BUFFS

[Private Moyse, with other prisoners, having fallen into the hands of the Chinese, was ordered to perform *kotou;* and refusing, was knocked upon the head. — TIMES CORRESPONDENT.]

LAST night, among his fellow roughs,
  He jested, quaffed, and swore;
A drunken private of the Buffs,
  Who never looked before.
To-day, beneath the foeman's frown,
  He stands in Elgin's place,
Ambassador from Britain's crown,
  And type of all her race.

Poor, reckless, rude, low-born, untaught,
  Bewildered, and alone,
A heart with English instinct fraught
  He yet can call his own.
Ay, tear his body limb from limb,
  Bring cord or axe or flame,
He only knows that not through him
  Shall England come to shame.

Far Kentish hop-fields round him seemed,
  Like dreams, to come and go;
Bright leagues of cherry-blossom gleamed,
  One sheet of living snow;
The smoke above his father's door
  In gray soft eddyings hung —
Must he then watch it rise no more,
  Doomed by himself so young?

Yes, honor calls! — with strength like steel
  He put the vision by;
Let dusky Indians whine and kneel,
  An English lad must die.
And thus, with eyes that would not shrink,
  With knee to man unbent,
Unfaltering on its dreadful brink,
  To his red grave he went.

Vain mightiest fleets of iron framed,
  Vain those all-shattering guns,

Unless proud England keep untamed
    The strong heart of her sons;
So let his name through Europe ring,—
    A man of mean estate,
Who died as firm as Sparta's king
    Because his soul was great.

SIR FRANCIS HASTINGS DOYLE.

RIDING TOGETHER

FOR many, many days together
    The wind blew steady from the east,
For many days hot grew the weather,
    About the time of Our Lady's feast.

For many days we rode together,
    Yet met we neither friend nor foe;
Hotter and clearer grew the weather,
    Steadily did the east wind blow.

We saw the trees in the hot, bright weather,
    Clear-cut, with shadows very black,
As freely we rode on together
    With helms unlaced and bridles slack.

And often as we rode together,
    We, looking down the green-banked stream,
Saw flowers in the sunny weather,
    And saw the bubble-making bream.

And in the night lay down together,
    And hung above our heads the rood,
Or watched night-long in the dewy weather,
    The while the moon did watch the wood.

Our spears stood bright and thick together,
    Straight out the banners streamed behind,
As we galloped on in the sunny weather,
    With faces turned towards the wind.

Down sank our threescore spears together,
    As thick we saw the pagans ride;

His eager face in the clear fresh weather
  Shone out that last time by my side.

Up the sweep of the bridge we dashed together,
  It rocked to the crash of the meeting spears;
Down rained the buds of the dear spring weather,
  The elm-tree flowers fell like tears.

There, as we rolled and writhed together,
  I threw my arms above my head;
For close by my side, in the lovely weather,
  I saw him reel and fall back dead.

I and the slayer met together:
  He waited the death-stroke there in his place;
With thoughts of death, in the lovely weather
  Gapingly mazed at my maddened face.

Madly I fought as we fought together;
  In vain,— the little Christian band
The pagans drowned, as in stormy weather
  The river drowns low-lying land.

They bound my blood-stained hands together,
  They bound his corpse to nod by my side;
Then on we rode in the bright March weather,
  With clash of cymbals did we ride.

We ride no more, no more together;
  My prison-bars are thick and strong;
I take no heed of any weather:
  The sweet saints grant I live not long.

WILLIAM WORKS.

ANTONY AND CLEOPATRA

I AM dying, Egypt, dying;—
    Ebbs the crimson life-tide fast;
  And the dark Plutonian shadows
    Gather on the evening blast.
  Let thine arms, O Queen, infold me;
    Hush thy sobs and bow thine ear;
  Listen to the great heart-secrets
    Thou, and thou alone, must hear.

Though my scarred and veteran legions
    Bear their eagles high no more,
And my wrecked and scattered galleys
    Strew dark Actium's fatal shore;
Though no glittering guards surround me,
    Prompt to do their master's will,
I must perish like a Roman,
    Die the great Triumvir still.

Let not Cæsar's servile minions
    Mock the lion thus laid low:
'Twas no foeman's arm that felled him,
    'Twas his own that struck the blow;
His who, pillowed on thy bosom,
    Turned aside from glory's ray,
His who, drunk with thy caresses,
    Madly threw a world away.

Should the base plebeian rabble
    Dare assail my name at Rome,
Where my noble spouse Octavia
    Weeps within her widowed home,
Seek her; say the gods bear witness —
    Altars, augurs, circling wings —
That her blood, with mine commingled,
    Yet shall mount the throne of kings.

As for thee, star-eyed Egyptian,
    Glorious sorceress of the Nile,
Light the path to Stygian horrors
    With the splendors of thy smile.
Give the Cæsar crowns and arches,
    Let his brow the laurel twine:
I can scorn the Senate's triumphs,
    Triumphing in love like thine.

I am dying, Egypt, dying; —
    Hark the insulting foeman's cry!
They are coming! quick, my falchion, —
    Let me front them ere I die.
Ah! no more amid the battle
    Shall my heart exulting swell;
Isis and Osiris guard thee!
    Cleopatra, Rome, farewell!

WILLIAM HAINES LYTLE.

THE CROWING OF THE RED COCK

ACROSS the eastern sky has glowed
    The flicker of a blood-red dawn;
  Once more the clarion cock has crowed,
    Once more the sword of Christ is drawn;
A million burning roof-trees light
The world-wide path of Israel's flight.

Where is the Hebrew's fatherland?
    The folk of Christ is sore bestead;
The Son of Man is bruised and banned,
    Nor finds whereon to lay his head.
His cup is gall, his meat is tears;
His passion lasts a thousand years.

Each crime that wakes in man the beast
    Is visited upon his kind:
The lust of mobs, the greed of priest,
    The tyranny of kings, combined
To root his seed from earth again;
His record is one cry of pain.

When the long roll of Christian guilt
    Against his sires and kin is known,
The flood of tears, the life-blood spilt,
    The agony of ages shown,
What oceans can the stain remove
From Christian law and Christian love?

Nay, close the book; not now, not here,
    The hideous tale of sin narrate,
Re-echoing in the martyr's ear:
    Even he might nurse revengeful hate;
Even he might turn in wrath sublime,
With blood for blood and crime for crime.

Coward? Not he who faces death,
    Who singly against worlds has fought,—
For what? A name he may not breathe,
    For liberty of prayer and thought.
The angry sword he will not whet,
His nobler task is—to forget.

EMMA LAZARUS.

LOYALIST LAYS

THE THREE TROOPERS

INTO the Devil tavern
    Three booted troopers strode,
From spur to feather spotted and splashed
    With the mud of a winter road.
In each of their cups they dropped a crust,
    And stared at the guests with a frown;
Then drew their swords, and roared for a toast,
    "God send this Crum-well down!"

A blue smoke rose from their pistol-locks,
    Their sword-blades were still wet;
There were long red smears on their jerkins of buff,
    As the table they overset.
Then into their cups they stirred the crusts,
    And cursed old London town;
Then waved their swords, and drank with a stamp,
    "God send this Crum-well down!"

The 'prentice dropped his can of beer,
    The host turned pale as a clout;
The ruby nose of the toping squires
    Grew white at the wild men's shout.
Then into their cups they flung the crusts,
    And showed their teeth with a frown:
They flashed their swords as they gave the toast,
    "God send this Crum-well down!"

The gambler dropped his dog's-eared cards,
    The waiting-women screamed,
As the light of the fire, like stains of blood,
    On the wild men's sabres gleamed.
Then into their cups they splashed the crusts
    And cursed the fool of a town,
And leaped on the table, and roared a toast,
    "God send this Crum-well down!"

Till on a sudden fire-bells rang,
    And the troopers sprang to horse;
The eldest muttered between his teeth
    Hot curses — deep and coarse.
In their stirrup-cups they flung the crusts,
    And cried as they spurred through town,

With their keen swords drawn and their pistols cocked,
  "God send this Crum-well down!"

Away they dashed through Temple Bar,
  Their red cloaks flowing free;
Their scabbards clashed, each back-piece shone,—
  None liked to touch the three.
The silver cups that held the crusts
  They flung to the startled town,
Shouting again with a blaze of swords,
  "God send this Crum-well down!"

THE CAVALIER'S ESCAPE

TRAMPLE! trample! went the roan,
  Trap! trap! went the gray;
But pad! *pad!* PAD! like a thing that was mad,
  My chestnut broke away:
It was just five miles from Salisbury town,
  And but one hour to day.

Thud! THUD! came on the heavy roan,
  Rap! RAP! the mettled gray;
But my chestnut mare was of blood so rare
  That she showed them all the way.
Spur on! spur on!—I doffed my hat,
  And wished them all good-day.

They splashed through miry rut and pool,
  Splintered through fence and rail;
But chestnut Kate switched over the gate —
  I saw them droop and tail:
To Salisbury town — but a mile of down,
  Once over this brook and rail.

Trap! trap! I heard their echoing hoofs,
  Past the walls of mossy stone:
The roan flew on at a staggering pace,
  But blood is better than bone;
I patted old Kate and gave her the spur,
  For I knew it was all my own.

But trample! trample! came their steeds,
  And I saw their wolf's eyes burn:
I felt like a royal hart at bay,
  And made me ready to turn;

I looked where highest grew the may,
  And deepest arched the fern.

I flew at the first knave's sallow throat—
  One blow and he was down;
The second rogue fired twice and missed—
  I sliced the villain's crown,
Clove through the rest, and flogged brave Kate,
  Fast, fast to Salisbury town.

Pad! pad! they came on the level sward,
  Thud! thud! upon the sand,
With a gleam of swords, and a burning match,
  And a shaking of flag and hand,
.But one long bound, and I passed the gate
  Safe from the canting band.

THE THREE SCARS

THIS I got on the day that Goring
  Fought through York, like a wild beast roaring.
  The roofs were black, and the streets were full,
The doors built up with the packs of wool:
But our pikes made way through a storm of shot
Barrel to barrel till locks grew hot;
Frere fell dead, and Lucas was gone,
But the drum still beat and the flag went on.

This I caught from a swinging sabre,—
All I had from a long night's labor.
When Chester flamed, and the streets were red,
In splashing shower fell the molten lead;
The fire sprang up, and the old roof split,
The fire-ball burst in the middle of it:
With a clash and a clang the troopers they ran,
For the siege was over ere well began.

This I got from a pistol butt
(Lucky my head's not a hazel-nut).
The horse they raced and scudded and swore;
There were Leicestershire gentlemen, seventy score:
Up came the "Lobsters," covered with steel—
Down we went with a stagger and reel;
Smash at the flag, I tore it to rag,
And carried it off in my foraging bag.

THE old men sat with hats pulled down,
    Their claret cups before them;
Broad shadows hid their sullen eyes,
    The tavern lamps shone o'er them,
As a brimming bowl, with crystal filled,
    Came borne by the landlord's daughter,
Who wore in her bosom the fair white rose
    That grew best over the water.

Then all leaped up, and joined their hands
    With hearty clasp and greeting;
The brimming cups, outstretched by all,
    Over the wide bowl meeting.
"A health," they cried, "to the witching eyes
    Of Kate, the landlord's daughter!
But don't forget the white, white rose
    That grows best over the water."

Each other's cups they touched all round,
    The last red drop outpouring;
Then with a cry that warmed the blood,
    One heart-born chorus roaring —
"Let the glass go round to pretty Kate,
    The landlord's black-eyed daughter;
But never forget the white, white rose
    That grows best over the water."

Then hats flew up and swords sprang out,
    And lusty rang the chorus:
"Never," they cried, "while Scots are Scots
    And the broad Frith's before us."
A ruby ring the glasses shine
    As they toast the landlord's daughter,
Because she wore the white, white rose
    That grew best over the water.

A poet cried, "Our thistle's brave,
    With all its stings and prickles;
The shamrock with its holy leaf
    Is spared by Irish sickles:
But bumpers round,— for what are these
    To Kate, the landlord's daughter,

Who wears at her bosom the rose as white
  That grows best over the water?"

They dashed the glasses at the wall—
  No lip might touch them after:
The toast had sanctified the cups
  That smashed against the rafter:
Their chairs thrown back, they up again
  To toast the landlord's daughter;
But never forgot the white, white rose
  That grew best over the water.

THE JACOBITES' CLUB

ONE threw an orange in the air,
  And caught it on his sword;
  Another crunched the yellow peel
    With his red heel on the board;
A third man cried, "When Jackson comes
  Into his large estate,
I'll pave the old hall down in Kent
  With golden bits of eight."

One, turning with a meaning wink,
  Fast double-locked the door,
Then held a letter to the fire—
  It was all blank before,
But now it's ruled with crimson lines,
  And ciphers odd and quaint:
They cluster round, and nod, and laugh,
  As one invokes a saint.

He pulls a black wig from his head—
  He's shaven like a priest;
He holds his finger to his nose,
  And smiles,—"The wind blows east;
The Dutch canals are frozen, sirs;—
  I don't say anything,
But when you play at ombre next,
  Mind that I lead a king."—

"Last night at Kensington I spent;
  'Twas gay as any fair:

Lord! how they stared to find that bill
  Stuck on the royal chair.
Some fools cried 'Treason!' some, 'A plot!'
  I slipped behind a screen,
And when the guards came fussing in,
  Sat chatting with the Queen.»

«I,» cried a third, «was printing songs
  In a garret in St. Giles's,
When I heard the watchman at the door,
  And flew up on the tiles.
The press was lowered into the vault,
  The types into a drain:
I think you'll own, my trusty sirs,
  I have a ready brain.»

A frightened whisper at the door,
  A bell rings — then a shot:
«Shift, boys, the Orangers are come!—
  Pity! the punch is hot.»
A clash of swords — a shout — a scream,
  And all abreast in force,
The Jacobites, some twenty strong,
  Break through and take to horse.

             GEORGE WALTER THORNBURY.

CURFEW MUST NOT RING TO-NIGHT

ENGLAND's sun was slowly setting o'er the hills so far away,
  Filling all the land with beauty at the close of one sad day:
  And the last rays kissed the forehead of a man and maiden fair,
He with step so slow and weakened, she with sunny, floating hair;
He with sad bowed head, and thoughtful, she with lips so cold and
      white,
Struggling to keep back the murmur, "Curfew must not ring to-night."

"Sexton,"—Bessie's white lips faltered, pointing to the prison old,
With its walls so dark and gloomy,—walls so dark and damp and
      cold,—
"I've a lover in that prison, doomed this very night to die
At the ringing of the curfew, and no earthly help is nigh.   [white,
Cromwell will not come till sunset:" and her face grew strangely
As she spoke in husky whispers, "Curfew must not ring to-night."

"Bessie," calmly spoke the sexton,—every word pierced her young
       heart
Like a thousand gleaming arrows, like a deadly poisoned dart,—
"Long, long years I've rung the curfew from that gloomy shadowed
       tower;
Every evening, just at sunset, it has told the twilight hour:
I have done my duty ever, tried to do it just and right;
Now I'm old, I will not miss it: girl, the curfew rings to-night!"

Wild her eyes and pale her features, stern and white her thoughtful
       brow,
And within her heart's deep centre, Bessie made a solemn vow.
She had listened while the judges read, without a tear or sigh,
"At the ringing of the curfew—Basil Underwood *must die.*"
And her breath came fast and faster, and her eyes grew large and
       bright—
One low murmur, scarcely spoken—"Curfew *must not* ring to-night!"

She with light step bounded forward, sprang within the old church
       door,
Left the old man coming slowly, paths he'd trod so oft before:
Not one moment paused the maiden, but with cheek and brow aglow,
Staggered up the gloomy tower, where the bell swung to and fro;
Then she climbed the slimy ladder, dark, without one ray of light,—
Upward still, her pale lips saying, "Curfew shall not ring to-night!"

She has reached the topmost ladder: o'er her hangs the great dark
       bell,
And the awful gloom beneath her, like the pathway down to hell!
See, the ponderous tongue is swinging! 'tis the hour of curfew now!
And the sight has chilled her bosom, stopped her breath and paled
       her brow.
Shall she let it ring? No, never! Her eyes flash with sudden light,
As she springs and grasps it firmly—"Curfew shall not ring to-night!"

Out she swung, far out; the city seemed a tiny speck below,
There, 'twixt heaven and earth suspended, as the bell swung to and
       fro,
And the half-deaf sexton ringing (years he had not heard the bell),
And he thought the twilight curfew rang young Basil's funeral knell:
Still the maiden clinging firmly, cheek and brow so pale and white,
Stilled her frightened heart's wild beating—"*Curfew shall not ring
       to-night!*"

It was o'er;—the bell ceased swaying, and the maiden stepped once
      more
Firmly on the damp old ladder, where for hundred years before
Human foot had not been planted: and what she this night had
      done
Should be told in long years after,—as the rays of setting sun
Light the sky with mellow beauty, aged sires with heads of white
Tell their children why the curfew did not ring that one sad night.

O'er the distant hills came Cromwell; Bessie saw him, and her brow,
Lately white with sickening terror, glows with sudden beauty now:
At his feet she told her story, showed her hands all bruised and
      torn;
And her sweet young face so haggard, with a look so sad and worn,
Touched his heart with sudden pity, lit his eyes with misty light—
"Go, your lover lives!" cried Cromwell: "curfew shall not ring to-
      night."

ROSA HARTWICK THORPE.

THE SONG OF THE WESTERN MEN

A GOOD sword and a trusty hand,
    A merry heart and true!
King James's men shall understand
    What Cornish lads can do.

And have they fixed the where and when?
    And shall Trelawny die?
Here's twenty thousand Cornishmen
    Will know the reason why!

Out spake their captain brave and bold,
    A merry wight was he:—
"If London Tower were Michael's hold,
    We'll set Trelawny free!

"We'll cross the Tamar, land to land,—
    The Severn is no stay,—
With 'one and all,' and hand in hand,
    And who shall bid us nay?

"And when we come to London wall,
    A pleasant sight to view,
Come forth! come forth, ye cowards all,—
    Here's men as good as you!

"Trelawny he's in keep and hold,
　Trelawny he may die;
But here's twenty thousand Cornish bold
　Will know the reason why!"

ROBERT STEPHEN HAWKER.

THE SONG OF HATRED

BRAVE soldier, kiss the trusty wife
　And draw the trusty blade!
Then turn ye to the reddening east,
　In freedom's cause arrayed.
Till death shall part the blade and hand,
　They may not separate:
We've practiced loving long enough,
　And come at length to hate!

To right us and to rescue us
　Hath Love essayed in vain;
O Hate! proclaim thy judgment-day,
　And break our bonds in twain.
As long as ever tyrants last,
　Our task shall not abate:
We've practiced loving long enough,
　And come at length to hate!

Henceforth let every heart, that beats
　With hate alone be beating;—
Look round! what piles of rotten sticks
　Will keep the flame a-heating!
As many as are free and dare,
　From street to street go say 't:
We've practiced loving long enough,
　And come at length to hate!

Fight tyranny, while tyranny
　The trampled earth above is;
And holier will our hatred be,
　Far holier than our love is.
Till death shall part the blade and hand,
　They may not separate:
We've practiced loving long enough,
　Let's come at last to hate!

GEORGE HERWEGH.

TO LUCASTA, ON GOING TO THE WARS

TELL me not, sweet, I am unkind,
   That from the nunnery
Of thy chaste breast and quiet mind
   To war and arms I fly.

True, a new mistress now I chase,—
   The first foe in the field;
And with a stronger faith embrace
   A sword, a horse, a shield.

Yet this inconstancy is such
   As you too should adore:
I could not love thee, dear, so much,
   Loved I not honor more.

RICHARD LOVELACE.

«IF DOUGHTY DEEDS»

IF DOUGHTY deeds my lady please,
   Right soon I'll mount my steed;
And strong his arm, and fast his seat,
   That bears frae me the meed.
I'll wear thy colors in my cap,
   Thy picture at my heart;
And he that bends not to thine eye
   Shall rue it to his smart!
     Then tell me how to woo thee, Love;
      Oh, tell me how to woo thee!
     For thy dear sake, nae care I'll take
     Though ne'er another trow me.

If gay attire delight thine eye,
   I'll dight me in array;
I'll tend thy chamber door all night,
   And squire thee all the day.
If sweetest sounds can win thine ear,
   These sounds I'll strive to catch;
Thy voice I'll steal to woo thysell,—
   That voice that nane can match.

But if fond love thy heart can gain,
   I never broke a vow;

Nae maiden lays her skaith to me,
  I never loved but you:
For you alone I ride the ring,
  For you I wear the blue;
For you alone I strive to sing,—
  Oh, tell me how to woo!
    Tell me how to woo thee, Love;
      Oh, tell me how to woo thee!
    For thy dear sake, nae care I'll take
      Though ne'er another trow me.

GRAHAM OF GARTMORE.

A SPINNING SONG

MY LOVE to fight the Saxon goes,
  And bravely shines his sword of steel;
A heron's feather decks his brows,
  And a spur on either heel;
His steed is blacker than a sloe,
  And fleeter than the falling star:
Amid the surging ranks he'll go
  And shout for joy of war.

Twinkle, twinkle, pretty spindle, let the white wool drift and dwindle;
  Oh! we weave a damask doublet for my love's coat of steel.
Hark! the timid, turning treadle, crooning soft old-fashioned ditties
  To the low, slow murmur of the brown, round wheel.

My love is pledged to Ireland's fight;
  My love would die for Ireland's weal,
To win her back her ancient right,
  And make her foemen reel.
Oh, close I'll clasp him to my breast
  When homeward from the war he comes;
The fires shall light the mountain's crest,
  The valley peal with drums.

Twinkle, twinkle, pretty spindle, let the white wool drift and dwindle;
  Oh! we weave a damask doublet for my love's coat of steel.
Hark! the timid, turning treadle, crooning soft old-fashioned ditties
  To the low, slow murmur of the brown, round wheel.

JOHN FRANCIS O'DONNELL.

LOVE'S WITHOUT REASON

'TIS not my lady's face that makes me love her,—
    Though beauty there doth rest,
    Enough to inflame the breast
  Of one that never did discover
    The glories of a face before;
    But I that have seen thousands more,
See naught in hers but what in others are;—
Only because I think she's fair, she's fair.

'Tis not her virtues, nor those vast perfections
    That crowd together in her,
    Engage my soul to win her,
  For those are only brief collections
    Of what's in man in folio writ;
    Which by their imitation wit,
Women, like apes and children, strive to do:
But we that have the substance slight the show.

'Tis not her birth, her friends, nor yet her treasure,
    My freeborn soul can hold;
    For chains are chains, though gold:
  Nor do I court her for my pleasure,
    Nor for that old morality
    Do I love her, 'cause she loves me:
For that's no love, but gratitude; and all
Loves that from fortunes rise with fortunes fall.

If friends or birth created love within me,
    Then princes I'd adore,
    And only scorn the poor;
  If virtue or good parts could win me,
    I'd turn platonic and ne'er vex
    My soul with difference of sex;
And he that loves his lady 'cause she's fair
Delights his eye, so loves himself, not her.

Reason and wisdom are to love high treason;
    Nor can he truly love,
    Whose flame's not far above
  And far beyond his wit or reason.
    Then ask no reason for my fires,
    For infinite are my desires:
Something there is moves me to love, and I
Do know I love, but know not how nor why.

ALEXANDER BROME.

TO ALTHEA

WHEN Love with unconfinèd wings
   Hovers within my gates,
And my divine Althea brings
   To whisper at the grates;
When I lie tangled in her hair,
   And fettered to her eye,—
The birds that wanton in the air
   Know no such liberty.

When flowing cups run swiftly round
   With no allaying Thames,
Our careless heads with roses crowned,
   Our hearts with loyal flames;
When thirsty grief in wine we steep,
   When healths and draughts go free,—
Fishes that tipple in the deep
   Know no such liberty.

When, like committed linnets, I
   With shriller throat shall sing
The sweetness, mercy, majesty,
   And glories of my King;
When I shall voice aloud how good
   He is, how great should be,—
Enlargèd winds that curl the flood
   Know no such liberty.

Stone walls do not a prison make,
   Nor iron bars a cage;
Minds innocent and quiet take
   That for an hermitage:
If I have freedom in my love,
   And in my soul am free,
Angels alone that soar above
   Enjoy such liberty.

              RICHARD LOVELACE.

AMYNTA

MY SHEEP I neglected, I broke my sheep-crook,
   And all the gay haunts of my youth I forsook;
    No more for Amynta fresh garlands I wove:
For ambition, I said, would soon cure me of love.

Oh! what had my youth with ambition to do?
Why left I Amynta? Why broke I my vow?
Oh! give me my sheep, and my sheep-crook restore,
And I'll wander from love and Amynta no more.

Through regions remote in vain do I rove,
And bid the wide ocean secure me from love!
O fool! to imagine that aught could subdue
A love so well founded, a passion so true!—
Alas! 'tis too late at thy fate to repine:
Poor shepherd, Amynta can never be thine;
Thy tears are all fruitless, thy wishes are vain,
The moments neglected return not again.

SIR GILBERT ELLIOT.

VISION OF A FAIR WOMAN

(AISLING AIR DHREACH MNA)

TELL us some of the charms of the stars!—
    Close and well set were her ivory teeth;
White as the canna upon the moor
    Was her bosom the tartan bright beneath.

Her well-rounded forehead shone
    Soft and fair as the mountain-snow:
Her two breasts were heaving full;
    To them did the hearts of heroes flow.

Her lips were ruddier than the rose;
    Tender and tunefully sweet her tongue;
White as the foam adown her side
    Her delicate fingers extended hung.

Smooth as the dusky down of the elk,
    Appeared her shady eyebrows to me;
Lovely her cheeks were, like berries red.
    From every guile she was wholly free.

Her countenance looked like the gentle buds
    Unfolding their beauty in early spring;
Her yellow locks like the gold-browed hills;
    And her eyes like the radiance the sunbeams bring.

Ancient Erse.

THE SONG OF ETHLENN STUART

His face was glad as dawn to me,
His breath was sweet as dusk to me,
His eyes were burning flames to me,
Shule, Shule, Shule, agràh!

The broad noonday was night to me,
The full-moon night was dark to me,
The stars whirled and the Poles span,
The hour God took him far from me.

Perhaps he dreams in heaven now,
Perhaps he doth in worship bow,
A white flame round his foam-white brow,
Shule, Shule, Shule, agràh!

I laugh to think of him like this,
Who once found all his joy and bliss
Against my heart, against my kiss,
Shule, Shule, Shule, agràh!

Star of my joy, art still the same
Now thou hast gotten a new name,
Pulse of my heart, my Blood, my Flame,
Shule, Shule, Shule, agràh?

FIONA MACLEOD.

UNNUMBERED

How many times do I love thee, dear?
Tell me how many thoughts there be
In the atmosphere
Of a new-fallen year,
Whose white and sable hours appear
The latest flake of Eternity:
So many times do I love thee, dear.

How many times do I love, again?
Tell me how many beads there are
In a silver chain
Of evening rain,
Unraveled from the tumbling main,
And threading the eye of a yellow star:
So many times do I love, again.

THOMAS LOVELL BEDDOES.

MOLLY ASTHORE

O MARY dear! O Mary fair!
    O branch of generous stem!
White blossom of the banks of Nair,
    Though lilies grow on them,—
You've left me sick at heart for love,
    So faint I cannot see;
The candle swims the board above,
    I'm drunk for love of thee!
O stately stem of maiden pride,
    My woe it is and pain
That I thus severed from thy side
    The long night must remain.

Through all the towns of Innisfail
    I've wandered far and wide;
But from Downpatrick to Kinsale,
    From Carlow to Kilbride,—
Many lords and dames of high degree,—
    Where'er my feet have gone,
My Mary, one to equal thee
    I never looked upon.
I live in darkness and in doubt
    Whene'er my love's away;
But were the gracious sun put out,
    Her shadow would make day.

'Tis she, indeed, young bud of bliss,
    As gentle as she's fair.
Though lily-white her bosom is,
    And sunny bright her hair,
And dewy azure her blue eye,
    And rosy red her cheek,
Yet brighter she in modesty,
    Most beautifully meek.
The world's wise men from north to south
    Can never cure my pain;
But one kiss from her honey mouth
    Would make me well again.

SIR SAMUEL FERGUSON.

KATHLEEN MAVOURNEEN

KATHLEEN MAVOURNEEN! the gray dawn is breaking,
 The horn of the hunter is heard on the hill;
 The lark from her light wing the bright dew is
  shaking,—
Kathleen mavourneen! what, slumbering still?
Oh, hast thou forgotten how soon we must sever?
 Oh! hast thou forgotten this day we must part?
It may be for years, and it may be forever!
 Oh, why art thou silent, thou voice of my heart?
Oh! why art thou silent, Kathleen mavourneen?

Kathleen mavourneen, awake from thy slumbers!
 The blue mountains glow in the sun's golden light;
Ah, where is the spell that once hung on my numbers?
 Arise in thy beauty, thou star of my night!
Mavourneen, mavourneen, my sad tears are falling,
 To think that from Erin and thee I must part!
It may be for years, and it may be forever!
 Then why art thou silent, thou voice of my heart?
Then why art thou silent, Kathleen mavourneen?

     LOUISA MACARTNEY CRAWFORD.

WAVE-WON

TO-NIGHT I hunger so,
 Belovèd one, to know
 If you recall and crave again the dream
 That haunted our canoe,
 And wove its witchcraft through
Our hearts as 'neath the northern night we sailed the northern stream.

 Ah! dear, if only we
 As yesternight could be
Afloat within that light and lonely shell,
 To drift in silence till
 Heart-hushed, and lulled and still
The moonlight through the melting air flung forth its fatal spell.

 The dusky summer night,
 The path of gold and white
The moon had cast across the river's breast,

The shores in shadows clad,
The far-away, half-sad
Sweet singing of the whippoorwill, all soothed our souls to rest.

You trusted I could feel
My arm as strong as steel,
So still your upturned face, so calm your breath,
While circling eddies curled,
While laughing rapids whirled
From bowlder unto bowlder, till they dashed themselves to death.

Your splendid eyes aflame
Put heaven's stars to shame;
Your god-like head so near my lap was laid
My hand is burning where
It touched your wind-blown hair,
As sweeping to the rapids' verge I changed my paddle blade.

The boat obeyed my hand,
Till wearied with its grand
Wild anger, all the river lay aswoon;
And as my paddle dipped,
Through pools of pearl it slipped
And swept beneath a shore of shade, beneath a velvet moon.

To-night, again dream you
Our spirit-winged canoe
Is listening to the rapids purling past?
Where in delirium reeled
Our maddened hearts that kneeled
To idolize the perfect world, to taste of love at last.

E. PAULINE JOHNSON ("Tekahionwake").

WHEN DID WE MEET?

WHEN did I know thee and not love thee?
How could I live and know thee not?
The look of thine that first did move me
I have forgot.

Canst thou recall thy life's beginning?
Will childhood's conscious wonder last?
Each glance from thee, so worth the winning,
Blots all the past.

ELAINE GOODALE.

SONG TO AITHNE

THY dark eyes to mine, Aithne,
   Lamps of desire!
Oh how my soul leaps,
   Leaps to their fire!

Sure now, if I in heaven,
   Dreaming in bliss,
Heard but the whisper,
But the lost echo even,
   Of one such kiss,

All of the Soul of me
   Would leap afar;
If that called me to thee,
Aye, I would leap afar,
   A falling star!

         IAN CAMERON (" Ian Mòr ").

GRACIE OG MACHREE

SONG OF THE " WILD GEESE "

I PLACED the silver in her palm
   By Inny's smiling tide,
And vowed, ere summer-time came on,
   To claim her as a bride.
But when the summer-time came on,
   I dwelt beyond the sea;
Yet still my heart is ever true
   To Gracie og machree.

Oh, bonnie are the woods of Targ,
   And green thy hills, Rathmore,
And soft the sunlight ever falls
   On Darre's sloping shore;
And there the eyes I love, in tears
   Shine ever mournfully,
While I am far and far away
   From Gracie og machree.

When battle-steeds were neighing loud,
   With bright blades in the air,

Next to my inmost heart I wore
  A bright tress of her hair.
When stirrup-cups were lifted up
  To lips, with soldier glee,
One toast I always fondly pledged,—
  'Twas Gracie og machree.

JOHN K. CASEY.

ROBIN ADAIR

WELCOME on shore again,
    Robin Adair!
  Welcome once more again,
    Robin Adair!
I feel thy trembling hand;
Tears in thy eyelids stand,
To greet thy native land,
    Robin Adair!

Long I ne'er saw thee, love,
    Robin Adair!
Still I prayed for thee, love,
    Robin Adair!
When thou wert far at sea
Many made love to me,
But still I thought on thee,
    Robin Adair!

Come to my heart again,
    Robin Adair!
Never to part again,
    Robin Adair!
And if you still are true,
I will be constant too,
And will wed none but you,
    Robin Adair!

LADY CAROLINE KEPPEL.

WISHES FOR THE SUPPOSED MISTRESS

WHOE'ER she be,
  That not impossible She
That shall command my heart and me;

  Where'er she lie,
  Locked up from mortal eye
In shady leaves of destiny

  Till that ripe birth
  Of studied Faith stand forth,
And teach her fair steps tread our earth;

  Till that divine
  Idea take a shrine
Of crystal flesh, through which to shine:

  Meet you her, my Wishes,
  Bespeak her to my blisses,
And be ye called, my absent kisses.

  I wish her beauty
  That owes not all its duty
To gaudy tire, or glist'ring shoe-tie,—

  Something more than
  Taffeta or tissue can,
Or rampant feather, or rich fan,—

  A face that's best
  By its own beauty drest,
And can alone commend the rest;

 . . . . .

  Soft silken hours,
  Open suns, shady bowers,—
'Bove all, nothing within that lowers;

 . . . . . .

  Days, that in spite
  Of darkness, by the light
Of a clear mind are day all night;

  Life, that dares send
  A challenge to his end,
And when it comes, say, "Welcome, friend."

I wish her store
Of worth may leave her poor
Of wishes; and I wish — no more.

Now, if Time knows
That Her, whose radiant brows
Weave them a garland of my vows;

.   .   .   .   .   .

Such worth as this is
Shall fix my flying wishes,
And determine them to kisses.

Let her full glory,
My fancies, fly before ye;
Be ye my fictions — but her story.

RICHARD CRASHAW.

AMATURUS

SOMEWHERE beneath the sun, —
    These quivering heart-strings prove it, —
Somewhere there must be one
    Made for this soul to move it:
Some one that hides her sweetness
    From neighbors whom she slights,
Nor can attain completeness,
    Nor give her heart its rights;
Some one whom I could court
    With no great change of manner,
Still holding reason's fort,
    Though waving fancy's banner:
A lady, not so queenly
    As to disdain my hand,
Yet born to smile serenely
    Like those that rule the land, —
Noble, but not too proud;
    With soft hair simply folded,
And bright face crescent-browed,
    And throat by Muses molded;
And eyelids lightly falling
    On little glistening seas,
Deep-calm, when gales are brawling,
    Though stirred by every breeze;

Swift voice, like flight of dove
    Through minster arches floating,
With sudden turns, when love
    Gets overnear to doting;
Keen lips, that shape soft sayings
    Like crystals of the snow,
With pretty half-betrayings
    Of things one may not know;
Fair hand, whose touches thrill
    Like golden rod of wonder,
Which Hermes wields at will
    Spirit and flesh to sunder;
Light foot to press the stirrup
    In fearlessness and glee,
Or dance till finches chirrup
    And stars sink to the sea.

Forth, Love, and find this maid,
    Wherever she be hidden:
Speak, Love, be not afraid,
    But plead as thou art bidden;
And say that he who taught thee
    His yearning want and pain,
Too dearly, dearly bought thee
    To part with thee in vain.

WILLIAM JOHNSON–CORY.

TELL ME, MY HEART, IF THIS BE LOVE

WHEN Delia on the plain appears,
    Awed by a thousand tender fears,
    I would approach, but dare not move; —
Tell me, my heart, if this be love.

Whene'er she speaks, my ravished ear
No other voice than hers can hear;
No other wit but hers approve; —
Tell me, my heart, if this be love.

If she some other swain commend,
Though I was once his fondest friend,
His instant enemy I prove; —
Tell me, my heart, if this be love.

When she is absent, I no more
Delight in all that pleased before,—
The clearest spring, the shadiest grove;—
Tell me, my heart, if this be love.

When fond of power, of beauty vain,
Her nets she spread for every swain,
I strove to hate, but vainly strove;—
Tell me, my heart, if this be love.

GEORGE, LORD LYTTELTON.

FAIR HELEN

I WISH I were where Helen lies;—
Night and day on me she cries:
Oh that I were where Helen lies
      On fair Kirconnell lea!

Curst be the heart that thought the thought,
And curst the hand that fired the shot—
And in my hands burd Helen dropt,
      And died to succor me!

O think na but my heart was sair
When my love dropt down and spak nae mair!
I laid her down wi' meikle care
      On fair Kirconnell lea.

As I went down the water-side,
None but my foe to be my guide,
None but my foe to be my guide,
      On fair Kirconnell lea,—

I lighted down my sword to draw,
I hackèd him in pieces sma',
I hackèd him in pieces sma',
      For her sake that died for me.

O Helen fair, beyond compare!
I'll make a garland of thy hair
Shall bind my heart for evermair
      Until the day I die.

Oh that I were where Helen lies!
Night and day on me she cries;
Out of my bed she bids me rise —
    Says, "Haste and come to me!"

O Helen fair! O Helen chaste!
If I were with thee I were blest,
Where thou lies low and takes thy rest
    On fair Kirconnell lea.

I wish my grave were growing green,
A winding-sheet drawn ower my een,
And I in Helen's arms lying,
    On fair Kirconnell lea.

I wish I were where Helen lies;—
Night and day on me she cries;
And I am weary of the skies,
    Since my Love died for me.

Author Unknown.

SALLY IN OUR ALLEY

OF ALL the girls that are so smart
    There's none like pretty Sally;
She is the darling of my heart,
    And she lives in our alley.
There is no lady in the land
    Is half so sweet as Sally:
She is the darling of my heart,
    And she lives in our alley.

Her father he makes cabbage-nets,
    And through the streets does cry 'em;
Her mother she sells laces long
    To such as please to buy 'em:
But sure such folks could ne'er beget
    So sweet a girl as Sally!
She is the darling of my heart,
    And she lives in our alley.

When she is by, I leave my work,
    I love her so sincerely:
My master comes like any Turk,
    And bangs me most severely;

But let him bang his bellyful,
  I'll bear it all for Sally:
She is the darling of my heart,
  And she lives in our alley.

Of all the days that's in the week,
  I dearly love but one day,
And that's the day that comes betwixt
  A Saturday and Monday;
For then I'm drest all in my best
  To walk abroad with Sally:
She is the darling of my heart,
  And she lives in our alley.

My master carries me to church,
  And often am I blamed
Because I leave him in the lurch
  As soon as text is named;
I leave the church in sermon-time
  And slink away to Sally:
She is the darling of my heart,
  And she lives in our alley.

When Christmas comes about again,
  Oh then I shall have money:
I'll hoard it up, and box it all,
  I'll give it to my honey.
I would it were ten thousand pound,
  I'd give it all to Sally:
She is the darling of my heart,
  And she lives in our alley.

My master and the neighbors all
  Make game of me and Sally;
And but for her, I'd better be
  A slave and row a galley:
But when my seven long years are out,
  Oh then I'll marry Sally;
Oh then we'll wed, and then we'll bed —
  But not in our alley.

                              HENRY CAREY.

SHEPHERD'S SONG

WE THAT have known no greater state
Than this we live in, praise our fate;
For courtly silks in cares are spent,
When country's russet breeds content.

The power of sceptres we admire,
But sheep-crooks for our use desire;
Simple and low is our condition,
For here with us is no ambition.

We with the sun our flocks unfold,
Whose rising makes their fleeces gold;
Our music from the birds we borrow,
They bidding us, we them, good-morrow.

Our habits are but coarse and plain,
Yet they defend us from the rain;
As warm too, in an equal eye,
As those bestained in scarlet dye.

The shepherd with his homespun lass
As many merry hours doth pass
As courtiers with their costly girls,
Though richly decked in gold and pearls.

THOMAS HEYWOOD.

A MADRIGAL

LOVE me not for comely grace,
For my pleasing eye or face,
Nor for any outward part,
No, nor for my constant heart;
For these may fail or turn to ill,
So thou and I shall sever:
Keep therefore a true woman's eye,
And love me still but know not why;
So hast thou the same reason still
To doat upon me ever.

JOHN WILBYE.

METEMPSYCHOSIS

THOU wert a shepherdess with fawn-like eyes;
   I but a linnet swinging on a spray,
   Who sang to thee of love the livelong day,
'Neath the deep azure of Ionian skies:
And thou didst throw me crumbs, and smile upon
The rustic wooing of some Corydon.

Thou wert a princess in Provençal towers;
   I but a hunchback minstrel of her train,
   Whose beauty tuned my lute's divinest strain
To sing its master's love to pitying flowers:
Yet once, led forth a monarch's bride to be,
Thou kissed the dead lips that had sung of thee.

And now again I see thee as of yore;
   In charms mysterious, fadeless, and supreme.
   Still must I chant the love-slain minstrel's dream,
Still weave in song the linnet's passion lore.
And thou?— hast thou yet nothing more to give?
Wilt thou not love me, sweet, while now I live?

DUFFIELD OSBORNE.

AN OPAL

A ROSE of fire shut in a veil of snow,
   An April gleam athwart a misted sky:
   A jewel — a soul! gaze deep if thou wouldst know
     The flame-wrought spell of its pale witchery;
And now each tremulous beauty lies revealed,
And now the drifted snow doth beauty shield.

So my shy love, aneath her kerchief white,
   Holdeth the glamour of the East in fee;
Warm Puritan — who fears her own delight,
   Who trembleth over that she yieldeth me.
And now her lips her heart's rich flame have told;
And now they pale that they have been so bold.

EDNAH PROCTER CLARKE.

HOLD, POETS!

HOLD, poets! Hear *me* tell
    Where Beauty's queen doth dwell!
    'Tis in no foreign land,
'Tis by no storied strand,
But here her sweet renown
Haunts an old fishing-town.

Not alone Beauty's queen,—
Virtue were proud, I ween,
Could she be known to fame
By this dear maiden's name,
Or could her ways so win
Followers to walk therein.

Wit's arrow on her lips
First into honey dips;
Lips at whose magic spell
Shamed Music breaks her shell.
All to bless, naught to blame,—
Blanche is her sweetest name.

Now, poets, spend your days
Piping in her pure praise;
Wake, when fond love inspires,
To her your happy lyres:
Not to my halting songs
Such a charmed theme belongs!

RICHARD S. SPOFFORD.

PANGLORY'S WOOING SONG

LOVE is the blossom where there blows
    Everything that lives or grows;
    Love doth make the heavens to move,
And the sun doth burn in love;
Love the strong and weak doth yoke,
And makes the ivy climb the oak,
Under whose shadows lions wild,
Softened by love, grow tame and mild.
Love no med'cine can appease:
He burns the fishes in the seas;

Not all the skill his wounds can stanch;
Not all the sea his fire can quench.
Love did make the bloody spear
Once a leafy coat to wear,
While in his leaves there shrouded lay
Sweet birds, for love that sing and play;
And of all love's joyful flame
I the bud and blossom am.
    Only bend thy knee to me —
    Thy wooing shall thy winning be.

See! see the flowers that below
Now freshly as the morning blow,
And of all, the virgin rose,
That as bright Aurora shows —
How they all unleavèd die,
Losing their virginity;
Like unto a summer shade,
But now born, and now they fade:
Everything doth pass away;
There is danger in delay.
Come, come, gather then the rose;
Gather it, or it you lose.
All the sand of Tagus's shore
In my bosom casts its ore;
All the valleys' swimming corn
To my house is yearly borne;
Every grape of every vine
Is gladly bruised to make me wine;
While ten thousand kings as proud
To carry up my train, have bowed;
And a world of ladies send me,
In my chambers to attend me;
All the stars in heaven that shine,
And ten thousand more, are mine.
    Only bend thy knee to me —
    Thy wooing shall thy winning be.

GILES FLETCHER.

LOVE IN THE VALLEY

UNDER yonder beech-tree standing on the greensward,
    Couched with her arms behind her little head,
Her knees folded up, her tresses on her bosom,
    Lies my young love sleeping in the shade.
Had I the heart to slide one arm beneath her,
    Press her dreaming lips as her waist I folded slow!
Waking on the instant she could not but embrace me —
    Ah! would she hold me, and never let me go?

Shy as the squirrel, and wayward as the swallow;
    Swift as the swallow when athwart the western flood
Circleting the surface he meets his mirrored winglets, —
    Is that dear one in her maiden bud.
Shy as the squirrel whose nest is in the pine-tops;
    Gentle — ah! that she were jealous as the dove!
Full of all the wildness of the woodland creatures,
    Happy in herself is the maiden that I love!

What can have taught her distrust of all I tell her?
    Can she truly doubt me when looking on my brows?
Nature never teaches distrust of tender love-tales,
    What can have taught her distrust of all my vows?
No, she does not doubt me! on a dewy eve-tide,
    Whispering together beneath the listening moon,
I prayed till her cheek flushed, implored till she faltered —
    Fluttered to my bosom — ah! to fly away so soon! .

When her mother tends her before the laughing mirror,
    Tying up her laces, looping up her hair,
Often she thinks, "Were this wild thing wedded,
    I should have more love, and much less care."
When her mother tends her before the bashful mirror,
    Loosening her laces, combing down her curls,
Often she thinks, "Were this wild thing wedded,
    I should lose but one for so many boys and girls."

Clambering roses peep into her chamber,
    Jasmine and woodbine breathe sweet, sweet;
White-necked swallows twittering of summer,
    Fill her with balm and nested peace from head to feet.
Ah! will the rose-bough see her lying lonely,
    When the petals fall and fierce bloom is on the leaves?
Will the autumn garners see her still ungathered,
    When the fickle swallows forsake the weeping eaves?

Comes a sudden question — should a strange hand pluck her!
  Oh what an anguish smites me at the thought,
Should some idle lordling bribe her mind with jewels! —
  Can such beauty ever thus be bought?
Sometimes the huntsmen prancing down the valley
  Eye the village lasses, full of sprightly mirth;
They see as I see, mine is the fairest!
  Would she were older, and could read my worth!

Are there not sweet maidens if she will deny me?
  Shów the bridal heavens but one bright star?
Wherefore thus then do I chase a shadow,
  Chattering one note like a brown eve-jar?
So I rhyme and reason till she darts before me —
  Through the milky meadows from flower to flower she flies,
Sunning her sweet palms to shade her dazzled eyelids
  From the golden love that looks too eager in her eyes.

When at dawn she wakens, and her fair face gazes
  Out on the weather through the window-panes,
Beauteous she looks! like a white water-lily
  Bursting out of bud on the rippled river-plains.
When from bed she rises, clothed from neck to ankle
  In her long nightgown, sweet as boughs of May,
Beauteous she looks! like a tall garden lily
  Pure from the night and perfect for the day!

Happy, happy time, when the gray star twinkles
  Over the fields all fresh with bloomy dew;
When the cold-cheeked dawn grows ruddy up the twilight,
  And the gold sun wakes, and weds her in the blue.
Then when my darling tempts the early breezes,
  She the only star that dies not with the dark!
Powerless to speak all the ardor of my passion,
  I catch her little hand as we listen to the lark.

Shall the birds in vain then valentine their sweethearts,
  Season after season tell a fruitless tale?
Will not the virgin listen to their voices?
  Take the honeyed meaning — wear the bridal veil?
Fears she frosts of winter, fears she the bare branches?
  Waits she the garlands of spring for her dower?
Is she a nightingale that will not be nested
  Till the April woodland has built her bridal bower?

Then come, merry April, with all thy birds and beauties!
  With thy crescent brows and thy flowery, showery glee;
With thy budding leafage and fresh green pastures:
  And may thy lustrous crescent grow a honeymoon for me!
Come, merry month of the cuckoo and the violet!
  Come, weeping Loveliness, in all thy blue delight!
Lo! the nest is ready, let me not languish longer!
  Bring her to my arms on the first May night.

GEORGE MEREDITH.

SING AGAIN

You sang me a song:
      'Twas the close of the year —
    Sing again!
I cannot remember the name
      Or the words:
      'Tis the same
  We listen to hear
When the windows are open in spring,
  And the air's full of birds;
One calls from the branch some sweet thing,
  And one sings on the wing
    The refrain.

  You sang me a song
  My heart thrilled to hear.
    The refrain
Has run like a filet of gold
    Through the woof
    Of the cold
  Dark days of a year.
To-night there's a year at its start,
  All the birds are aloof,
Your eyes hold the sun for my part,
  And the Spring's in your heart —
    Sing again!

MARIE LOUISE VAN VORST.

WHAT MY LOVER SAID

BY THE merest chance, in the twilight gloom,
  In the orchard path he met me—
In the tall, wet grass, with its faint perfume;
And I tried to pass, but he made no room—
  Oh I tried, but he would not let me.
So I stood and blushed till the grass grew red,
  With my face bent down above it,
While he took my hand as he whispering said—
(How the clover lifted each pink, sweet head,
To listen to all that my lover said;
  Oh, the clover in bloom, I love it!)

In the high, wet grass went the path to hide,
  And the low wet leaves hung over;
But I could not pass upon either side,
For I found myself, when I vainly tried,
  In the arms of my steadfast lover.
And he held me there and he raised my head,
  While he closed the path before me,
And he looked down into my eyes and said—
(How the leaves bent down from the boughs o'erhead,
To listen to all that my lover said,
  Oh, the leaves hanging lowly o'er me!)

Had he moved aside but a little way,
  I could surely then have passed him;
And he knew I never could wish to stay,
And would not have heard what he had to say,
  Could I only aside have cast him.
It was almost dark, and the moments sped,
  And the searching night wind found us,
But he drew me nearer and softly said—
(How the pure, sweet wind grew still, instead,
To listen to all that my lover said;
  Oh, the whispering wind around us!)

I am sure he knew when he held me fast,
  That I must be all unwilling;
For I tried to go, and I would have passed,
As the night was come with its dew at last,
  And the sky with its stars was filling.
But he clasped me close when I would have fled,
  And he made me hear his story,

And his soul came out from his lips and said —
(How the stars crept out where the white moon led,
To listen to all that my lover said;
  Oh, the moon and the stars in glory!)

I know that the grass and the leaves will not tell,
  And I'm sure that the wind, precious rover,
Will carry my secret so safely and well
  That no being shall ever discover
One word of the many that rapidly fell
  From the soul-speaking lips of my lover;
  And the moon and the stars that looked over
Shall never reveal what a fairy-like spell
They wove round about us that night in the dell,
  In the path through the dew-laden clover,
Nor echo the whispers that made my heart swell
  As they fell from the lips of my lover.

HOMER G. GREENE.

TWO DREAMS

HIS

IF A Rose could sing
  In just one song
All it dreamed of spring
  Through the winter long,
Would it pray the zephyr to lend its tone,
Or the brook, that maketh a mimic moan
Over some cruel hard-hearted stone?
Or the mating bird, who sings his best
On the bough that shadows his covert nest?
Ah, no, my Beautiful! thine alone
Of all the music to Echo known,
Thy sweet soprano, with silvery ring,
  Would be the voice
  Of its loving choice,
   If a Rose could sing!

HERS

Could I be a Rose for a sweet, swift hour, —
A passionate, purple, perfect flower, —
Not a breath would I spare to the vagrant air,
For the woodland warbler I would not care:

But oh! if my human lover came,
Then would I blush like a heart of flame,—
Like a heart of flame I would send a sigh,
A note of perfume, when he drew nigh,
That should make him take me ere bees could sip,
That should woo him to me with bloomy lip;
Till, his kisses culling the flower of me,
　My petals close on his lips would close,
And — once more a Woman I think I'd be
　　　Could I be a Rose!

HENRY W. AUSTIN.

JUNE IN LONDON

(WITH PUPILS)

BOOKS and heat, the dullard mind
　　Reeling under Cicero;
　London landscape, roof and blind
　Blacker e'en than London snow;
Pupils coming all day long,
　All my pause the thought that she,
She I love, my joy and song,
　Dreams by day and night of me.
Ah, might I gather a rose with its dew
For her heart on this bright June morning!

Doric of the roughest mold
　　Planned to make a Master sour;
Thirty lines of Virgil's gold
　Slowly melting in an hour!
Ovid's ingots and the gems
　Horace polished for our eyes
In a maze of roots and stems,
　Hurdy-gurdies, cabmen's cries!
Ah, might I gather a rose in its dew
For her heart on this bright June morning!

Envious twigs in leafy nook
　　Catch my love's long tresses fair,
E'en as Grecian branches shook
　Down Diana's crown of hair!
While on Cæsar's bridge I stand,
　Fancy brings (but could they speak!)

Laura's lips, and, faintly tanned,
Peachy glimpses of her cheek!
Ah, might I gather a rose in its dew
For her heart on this bright June morning!

NORMAN R. GALE.

TO PHILLIS

TO ABANDON THE COURT

FIE on this courtly life, full of displeasure!
Where neither frowns nor smiles keep any measure,
But every passion governs in extreme:
Free love and faith from hence falsehood doth banish,
And vows of friendship here like vapors vanish;
Loyalty's counted but a dream;
Inconstant favors like rivers gliding;
Truth is despised
Whilst flattery's prized;
Poor virtue here hath no certain abiding.

Then let's no longer stay, my fairest Phillis;
But let us fly from hence, where so much ill is,
Into some desert place there to abide; —
True love shall go with us, and faith unfeigned,
Pure thoughts, embraces chaste, and vows unstained.
Virtue herself shall ever be our guide; —
In cottage poor, where neither frowning fortune
Nor change of fate
Can once abate
Our sweet content, or peace at all importune.

There will we drive our flocks from hill and valley,
And whilst they feeding are, we'll sit and dally;
And thy sweet voice to sing birds shall invite;
Whilst I with roses, violets, and lilies
Will flowery garlands make to crown my Phillis,
Or numbered verses to thy praise indite.
And when the sun is westwardly declining,
.   Our flocks and we
Will homeward flee
And rest ourselves until the sun's next shining.

Author Unknown.

WINIFREDA

Away! let naught to love displeasing,
　　My Winifreda, move your care;
Let naught delay the heavenly blessing —
　　Nor squeamish pride nor gloomy fear.

What though no grants of royal donors
　　With pompous title grace our blood?
We'll shine in more substantial honors,
　　And to be noble we'll be good.

Our name, while virtue thus we tender,
　　Will sweetly sound where'er 'tis spoke;
And all the great ones they shall wonder
　　How they respect such little folk.

What though from Fortune's lavish bounty
　　No mighty treasures we possess?
We'll find within our pittance plenty,
　　And be content without excess.

Still shall each kind returning season
　　Sufficient for our wishes give;
For we will live a life of reason,
　　And that's the only life to live.

Through youth and age in love excelling,
　　We'll hand in hand together tread;
Sweet smiling peace shall crown our dwelling,
　　And babes, sweet smiling babes, our bed.

How should I love the pretty creatures,
　　While round my knees they fondly clung,
To see them look their mother's features,
　　To hear them lisp their mother's tongue!

And when with envy Time transported
　　Shall think to rob us of our joys,
· You'll in your girls again be courted,
　　And I'll go wooing in my boys.

Author Unknown.

PRISCILLA

PRISCILLA hath come back to town
    A little bandit queen;
  Her cheek hath robbed the berry's brown,
    Her eye the dewdrop's sheen.
Upon her lips there brightly glows
    The poppy's crimson hue;
With autumn music in her toes
    She charms the avenue.

Alas! how wildly hearts will beat
    That late kept slowest time;
Alas! how many a snowy sheet
    Will meet its fate in rhyme!
Laugh, Cupid, laugh, with saucy glee
    At all the pangs in store;
But never point thy dart at me,—
    My heart was hers before.

SAMUEL MINTURN PECK.

PEPITA

UP IN her balcony where
    Vines through the lattices run,
  Spilling a scent on the air,
    Setting a screen to the sun,
Fair as the morning is fair,
    Sweet as a blossom is sweet,
    Dwells in her rosy retreat
        Pepita.

Often a glimpse of her face,
    When the wind rustles the vine,
Parting the leaves for a space,
    Gladdens this window of mine:
Pink in its leafy embrace,
    Pink as a roseleaf is pink,
    Sweet as a blossom I think
        Pepita.

I who dwell over the way
    Watch where Pepita is hid,
Safe from the glare of the day
    Like an eye under its lid:

Over and over I say —
    Name like the song of a bird,
    Melody shut in a word —
        "Pepita."

Look where the little leaves stir!
    Look, the green curtains are drawn!
There in a blossomy blur
    Breaks a diminutive dawn —
Dawn and the pink face of her;
    Name like the lisp of the South,
    Fit for a rose's small mouth, —
        Pepita!

          FRANK DEMPSTER SHERMAN.

THE WITCH

CHILD! attend to what I say:
    Do not turn nor look away.
    Roguish eye! you must not wink —
I shall tell you all I think.
Here! Hallo! Don't look away.
Child! attend to what I say!

You're not homely, that is true!
You've an eye that's clear and blue;
Cunning mouth and little nose
Have their merits, I suppose.
Charming is the word to fit it, —
Yes, you're charming; I admit it.

Charming here and charming there,
But no *empress* anywhere.
No! I cannot quite allow
Beauty's crown would suit your brow.
Charming there and charming here
Do not make a queen, my dear.

For I know a hundred girls,
Brown as berries, fair as pearls,
Each of whom might claim the prize
Given to loveliest lips and eyes —
Yes, a hundred might go in,
Challenge you, sweet child, and win.

A hundred beauties, did I say?
Why, what a number! Yet there may
A hundred thousand girls combine
To drive thee from this heart of mine;
May try together, try alone,—
My empress they cannot dethrone.

Whence, then, this imperial right
Over me, your own true knight?
Like an empress is your reign
In my heart for joy or pain;
Death or life, your royal right,
He accepts—your own true knight.

Roguish lip and roguish eye,
Look at me and make reply.
Witch! I wish to understand
How I came into your hand.
Look at me and make reply:
Tell me, roguish lip and eye.

Up and down I search to see
The meaning of this mystery.
Tied so tight by *nothing*, dear?
Ah! there must be magic here!
Up and down, sweet sorceress, tell!
Where's your wand, and what's your spell?

GOTTFRIED AUGUST BÜRGER.

Translation of James Freeman Clarke.

I WONDER

I WONDER, in those dear old days departed,
　Whose was the foot that wore this tiny shoe;—
A slipper just as small as Cinderella's,
　But not of glass—of faded satin blue.

I'll say it was a princess, tall and stately,
　And rather haughty, but not overmuch.
I see her walking through her garden alleys:
　How rose-hearts beat to feel that light foot's touch!

I see her treading through her row of pages,
　That small foot lifted high with haughty grace;

A knight beside her, whispering tender speeches,—
   She hears them all, with silent, downcast face.

I see her in the dazzling ball-room stepping
   Through stately minuet or swifter dance,
Her small foot slipping through her rich robes sweeping,
   Or even not perceived—divined, perchance.

How many knights adored you, little slipper,
   And knelt before you—fine and fair and blue!
How many you have fled from—too bold suitors!
   How many hearts you've trod on, tiny shoe!

                                        CORA FABBRI.

A TWELFTH-CENTURY LYRIC

WILL ye attend me, while I sing
      A song of love,—a pretty thing,
         Not made on farms:
Nay, by a gentle knight 'twas made,
Who lay beneath an olive's shade
         In his love's arms.

A linen undergown she wore,
And a white ermine mantle, o'er
         A silken coat;
With flowers of May to keep her feet,
And round her ankles leggings neat,
         From lands remote.

Her girdle was of leafage green,—
Spring foliage, with a fringing sheen
         Of gold above;
And underneath a love-purse hung,
By bloomy pendants featly strung,
         A gift of love.

Upon a mule the lady rode,
The which with silver shoes was shod;
         Saddle gold-red;
And behind rose-bushes three
She had set up a canopy
         To shield her head.

As so she passed adown the meads,
A gentle childe in knightly weeds
    Cried, "Fair one, wait!
What region is thy heritance?"
And she replied: "I am of France,
    Of high estate.

"My father is the nightingale,
Who high within the bosky pale,
    On branches sings;
My mother's the canary; she
Sings on the high banks where the sea
    Its salt spray flings."

"Fair lady, excellent thy birth;
Thou comest from the chief of earth,
    Of high estate:
Ah, God our Father, that to me
Thou hadst been given, fair ladye,
    My wedded mate!"

Author Unknown.

Translation of Edward T. McLaughlin.

A NINETEENTH-CENTURY LYRIC

COULD I answer love like thine,
    All earth to me were heaven anew;
  But were thy heart, dear child, as mine,
    What place for love between us two?
Bright things for tired eyes vainly shine:
    A grief the pure heaven's simple blue.
Alas, for lips past joy of wine,
    That find no blessing in God's dew!
From dawning summits crystalline
Thou lookest down; thou makest sign
    Toward this bleak vale I wander through.
I cannot answer: that pure shrine
    Of childhood, though my love be true,
Is hidden from my dim confine;
    I must not hope for clearer view.
The sky, the earth, the wrinkled brine,
    Would wear to me a fresher hue,
And all once more be half divine,
Could I answer love like thine.

Author Unknown.

A MODERN PSYCHE

She Speaks

BUT do not go—I like to have you near me;
    Not quite so near—sit there, sir, if you please.
  The orchestra is silent; you can hear me:
    And distance puts us both more at our ease.

I missed you yesterday past all expression,
    Though winged with song and mirth the bright hours flew;
Because I think—pray mark my frank confession—
    That no one loves me quite so well as you.

It may be as you say, that I am taking
    A false step that I never can retrace;
Perhaps some day will come a bitter waking,
    When love has fled with youth and youth's sweet grace.

Listen! there's some one singing 'Traviata':
    "Gayly through life"—ah, yes! 'tis apropos!
Your arm, *mon ami*. A swift waltz will scatter
    And turn to blissful breath those sighs of woe.

'Tis strange! I do not care to take your heart, sir,
    In fair exchange; and yet, strong jealous wrath
Would kindle all my soul should you depart, sir,
    To lay it in some other woman's path.

"Selfish," am I, and "void of feelings tender"?
    Perhaps; but then, I'm sure you can but own
That for a foot so finely arched and slender
    A heart is just the fittest stepping-stone.

And if you bade me cease my idle playing
    On the tired chords my hands have swept for years,
I think the moonlight o'er my pillow straying
    Would find it slightly wet with "idle tears."

And yet I love you not. Nay, do not start!
    The reason, sir, you never could discover:
Another mystery of a woman's heart,—
    I love the love, but cannot love the lover.

ELIZA CALVERT HALL.

PHILLIDA FLOUTS ME

OH WHAT a plague is love!
    I cannot bear it.
  She will inconstant prove,
    I greatly fear it;   ·
It so torments my mind
  That my heart faileth.
She wavers with the wind
  As a ship saileth;
Please her the best I may,
She looks another way:
Alack and well-a-day!
  Phillida flouts me.

I often heard her say
  That she loved posies:
In the last month of May
  I gave her roses,
Cowslips and gilliflowers,
  And the sweet lily,
I got to deck the bowers
  Of my dear Philly;
She did them all disdain,
And threw them back again;
Therefore 'tis flat and plain,
  Phillida flouts me.

Which way soe'er I go,
  She still torments me;
And whatsoe'er I do,
  Nothing contents me:
I fade and pine away
  With grief and sorrow;
I fall quite to decay,
  Like any shadow:
Since 'twill no better be,
I'll bear it patiently;
Yet all the world may see
  Phillida flouts me.

Author Unknown.

TO HIS COY MISTRESS

Had we but world enough, and time,
This coyness, lady, were no crime.
We would sit down, and think which way
To walk, and pass our long love's day.
Thou by the Indian Ganges's side
Shouldst rubies find: I by the tide
Of Humber would complain. I would
Love you ten years before the Flood,
And you should, if you please, refuse
Till the conversion of the Jews;
My vegetable love should grow
Vaster than empires, and more slow:
An hundred years should go to praise
Thine eyes, and on thy forehead gaze;
Two hundred to adore each breast,
But thirty thousand to the rest—
An age at least to every part,
And the last age should show your heart.
For, lady, you deserve this state,
Nor would I love at lower rate.
But at my back I always hear
Time's wingèd chariot hurrying near,
And yonder all before us lie
Deserts of vast eternity.
Thy beauty shall no more be found,
Nor, in thy marble vault, shall sound
My echoing song; then worms shall try
That long-preserved virginity,
And your quaint honor turned to dust,
And into ashes all my lust:
The grave's a fine and private place,
But none, I think, do there embrace.

ANDREW MARVELL.

ALL ON ONE SIDE

She is like Nature: and I love
Her ever-changing, wayward moods,
As I adore the sky above;
The far blue hills; the dark, green woods;

The noisy brook; the torrent's roar;
  The glamour of a moonlight night;
The never-ending ocean's shore;
  The fleecy cloud-heads, soft and white.

She is like Nature. Much she cares,
  Though I should love a thousand years!
If I am sad when sunlight glares,
  Will cloudless skies weep scalding tears?
And will my gladness dry the rain?
  Will Nature smile and join my glee?
Will Nature love me back again?
  I think not—and no more will She!

HARRY ROMAINE.

DELAY

TASTE the sweetness of delaying,
  Till the hour shall come for saying
    That I love you with my soul:
Have you never thought your heart
Finds a something in the part,
    It would miss from out the whole?

In this rosebud you have given,
Sleeps that perfect rose of heaven
  That in Fancy's garden blows:
Wake it not by touch or sound,
Lest perchance 'twere lost, not found,
  In the opening of the rose.

Dear to me is this reflection,
Of a fair and far perfection,
  Shining through a veil undrawn:
Ask no question then of fate;
Yet a little longer wait
  In the beauty of the dawn.

Through our mornings, veiled and tender,
Shines a day of golden splendor,
  Never yet fulfilled by day:
Ah! if love be made complete,
Will it, can it, be so sweet
  As this ever sweet delay?

LOUISA BUSHNELL.

SONG WRITTEN AT SEA

IN THE FIRST DUTCH WAR, JUNE 2D, 1665, THE NIGHT BEFORE AN
ENGAGEMENT

To ALL you ladies now on land,
    We men, at sea, indite;
But first would have you understand
    How hard it is to write:
The Muses now, and Neptune too,
We must implore to write to you,
    With a Fa, la, la, la, la.

For though the Muses should prove kind,
    And fill our empty brain,
Yet if rough Neptune rouse the wind
    To wave the azure main,
Our paper, pen, and ink, and we,
Roll up and down our ships at sea,
    With a Fa, la, la, la, la.

Then if we write not by each post,
    Think not we are unkind;
Nor yet conclude our ships are lost,
    By Dutchmen or by wind:
Our tears we'll send a speedier way,—
The tide shall bring 'em twice a day,
    With a Fa, la, la, la, la. . . .

Let wind and weather do its worst,
    Be you to us but kind;
Let Dutchmen vapor, Spaniards curse,
    No sorrow we shall find:
'Tis then no matter how things go,
Or who's our friend, or who's our foe,
    With a Fa, la, la, la, la. . . .

But now our fears tempestuous grow,
    And cast our hopes away:
Whilst you, regardless of our woe,
    Sit careless at a play;
Perhaps permit some happier man
To kiss your hand, or flirt your fan,
    With a Fa, la, la, la, la. . . .

In justice you cannot refuse
    To think of our distress,

When we for hopes of honor lose
  Our certain happiness:
All those designs are but to prove
Ourselves more worthy of your love,
  With a Fa, la, la, la, la.

And now we've told you all our loves,
  And likewise all our fears;
In hopes this declaration moves
  Some pity from your tears:
Let's hear of no inconstancy,—
We have too much of that at sea,
  With a Fa, la, la, la, la.

CHARLES SACKVILLE (Earl of Dorset).

GLEE

A BLOSSOM wreath of rich perfume
  I for my fairest wove:
She to her beauty gave its bloom,
  Its transience to her love.

I sent her then a pearl to prize:
  With much she soon did part,
But kept its brilliance in her eyes,
  Its hardness in her heart.

T. M. DOVASTON.

THE WHITE ROSE

SENT BY A YORKSHIRE LOVER TO HIS LANCASTRIAN MISTRESS

IF THIS fair rose offend thy sight,
  Placed in thy bosom bare,
'Twill blush to find itself less white,
  And turn Lancastrian there.

But if thy ruby lip it spy,
  As kiss it thou mayst deign,
With envy pale 'twill lose its dye,
  And Yorkshire turn again.

Author Unknown.

MY LOVE IN HER ATTIRE DOTH SHEW HER WIT

MY LOVE in her attire doth shew her wit,
   It doth so well become her:
For every season she hath dressings fit,
   For winter, spring, and summer.
No beauty she doth miss
   When all her robes are on;
But Beauty's self she is
   When all her robes are gone.

Author Unknown.

WHENAS IN SILKS MY JULIA GOES

WHENAS in silks my Julia goes,
   Then, then (methinks) how sweetly flows
   That liquefaction of her clothes!

Next, when I cast mine eyes and see
That brave vibration each way free —
O how that glittering taketh me!

ROBERT HERRICK.

THE TIME O' DAY

IF I SHOULD look for the time o' day
   On the rose's dial red,
I should think it was just the sunrise hour,
   From the flush of its petals spread.

And if I would tell by the lily-bell,
   I should think it was calm, white noon;
And the violet's blue would tell by its hue
   Of the evening coming soon.

But when I would know by my lady's face,
   I am all perplexed the while;
For it's always starlight by her eyes,
   And sunlight by her smile.

ALBION FELLOWS BACON.

DEFIANCE

CLOTHO, Lachesis, Atropos!
    All your gain is not my loss.
    Spin your black threads if you will;
Twist them, turn, with all your skill.
Hold! there's one you cannot sever!
One bright thread shall last forever.

You are defied, you, Atropos!
Draw your glittering shears across,—
One still mocks your cruel art!
From the fibres of my heart
Did I spin the shining thread
That will live when you are dead.

Fate, but hark! one thing I'll teach:
There are wonders past your reach,
Of the heart and of the soul,—
Woman's love's past your control!
These are not threads of your spinning,
No, nor shall be of your winning.

                    ANNIE FIELDS.

IF LOVE WERE NOT

IF LOVE were not, the wilding rose
    Would in its leafy heart inclose
        No chalice of perfume.

By mossy bank in glen or grot,
No bird would build, if love were not,
    No flower complacent bloom.

The sunset clouds would lose their dyes,
The light would fade from beauty's eyes,
    The stars their fires consume.

And something missed from hall and cot
Would leave the world, if love were not,
    A wilderness of gloom.

                    FLORENCE EARLE COATES.

PRAISE OF LITTLE WOMEN

IN A little precious stone what splendor meets the eyes!
   In a little lump of sugar, how much of sweetness lies!
   So in a little woman love grows and multiplies:
You recollect the proverb says, A word unto the wise.

A peppercorn is very small, but seasons every dinner
More than all other condiments, although 'tis sprinkled thinner:
Just so a little woman is, if love will let you win her,—
There's not a joy in all the world you will not find within her.

And as within the little rose you find the richest dyes,
And in a little grain of gold much price and value lies,
As from a little balsam much odor doth arise,
So in a little woman there's a taste of paradise.

The skylark and the nightingale, though small and light of
      wing,
Yet warble sweeter in the grove than all the birds that sing;
And so a little woman, though a very little thing,
Is·sweeter far than sugar and flowers that bloom in spring.

JUAN RUIZ DE HITA (Spanish).

THE HEART OF A SONG

DEAR love, let this my song fly to you: :
   Perchance forget it came from me.
It shall not vex you, shall not woo you;
   But in your breast lie quietly.

Only beware — when once it tarries,
   I cannot coax it from you then:
This little song my whole heart carries,
   And ne'er will bear it back again.

For if its silent passion grieve you,
   My heart would then too heavy grow;—
And it can never, never leave you,
   If joy of yours must with it go!

GEORGE PARSONS LATHROP.

« BRING ME WORD HOW TALL SHE IS »

WOMAN IN 1873

« How tall is your Rosalind ? » — « Just as high as my heart. »
— 'As You Like It.'

WITHIN a garden shade,
     A garden sweet and dim,
   Two happy children played
Together   he was made
   For God, and she for him.

Beyond the garden's shade,
   In deserts drear and dim,
Two outcast children strayed
Together — he betrayed
   By her, and she by him.

Together, girl and boy,
   They wandered, ne'er apart;
Each wrought to each annoy,
Yet each knew never joy
   Save in the other's heart.

By her so oft deceived,
   By him so sore opprest,
They each the other grieved;
   Yet each of each was best
   Beloved, and still caressed.

And she was in his sight
   Found fairest — still his prize,
His constant chief delight;
   She raised to him her eyes
That led her not aright,

And ever by his side
   A patient huntress ran
Through forests dark and wide,
And still the Woman's pride
   And glory was the Man.

When her he would despise,
   She kept him captive bound;

Forbidding her to rise,
By many cords and ties
    She held him to the ground.

At length, in stature grown,
    He stands erect and free;
Yet stands he not alone,
    For his beloved would be
Like him she loveth, wise, like him she loveth, free.

So wins she her desire;
    Yet stand they not apart:
For as *she* doth aspire
He grows; nor stands she higher
    Than her Belovèd's heart.

DORA GREENWELL.

UNDER THE KING

LOVE with the deep eyes and soft hair,
    Love with the lily throat and hands,
Is done to death, and free as air
    Am I of all my King's commands.

How shall I celebrate my joy?
    Or dance with feet that once were fleet
In his adorable employ?
    Or laugh with lips that felt his sweet?

How can I at his lifeless face
    Aim any sharp or bitter jest,
Since roguish destiny did place
    That tender target in my breast?

Nay, let me be sincere and strong:
    I cannot rid me of my chains,
I cannot to myself belong:
    My King is dead—his soul still reigns.

ETHELWYN WETHERALD.

LIGHT

THE night has a thousand eyes,
    The day but one;
Yet the light of the bright world dies
    With the dying sun.

The mind has a thousand eyes,
    And the heart but one;
Yet the light of a whole life dies
    When love is done.

                            · F. W. BOURDILLON.

«A THOUSAND YEARS IN THY SIGHT ARE BUT AS ONE DAY»

NEITHER joy nor sorrow move
    The figure at the feet of Love;
    Light of breathing life is she,
Spirit of immortality.

Lead me up thy stony stair,
O Spirit, into thy great air!
For his day of pain and tears
Is to man a thousand years.

                            ANNIE FIELDS.

FOR A NOVEMBER BIRTHDAY

WHEN first our rose of love disclosed its heart,
    Thy natal day (I thought) comes with the spring,
When from the sky the doubting clouds depart,
    And rare, rathe blossoms o'er the woodland fling

A mystic sense of joy.
                    Yet bitter tears
Will start unbidden at the touch of May.
Love's ecstasy begets love's longing and love's fears,
    And naught of these may mar thy natal day.

When I had learned the richness of thy gift,
   Surely the happy month (I thought) is June,
When full and strong the waves of life uplift
   The heart upon their surges.
                        Yet too soon

The ebbing tide will leave the lonely shore;
   Full soon the rose must let her beauty fall;
Love's torch will burn to ashes. But no more
   May any change our changeless love befall.

Lo! spring and summer faded, and the year
   In all their sunny round brought not the morn;
But now, 'mid autumn's melancholy cheer,
   'Mid soughing boughs and pallid light, 'tis born.

So drear, thou sayest?
                  —Love may the clouds dispel.
   So brief?
              —With eve our passion shall not cease.
So still?
          —Oh let the day this message tell:
Not rapture is love's crowning gift, but peace.

                        GEORGE M. WHICHER.

THE SURFACE AND THE DEPTHS

LOVE took my life and thrilled it
    Through all its strings,
  Played round my mind and filled it
    With sound of wings;
But to my heart he never came
To touch it with his golden flame.

Therefore it is that singing
    I do rejoice,
Nor heed the slow years bringing
    A harsher voice;
Because the songs which he has sung
Still leave the untouched singer young.

But whom in fuller fashion
    The Master sways,

For him, swift-winged with passion,
Fleet the brief days.
Betimes the enforced accents come,
And leave him ever after dumb.

LEWIS MORRIS.

LOVE BRINGETH LIFE

FOND hands laid sweet Ophelia softly low
In that small straitened grave beneath the yew;
Thenceforth the world a little sadder grew,
Seeing one lover's footsteps come and go,
And wander in a sudden drear amaze
Through all the winter days.

In darkness lies white-robèd Juliet,
With slender hands close folded on her breast,
On the quick-throbbing heart at length at rest
In the forsaken tomb of Capulet;
And earth hath one more mourning for a bride,
One other grief to hide.

And what of thee, O tender Marguerite?
Long dead thou art, and thy lone grave is deep,
But scant to hide from us thy maiden sleep
Loose held within a moldered winding-sheet;
Thou still awakest, and canst not forget,
And pray'st assoilment yet.

And thou, Francesca? On the open page
Of thy dark history a rose-spray lies,
As though to hide thee from unrighteous eyes,
Whose evil looks are all thy heritage.
Thou art love's victim. On thy pensive face
Grief finds abiding place.

These died for love's sake. Many such there be:
Yet best for thee, O little maid, whose vows
Were made last eve 'neath blossomed cherry-boughs,
Were love, though death shall follow. Best for thee!
Love bringeth sorrow, yet unto our need
Love bringeth life indeed.

CAROLINE WILDER FELLOWES.

THE POWER OF BEAUTY

THOU needst not weave nor spin,
   Nor bring the wheat-sheaves in,
   Nor, forth afield at morn,
At eve bring home the corn,
Nor on a winter's night
Make blaze the fagots bright.

So lithe and delicate,
So slender is thy state,
So pale and pure thy face,
So deer-like in their grace
Thy limbs, that all do vie
To take and charm the eye.

Thus, toiling where thou'rt not
Is but the common lot:
Three men mayhap alone
By strength may move a stone —
But, toiling near to thee,
One man may work as three,

If thou but bend a smile
To fall on him the while;
Or if one tender glance —
Though coy and shot askance —
His eyes discover, then
One man may work as ten.

Men commonly but ask,
"When shall I end my task?"
But seeing thee come in,
'Tis, "When may I begin?"
Such power does beauty bring
To take from toil its sting.

If then thou'lt do but this, —
Fling o'er the work a bliss
From thy mere presence, — none
Shall think thou'st nothing done:
Thou needst not weave nor spin,
Nor bring the wheat-sheaves in.

JAMES HERBERT MORSE.

A DANCER

IN THE lamplight's glare she stood,—
   The dancer, the octoroon,—
On a space of polished wood
   With glittering sand-grains strewn;
   And a rapid rhythmic tune
From the strings of a mandolin   [din.
Leaped up through the air in viewless flight and passed in a strident

Her eyes like a fawn's were dark,
   But her hair was black as night,
And a diamond's bluish spark
   From its masses darted bright,
   While around her figure slight
Clung a web of lace she wore,
In curving lines of unhidden grace as she paused on the sanded floor

Then the clashing music sprang
   From the frets of the mandolin,
While the shadowy arches rang
   With insistent echoes thin;
   And there, as the spiders spin
Dim threads in a ring complete,
A labyrinthine wheel she wove with the touch of her flying feet.

To the right she swayed,—to the left,—
   Then swung in a circle round,
Fast weaving a changing weft
   To the changing music's sound,
   As light as a leaf unbound
From the grasp of its parent tree,
That falls and dips with the thistle-down afloat on a windy sea.

And wilder the music spell
   Swept on in jarring sound,—
Advanced and rose and fell,
   By gathering echoes crowned;
   And the lights whirled round and round
O'er the woman dancing there,
With her Circe grace and passionate face and a diamond in her hair.

ERNEST McGAFFEY.

THE LONGING OF CIRCE

THE rapid years drag by, and bring not here
    The man for whom I wait;
All things pall on me: in my heart grows fear
    Lest I may miss my fate.

I weary of the heavy wealth and ease
    Which all my isle enfold;
The fountain's sleepy plash, the summer breeze
    That bears not heat nor cold.

With dull, unvaried mien, my maid and I
    Plod through our daily tasks:
Gather strange herbs, weave purple tapestry,
    Distill in magic flasks.

Most weary am I of these men who yield
    So quickly to my spell,—
The beastly rout now wandering afield,
    With grunt and snarl and yell.

Ah, when, in place of tigers and of swine,
    Shall he confront me whom
My song cannot enslave, nor that bright wine
    Where rank enchantments fume?

Then with what utter gladness will I cast
    My sorceries away,
And kneel to him, my lord revealed at last,
    And serve him night and day!

CAMERON MANN.

CIRCE

WHAT fate is mine, who, far apart from pains
    And fears and turmoils of the cross-grained world,
    Dwell, like a lonely god, in a charmed isle
Where I am first and only, and like one
Who should love poisonous savors more than mead,
Long for a tempest on me, and grow sick
Of resting and divine free carelessness!
O me! I am a woman, not a god;
Yea, those who tend me even are more than I,—

My nymphs who have the souls of flowers and birds
Singing and blossoming immortally.

Ah me! these love a day and laugh again,
And loving, laughing, find a full content;
But I know naught of peace, and have not loved.

Where is my love? Does some one cry for me,
Not knowing whom he calls? does his soul cry
For mine to grow beside it, grow in it?
Does he beseech the gods to give him me,—
The yet unknown rare woman by whose side
No other woman, thrice as beautiful,
Should once seem fair to him; to whose voice heard
In any common tones no sweeter sound
Of love made melody on silver lutes,
Or singing like Apollo's when the gods
Grow pale with happy listening, might be peered
For making music to him; whom once found
There will be no more seeking anything?

O love, O love, O love, art not yet come
Out of the waiting shadows into life?
Art not yet come after so many years
That I have longed for thee? Come! I am here. . . .

Nay, but he *will* come. Why am I so fair,
And marvelously minded, and with sight
Which flashes suddenly on hidden things,
As the gods see who do not need to look?
Why wear I in my eyes that stronger power
Than basilisks, whose gaze can only kill,
To draw men's souls to me to live or die
As I would have them? Why am I given pride
Which yet longs to be broken, and this scorn
Cruel and vengeful for the lesser men
Who meet the smiles I waste for lack of him,
And grow too glad? Why am I who I am,
But for the sake of him whom fate will send
One day to be my master utterly,
That he should take me, the desire of all,
Whom only he in all the world could bow to him?
O sunlike glory of pale glittering hairs,
Bright as the filmy wires my weavers take
To make me golden gauzes; O deep eyes,

Darker and softer than the bluest dusk
Of August violets, darker and deep
Like crystal fathomless lakes in summer moons;
O sad sweet longing smile; O lips that tempt
My very self to kisses; O round cheeks,
Tenderly radiant with the even flush
Of pale smoothed coral; perfect lovely face
Answering my gaze from out this fleckless pool;
Wonder of glossy shoulders, chiseled limbs,—
Should I be so your lover as I am,
Drinking an exquisite joy to watch you thus
In all a hundred changes through the day,
But that I love you for him till he comes,
But that my beauty means his loving it? . . .

Too cruel am I? . And the silly beasts,
Crowding around me when I pass their way,
Glower on me, and although they love me still
(With their poor sorts of love such as they could),
Call wrath and vengeance to their humid eyes
To scare me into mercy, or creep near
With piteous fawnings, supplicating bleats.
Too cruel? Did I choose them what they are?
Or change them from themselves by poisonous charms?
But any draught — pure water, natural wine —
Out of my cup, revealed them to themselves
And to each other. Change? There was no change;
Only disguise gone from them unawares:
And had there been one right true man of them,
He would have drunk the draught as I had drunk,
And stood unchanged, and looked me in the eyes,
Abashing me before him. But these things—
Why, which of them has ever shown the kind
Of some one nobler beast? Pah! yapping wolves
And pitiless stealthy wild-cats, curs and apes
And gorging swine and stinking venomous snakes,—
All false and ravenous and sensual brutes
That shame the earth that bore them,— these they are.

AUGUSTA WEBSTER.

A FORECAST

WHAT days await this woman, whose strange feet
    Breathe spells; whose presence makes men dream
      like wine;
  Tall, free, and slender as the forest pine;
Whose form is molded music; through whose sweet
Frank eyes I feel the very heart's least beat,
  Keen, passionate, and full of dreams and fire:
  How in the end, and to what man's desire,
Shall all this yield—whose lips shall these lips meet?
One thing I know: if he be great and pure,
This love, this fire, this beauty, shall endure;
  Triumph and hope shall lead him by the palm:
But if not this, some differing thing he be,
That dream shall break in terror; he shall see
  The whirlwind ripen, where he sowed the calm.

ARCHIBALD LAMPMAN.

CROSS OF GOLD

THE fifth from the north wall;
  Row innermost; and the pall
  Plain black—all black—except
The cross on which she wept,
Ere she lay down and slept.

This one is hers, and this—
The marble next it—his:
So lie in brave accord
The lady and her lord,
Her cross and his red sword.

And now, what seek'st thou here,
Having no care nor fear
To vex with thy hot tread
These halls of the long dead,—
To flash the torch's light
Upon their utter night?
What word hast thou to thrust
Into her ear of dust?

Spake then the haggard priest:—
In lands of the far East

I dreamed of finding rest —
What time my lips had prest
The cross on this dead breast.

And if my sin be shriven,
And mercy live in heaven,
Surely this hour, and here,
My long woe's end is near —
Is near — and I am brought
To peace, and painless thought
Of her who lies at rest,
This cross upon her breast, —

Whose passionate heart is cold
Beneath this cross of gold;
Who lieth, still and mute,   ·
In sleep so absolute.
Yea, by the precious sign
Shall sleep most sweet be mine;
And I at last am blest,
Knowing she went to rest
This cross upon her breast.

DAVID GRAY.

THE WEB

O MOONLIGHT spider-web,
        Filmy and fine and fair!
     A cloud of dewdrops blown
From rose-hearts overgrown —
Transfixed upon the bosom of the air.

     O moonlight-colored web,
        That some rude hand has torn!
     Each broken, lifeless thread
     Hangs downward, gray and dead,
Caught on the sharp edge of a red-rose thorn.

     O frail, fine web of Life,
        Woven 'mid stars above,
     Shattered on earth one day!
     Mine lieth dead and gray,
Caught on the sharp edge of the Thorn of Love.

CORA FABBRI

DOUBT

THOUGH that which made my life is fled,
  I still could live and still could smile,
Were I but sure thy love now dead
  Once lived a little while.

The future I can bear to lose,
  But not the past—oh, not the past!
Ah, love! do not this prayer refuse,
  And it shall be my last.

Ah, love! when 'neath the oak we stood,
  The moon pale-gleaming through her tears
Showed your stern face and altered mood,
  Which first awoke my fears.

As grows the storm-cloud on the blast,
  My darkening fears have grown and grown;
But let, oh, let me keep the past,
  Though hope and love have flown.

Again in dreams I silent stand,
  As that pale night, black leaves beneath;
Against your side you press my hand,
  I feel each throbbing breath.

The night wind moans in the long grass;
  By it, or thee, was the tale told
Which made the ghost of true love pass
  Wringing her white hands cold?

Though side by side, arm linked in arm,
  It swept between us bitter chill;
And now in blinding sunshine warm
  I shiver with it still.

Here in the same long grass I lie,
  The selfsame branches overhead;
I watch the pitiless blue sky;
  Would it shone o'er me dead!

Author Unknown.

TWO ROBBERS

WHEN Death from some fair face
    Is stealing life away,
All weep, save her, the grace
    That earth shall lose to-day.

When Time from some fair face
    Steals beauty, year by year,
For her slow-fading grace
    Who sheds, save her, a tear?

And Death not often dares
    To wake the world's distress;
While Time, the cunning, mars
    Surely all loveliness.

Yet though by breath and breath
    Fades all our fairest prime,
Men shrink from cruel Death,
    And honor crafty Time.

F. W. BOURDILLON

LOVE AND DEATH

ALAS! that men must see
    Love, before Death!
Else they content might be
    With their short breath;
Aye, glad when the pale sun
Showed restless Day was done,
And endless Rest begun!

Glad when with strong, cool hand
    Death clasped their own,
And with a strange command
    Hushed every moan;
Glad to have finished pain
And labor wrought in vain,
Blurred by Sin's deepening stain.

But Love's insistent voice
    Bids Self to flee:—
« Live that I may rejoice;
    Live on for me! »

So, for Love's cruel mind,
Men fear this Rest to find,
Nor know great Death is kind!

MARGARET DELAND.

THE MAID OF NEIDPATH

OH, LOVERS' eyes are sharp to see,
 And lovers' ears in hearing;
And love, in life's extremity,
 Can lend an hour of cheering.
Disease had been in Mary's bower,
 And slow decay from mourning,
Though now she sits in Neidpath's tower,
 To watch her love's returning.

All sunk and dim her eyes so bright,
 Her form decayed by pining,
Till through her wasted hand, at night,
 You saw the taper shining.
By fits a sultry hectic hue
 Across her cheek was flying;
By fits so ashy pale she grew
 Her maidens thought her dying.

Yet keenest powers to see and hear
 Seemed in her frame residing:
Before the watch-dog pricked his ear
 She heard her lover's riding;
Ere scarce a distant form was kenned
 She knew and waved to greet him,
And o'er the battlement did bend
 As on the wing to meet him.

He came — he passed — an heedless gaze
 As o'er some stranger glancing;
Her welcome, spoke in faltering phrase,
 Lost in his courser's prancing.—
The castle arch, whose hollow tone
 Returns each whisper spoken,
Could scarcely catch the feeble moan
 Which told her heart was broken.

SIR WALTER SCOTT

MADRIGAL TRISTE

I

IF WE should meet,
　　You and I,
　　My sweet,
In some fair land where under the blue sky
The scents of the fresh violets never die,
And Spring is deathless under deathless feet,
　　Should we clasp hands and kiss,
　　　My sweet,
　　With the old bliss?
　　Would our eyes meet
With the same passionate frankness as of old,
When the fresh Spring was in the Summer's gold?
　　Ah, no, my dear!
　　Woe's me! our kisses are but frore;
The blossoms of our early love are sere,
　　And will be fresh no more.

II

If we should stand,
　　You and I,
　　My sweet,
On that bright strand
Where day fades never, and the golden street
Rings to the music of the angels' feet,
Would our rent hearts find solace in the sky?
　　Should we lose heed,
　　My dear,
　　Of the sad years?
　　Would our souls cease to bleed
For the past anguish, and our eyes grow clear
In heaven from all the furrows of the tears?
　　Ah, no, my dear!
Needs must we sigh and stand aloof!
　　Once riven,
God could not heal our love,
　　Even in heaven.

JOHN PAYNE.

PARTING OF GODFRID AND OLYMPIA

From 'Madonna's Child'

So ONCE again they fled without delay,
    On wings of wind through leagues of dim-seen land;
Night and the stars accompanying their way,
    And roar and blackness close on either hand:
Until the dark drew off, and with the day
    They saw the sparkling bay and joyous strand,
White sails, brown oars, huge coils of briny ropes,
And fair proud city throned on regal slopes.

And soon the road they came by, which doth run
    'Twixt hill and sea, now smooth as woodland pond,
Saw them once more, with all their dreams unspun,
    Facing farewell. A little way beyond,
A big brown mule stood blinking in the sun,
    For a long march rudely caparisoned;
And at its side a gentle mountaineer,
Who to their grief lent neither eye nor ear.

"Hear me once more, Olympia! Must we part?
    Is Heaven so stern, and can a gentle breast
Inflict and aye endure so keen a smart,
    When pity's voice could lull our pain to rest?
Is there no common Eden of the heart,
    Where each fond bosom is a welcome guest?
No comprehensive paradise to hold
All loving souls in one celestial fold?

"For Love is older far than all the gods,
    And will survive both gods and men, and be
The sovereign ruler still, when Nature nods,
    And the scared stars through misty chaos flee.
Take love away, and we are brutish clods,
    Blind, spelling out our fate without the key;
Love, love is our immortal part, and they
Who own it not are only walking clay.

"But they who in this cold contentious sphere
    Deep in their heart cherish love's sacred fire,
Can smile at pain, and all that mortals fear,
    And tranquil keep when time and death conspire.

Though fickle winds should vex, they do not veer;
   No threats can daunt them, weary waitings tire:
Their feet are planted on the clouds; their eyes
Glare cannot blind, scan the eternal skies.

"This is my creed, and that the heaven I seek;
   Which even here, Olympia! may be ours,
Unless my lips, or else thine ears, be weak,
   Or we have outraged the supernal powers.
Oh, but that cannot be! Would Nature wreak
   Her wrath on thee, most precious of her flowers?
The sin, if sin there be, is mine, is mine;—
Wrong never was, can pain be ever, thine?

"Here 'twixt the mountains and the sea I swear
   That I thy faith will reverence as thy soul;
And as on that bright morning when thy fair
   Entrancing form upon my senses stole,
Still every dewy dawn fresh gifts will bear
   Unto Madonna's shrine,—that happy goal
Where our first journey ended, and I fain
Would have this end—not snapped, as now, in pain!"

The foam-fringe at their feet was not more white
   Than her pale cheeks, as downcast she replied:—
"No, Godfrid! no. Farewell, farewell! You might
   Have been my star;—a star once fell by pride;—
But since you furl your wings, and veil your light,
   I cling to Mary and Christ crucified.
Leave me, nay, leave me, ere it be too late!
Better part here than part at heaven's gate!"

Thereat he kissed her forehead, she his hand,
   And on the mule he mounted her, and then,
Along the road that skirts the devious strand,
   . Watched her, until she vanished from his ken.
Tears all in vain as water upon sand,
   Or words of grace to hearts of hardened men,
Coursed down her cheeks, whilst, half her grief divined,
The mountain guide walked sad and mute behind.

But never more as in the simple days
   When prayer was all her thought, her heart shall be;
For she is burdened with the grief that stays,
   And by a shadow vexed that will not flee.

Pure, but not spared, she passes from our gaze,—
　Victim, not vanquisher, of love.　And he?
Once more a traveler o'er land and main;—
Ah! life is sad and scarcely worth the pain!

　　　　　　　　　　　ALFRED AUSTIN.

THE LADY BLANCHE

THE Lady Blanche was saintly fair;
　　Not proud, but meek, her look;
　In her hazel eyes her thoughts lay clear
　　As pebbles in a brook.

Her father's veins ran noble blood,
　His hall rose 'mid the trees;
Like a sunbeam she came and went
　'Mong the white cottages.

The peasants thanked her with their tears
　When food and clothes were given:
"This is a joy," the lady said,
　"Saints cannot taste in heaven."

They met: the poet told his love,
　His hopes, despairs, and pains;
The lady with her calm eyes mocked
　The tumult in his veins.

He passed away;—a fierce song leapt
　From cloud of his despair,
As lightning like a bright wild beast
　Leaps from its thunder-lair.

He poured his frenzy forth in song,—
　Bright heirs of tears and praises!
Now resteth that unquiet heart
　Beneath the quiet daisies.

The world is old,—oh! very old,—
　The wild winds weep and rave;
The world is old, and gray, and cold,—
　Let it drop into its grave.

　　　　　　　　　　　ALEXANDER SMITH.

THE KING OF DENMARK'S RIDE

Word was brought to the Danish king
   (Hurry!)
 That the love of his heart lay suffering,
And pined for the comfort his voice would bring;
 (Oh, ride as though you were flying!)
Better he loves each golden curl
On the brow of that Scandinavian girl
Than his rich crown jewels of ruby and pearl;
 And his rose of the isles is dying!

Thirty nobles saddled with speed,
   (Hurry!)
Each one mounting a gallant steed
Which he kept for battle and days of need:
 (Oh, ride as though you were flying!)
Spurs were struck in the foaming flank;
Worn-out chargers staggered and sank;
Bridles were slackened, and girths were burst;
But ride as they would, the king rode first,
 For his rose of the isles lay dying!

'His nobles are beaten, one by one;
   (Hurry!)
They have fainted and faltered, and homeward gone:
His little fair page now follows alone,
 For strength and for courage trying.
The king looked back at that faithful child;
Wan was the face that answering smiled:
They passed the drawbridge with clattering din,
Then he dropped; and only the king rode in
 Where his rose of the isles lay dying!

The king blew a blast on his bugle horn:
   (Silence!)
No answer came; but faint and forlorn
An echo returned on the cold gray morn,
 Like the breath of a spirit sighing.
The castle portal stood grimly wide;
None welcomed the king from that weary ride:
For dead, in the light of the dawning day,
The pale sweet form of the welcomer lay,
 Who had yearned for his voice while dying!

The panting steed, with a drooping crest,
          Stood weary.
The king returned from her chamber of rest,
The thick sobs choking in his breast;
     And, that dumb companion eyeing,
The tears gushed forth which he strove to check;
He bowed his head on his charger's neck:—
"O steed — that every nerve didst strain,
Dear steed, our ride hath been in vain
     To the halls where my love lay dying!"

CAROLINE ELIZABETH NORTON.

HANNAH BINDING SHOES

Poor lone Hannah,
     Sitting at the window, binding shoes!
          Faded, wrinkled,
Sitting, stitching, in a mournful muse!
     Bright-eyed beauty once was she,
     When the bloom was on the tree:
          Spring and winter
Hannah's at the window, binding shoes.

     Not a neighbor
Passing nod or answer will refuse
          To her whisper,
"Is there from the fishers any news?"
     Oh, her heart's adrift with one
     On an endless voyage gone!
          Night and morning
Hannah's at the window, binding shoes.

     Fair young Hannah,
Ben, the sunburnt fisher, gayly wooes;
          Hale and clever,
For a willing heart and hand he sues.
     May-day skies are all aglow,
     And the waves are laughing so!
          For her wedding
Hannah leaves her window and her shoes.

     May is passing:
Mid the apple-boughs a pigeon cooes.

Hannah shudders,
For the mild southwester mischief brews.
Round the rocks of Marblehead,
Outward bound a schooner sped:
Silent, lonesome,
Hannah's at the window, binding shoes.

'Tis November.
Now no tear her wasted cheek bedews.
From Newfoundland
Not a sail returning will she lose,
Whispering hoarsely, "Fisherman,
Have you, have you heard of Ben?"
Old with watching,
Hannah's at the window, binding shoes.

Twenty winters
Bleach and tear the ragged shore she views,
Twenty seasons;—
Never one has brought her any news.
Still her dim eyes silently
Chase the white sail o'er the sea:
Hopeless, faithful,
Hannah's at the window, binding shoes.

LUCY LARCOM.

EILY CONSIDINE

AT THE barrack gate she sits,
Eily Considine;
Now she dozes, now she knits,
While the sunshine, through the slits
In the trellised trumpet-vine,
Warms old Eily Considine—
Warms her heart that long ago
Set the Regiment aglow!
Sweeter colleen ne'er was seen
Than Eileen;
Lips that flamed like scarlet wine,
Eyes of azure, smile divine—
Is that you,
Selling apples
Where the golden sunlight dapples,
Eily Considine?

I remember your first beau,
　　　　　Eily Considine;
That was years ago, I know.
Do you ever think of Stowe —
Stowe, lieutenant in the line —
Shot by Sioux in '59?
Do you sometimes think of Gray?
I can almost hear him say: —
　　"Sweeter colleen ne'er was seen
　　　　　　Than Eileen;
　　Lips that flame like scarlet wine,
　　Eyes of azure, smile divine — "
　　　　　Is that you,
　　　　　Selling apples
　　Where the golden sunlight dapples,
　　　　　Eily Considine?

First came Fairfax of the Staff,
　　　　　Eily Considine:
You forgave him with a laugh —
You're too generous by half.
Years ago he died — 'twas wine
Killed him, Eily Considine —
Killed him — 'twas a death of shame,
Yet in death he cried your name!
　　Sweeter colleen ne'er was seen
　　　　　　Than Eileen;
　　Lips of flame, like scarlet wine,
　　Eyes of azure, smile divine —
　　　　　Is that you,
　　　　　Selling apples
　　Where the golden sunlight dapples,
　　　　　Eily Considine?

If you wept when Fairfax left,
　　　　　Eily Considine,
Surely Donaldson was deft
To console a soul bereft
In so very brief a time —
Lonely Eily Considine.
After Donaldson came Hurse;
He it was who wrote this verse: —
　　"Sweeter colleen ne'er was seen
　　　　　　Than Eileen;

Lips that flame like scarlet wine,
Eyes of azure, smile divine—»
      Is that you,
      Selling apples
Where the golden sunlight dapples,
         Eily Considine?

Santa Anna settled Hurse,
         Eily Considine;
Then it went from bad to worse.
Yet if loving was your curse,
Bless me with this curse divine,—
Bless me, Eily Considine!
Phantom dim of long ago,
Misty, faint, and sweet—I know
   Sweeter colleen ne'er was seen
         Than Eileen;
Lips that flamed like scarlet wine,
Eyes of azure, smile divine—
      Is that you,
      Selling apples
Where the golden sunlight dapples,
         Eily Considine?

At the barrack gate she sits,
         Eily Considine;
Now she dozes, now she knits,
And the sunshine through the slits
In the trellised trumpet-vine
Falls on Eily Considine,
On her thin hair, silver-bright;—
God may wash her soul as white.
   Sweeter colleen ne'er was seen
         Than Eileen;
Lips that flamed like scarlet wine,
Eyes of azure, smile divine—
      Peace to you
      Selling apples
Where the golden sunlight dapples,
         Eily Considine!

ROBERT W. CHAMBERS.

THE BRIDAL OF ANDALLA

"RISE up, rise up, Xarifa! lay the golden cushion down;
 Rise up, come to the window, and gaze with all the town!
From gay guitar and violin the silver notes are flowing,
And the lovely lute doth speak between the trumpets' lordly
  blowing;
And banners bright from lattice light are waving everywhere,
And the tall, tall plume of our cousin's bridegroom floats proudly
  in the air:
Rise up, rise up, Xarifa! lay the golden cushion down;
Rise up, come to the window, and gaze with all the town!

"Arise, arise, Xarifa! I see Andalla's face;
He bends him to the people with a calm and princely grace:
Through all the land of Xeres and banks of Guadalquivir
Rode forth bridegroom so brave as he, so brave and lovely, never.
Yon tall plume waving o'er his brow, of purple mixed with white,
I guess 'twas wreathed by Zara, whom he will wed to-night.
Rise up, rise up, Xarifa! lay the golden cushion down;
Rise up, come to the window, and gaze with all the town!

"What aileth thee, Xarifa? what makes thine eyes look down?
Why stay ye from the window far, nor gaze with all the town?
I've heard you say on many a day — and sure you said the
  truth —
Andalla rides without a peer 'mong all Granada's youth;
Without a peer he rideth, and yon milk-white horse doth go,
Beneath his stately master, with a stately step and slow.
Then rise — oh rise, Xarifa! lay the golden cushion down:
Unseen here through the lattice, you may gaze with all the town!"

The Zegri lady rose not, nor laid her cushion down,
Nor came she to the window to gaze with all the town;
But though her eyes dwelt on her knee, in vain her fingers strove,
And though her needle pressed the silk, no flower Xarifa wove:
One bonny rosebud she had traced before the noise drew nigh, —
That bonny bud a tear effaced, slow dropping from her eye.
"No — no," she sighs: "bid me not rise, nor lay my cushion down,
To gaze upon Andalla with all the gazing town!" —

"Why rise ye not, Xarifa, nor lay your cushion down?
Why gaze ye not, Xarifa, with all the gazing town?
Hear, hear the trumpet how it swells, and how the people cry!
He stops at Zara's palace-gate; — why sit ye still — oh why?" —

"At Zara's gate stops Zara's mate: in him shall I discover
The dark-eyed youth pledged me his truth with tears, and was
    my lover?
I will not rise, with weary eyes, nor lay my cushion down,
To gaze on false Andalla with all the gazing town!"

                    Spanish: Author Unknown.
    Translation of John Gibson Lockhart.

RIVALS

G<small>RAY</small> in the east,
    Gray in the west, and a moon.
Dim gleam the lamps of the ended feast
    Through the misty dawn of June;
And I turn to watch her go
    Swift as the swallows flee,
Side by side with Joaquin Castro,
    Heart by heart with me.

    Jasmine star afloat
    In her soft hair's dusky strands;
Jasmine white is her swelling throat,
    And jasmine white her hands.
Ah, the plea of that clinging hand
    Through the whirl of that wild waltz tune!
Lost — lost for a league of land,
    Lying dark 'neath the sinking moon!

    Over yon stream
    The casa rests on its hard clay floor,
Its red tiles dim in the misty gleam;
    Old Pedro Vidal at the door,
And his small eye ranges keen
    Over vistas of goodly land —
Brown hills, with wild-oat sweeps between,
    Bought with his daughter's hand.

    Tangled and wreathed,
    The wild boughs over the wild streams meet;
And over the swamp flowers musky-breathed,
    And the cresses at their feet;
And over the dimpled springs,
    Where the deep brown shadows flaunt,

And the heron folds his ivory wings
And waits in his ferny haunt.

Side-scarred peaks
Where the gray sage hangs like a smoke,
And the vultures wipe their bloody beaks,
From the feast in the crotchèd oak,—
You are Castro's, hemming his acres in;
And I his vaquero, who o'er you rove,
Hold wealth he would barter you all to win,—
The wealth of her broad sweet love.

Joaquin Castro
Rides up from her home where the stream-mists hang,
And the cañon sides toss to and fro
The tread of his black mustang—
Half wild, a haughty beast,
Scarce held by the taut-drawn rein:
And a madness leaps into my breast,
And that wild waltz whirls in my brain.

By his mountain streams
We meet, and the waves glint through the shades;
And we light the morn with long thin gleams,
And wake it with clash of blades.
From some pale crag is borne
The owl's derisive laugh:
And the gray deer flies, like a shadow of dawn,
From the tide it fain would quaff.

A sudden wheel,
Then away, away, and the far hush rings
With hoof-beat, and chime of spurrèd heel;
And the blue air winds and sings
In the coils from each round gathering strength,
Ere I rise in my saddle for truer throw,
That the rope may spring its serpent length,
And drag from his seat my foe.

Was it an owl
Speedily flitting the trail across,
Or a twisted bough in its monk-like cowl
And robe of the long gray moss?
Or the race has frenzied the black's wild brain?
He rears, to the stout rein gives no heed,

Then backward, backward — curls and mane
  Intermingled, necks broken, rider and steed.

       Ah, señor,
  She is mine. It was all long years ago:
And at eve, when we sit in our vine-hung door,
  She speaks of Joaquin Castro,
How they found him there; and sweet drops start
  From sweeter eyes. And who shall know
That the brand of Cain burns red on my heart,
  Since the scar was spared my brow?

          VIRGINIA PEYTON FAUNTLEROY.

CARMEN

LA GITANILLA! Tall dragoons,
  In Andalusian afternoons,
   With ogling eye and compliment
Smiled on you, as along you went
Some sleepy street of old Seville —
Twirled with military skill
Mustaches; buttoned uniforms
Of Spanish yellow bowed your charms.

Proud, wicked head, and hair blue-black!
Whence your mantilla, half thrown back,
Discovered shoulders and bold breast
Bohemian brown! And you were dressed
In some short skirt of gipsy red
Of smuggled stuff; thence stockings dead
White silk, exposed with many a hole,
Through which your plump legs roguish stole
A fleshly look; and tiny toes
In red morocco shoes with bows
Of scarlet ribbons. Daintily
You walked by me, and I did see
Your oblique eyes, your sensuous lip,
That gnawed the rose you once did flip
At bashful José's nose, while loud
Laughed the gaunt guards among the crowd.
And in your brazen chemise thrust,
Heaved with the swelling of your bust,

The bunch of white acacia blooms
Whiffed past my nostrils hot perfumes.
As in a cool *neveria*
I ate an ice with Mérimée,
Dark Carmencita, you passed gay,
All holiday-bedizenèd,
A new mantilla on your head;
A crimson dress bespangled fierce;
And crescent gold hung in your ears,
Shone, wrought morisco; and each shoe,
Cordovan leather spangled blue,
Glanced merriment; and from large arms
To well-turned ankles all your charms
Blew flutterings and glitterings
Of satin bands and beaded strings;
And round each arm's fair thigh one fold,
And graceful wrists, a twisted gold
Coiled serpents' tails fixed in each head,
Convulsive-jeweled glossy red.
In flowers and trimmings, to the jar
Of mandolin and low guitar,
You in the grated *patio*
Danced: the curled coxcombs' flirting row
Rang pleased applause. I saw you dance,
With wily motion and glad glance
Voluptuous, the wild *romalis*,
Where every movement was a kiss
Of elegance delicious, wound
In your Basque tambourine's dull sound;
Or as the ebon castanets
Clucked out dry time in unctuous jets,
Saw angry José through the grate
Glare on us a pale face of hate,
When some indecent colonel there
Presumed too lewdly for his ear.

Some still night in Seville, the street
Candilejo, two shadows meet —
Flash sabres crossed within the moon —
Clash rapidly — a dead dragoon.

MADISON J. CAWEIN.

À OUTRANCE

(FRANCE, SEVENTEENTH CENTURY)

HEIGHO! Why the plague did you wake me?
    It's barely a half after four;
  My head, too, is — ah! I remember
    That little affair at the shore.
Well, I had forgotten completely!
  I must have been drinking last night.—
Rapiers, West Sands, and sunrise;—
  But whom, by the way, do I fight?

De Genlis! Ah, now I recall it!—
  He started it all, did he not?
I drank to his wife — but, the devil!
  He needn't have gotten so hot.
Just see what a ruffler that man is,
  To give me a challenge to fight,
And only for pledging milady
  A half-dozen times in a night.

Ah, well! it's a beautiful morning,—
  The sun just beginning to rise,—
A glorious day for one's spirit
  To pilgrimage off to the skies —
God keep mine from any such notion;—
  This dual's *à outrance*, you see.—
I haven't confessed for a month back,
  And haven't had breakfast, *tant pis!*

Well, here we are, first at the West Sands!
  The tide is well out; and how red
The sunrise is painting the ocean;—
  Is that a sea-gull overhead?
And here come De Genlis and Virron:
  Messieurs, we were waiting for you
To complete, with the sea and the sunrise,
  The charming effect of the view.

Are we ready? Indeed we were waiting
  Your orders, Marigny and I.
On guard then it is,—we must hasten:
  The sun is already quite high.

Where now would you like me to pink you?
　I've no choice at all, don't you see;
And any spot you may desire
　Will be *convenable* for me.

From this hand-shake I judge I was drinking
　Last night, with the thirst of a fish;
I've vigor enough though to kill you,
　Mon ami, and that's all I wish.
Keep cool, keep your temper, I beg you,—
　Don't fret yourself— Now by your leave
I'll finish you off— Help, Marigny!
　His sword's in my heart, I believe.

God! God! What a mortification!
　The Amontillado last night—
Was drinking, you know, and my hand shook;—
　My head, too, was dizzy and light.
And I the best swordsman in Paris!
　No priest, please, for such as I am—
I'm going— Good-by, my Marigny;
　De Genlis, my love to Madame.

ROBERT CAMERON ROGERS.

A CONQUEST

I FOUND him openly wearing her token;
　I knew that her troth could never be broken:
　I laid my hand on the hilt of my sword,—
He did the same, and he spoke no word.
I faced him with his villainy;
He laughed, and said, "She gave it me."
We searched for seconds, they soon were found:
They measured our swords; they measured the ground:
They held to the deadly work too fast—
They thought to gain our place at last.
We fought in the sheen of a wintry wood;
The fair white snow was red with his blood:
But his was the victory, for, as he died,
He swore by the rood that he had not lied.

WALTER HERRIES POLLOCK.

BALLAD OF A BRIDAL

"OH, FILL me flagons full and fair
 Of red wine and of white,
And, maidens mine, my bower prepare:
 It is my wedding night!

"Braid up my hair with gem and flower,
 And make me fair and fine:
The day has dawned that brings the hour
 When my desire is mine!"

They decked her bower with roses blown,
 With rushes strewed the floor;
And sewed more jewels on her gown
 Than ever she wore before.

She wore two roses in her face,
 Two jewels in her e'en;
Her hair was crowned with sunset rays,
 Her brows shone white between.

"Tapers at the bed's foot," she saith,
 "Two tapers at the head!"
(It seemed more like the bed of death
 Than like a bridal bed.)

He came. He took her hands in his;
 He kissed her on the face:
"There is more heaven in thy kiss
 Than in Our Lady's grace!"

He kissed her once, he kissed her twice,
 He kissed her three times o'er,
He kissed her brow, he kissed her eyes,
 He kissed her mouth's red flower.

"O love! What is it ails thy knight?
 I sicken and I pine:
Is it the red wine or the white,
 Or that sweet kiss of thine?"

"No kiss, no wine or white or red
 Can make such sickness be:
Lie down and die on thy bride-bed,
 For I have poisoned thee!"

"And though the curse of saints and men
    Be for the deed on me,
I would it were to do again,
    Since thou wert false to me!

" Thou shouldst have loved or one or none,—
    Nor *she* nor I loved twain;
But we are twain thou hast undone
    And therefore art thou slain.

"And when before my God I stand,
    With no base flesh between,
I shall hold up my guilty hand,
    And he shall judge it clean!"

He fell across the bridal bed,
    Between the tapers pale.
" I first shall see our God," he said,
    "And *I* will tell thy tale:

"And if God judge thee as I do,
    Then art thou justified;
I love thee, and I was not true,
    And that was why I died.

" If I might judge thee, thou shouldst be
    First of the saints on high;
But ah, I fear God loveth thee
    Not half so dear as I!"

EDITH (NESBIT) BLAND.

HER CREED

SHE stood before a chosen few,
    With modest air and eyes of blue;
        A gentle creature, in whose face
Were mingled tenderness and grace.

" You wish to join our fold," they said:
" Do you believe in all that's read
From ritual and written creed,
Essential to our human need?"

A troubled look was in her eyes;
She answered, as in vague surprise,
As though the sense to her were dim,
"I only strive to follow Him."

They knew her life; how, oft she stood,
Sweet in her guileless maidenhood,
By dying bed, in hovel lone,
Whose sorrow she had made her own.

Oft had her voice in prayer been heard,
Sweet as the voice of singing bird;
Her hand been open in distress;
Her joy to brighten and to bless.

Yet still she answered, when they sought
To know her inmost earnest thought,
With look as of the seraphim,
"I only strive to follow Him."

Creeds change as ages come and go;
We see by faith, but little know:
Perchance the sense was not so dim
To her who "strove to follow Him."

SARAH KNOWLES BOLTON.

A SAINT OF YORE

In Mem., E. V.

WHO brings it, now, her sweet accord
To every precept of her Lord?
In quaintly fashioned bonnet
With simplest ribbons on it,
The older folk remember well
How prompt she was at Sabbath bell.

I see her yet; her decent shawl,
Her sober gown, silk mitts, and all.
The deacons courtly meet her,
The pastor turns to greet her,
And maid and matron quit their place
To find her fan or smooth her lace.

I see her yet, with saintly smile,
Pass slowly up the quiet aisle:
Her mien, her every motion,
Is melody, devotion;
Contagious grace spreads round her way,
The prayer that words can never pray.

Old Groveland Church! the good folk fill
It yet, up on the windy hill:
The grass is round it growing
For nearest neighbors' mowing;
The weathered, battered sheds, behind,
Still rattle, rattle, with the wind.

All is the same; but in yon ground
Have thickened fast the slab and mound.
Hark! Shall I join the praises?
Rather, among the daisies,
Let me, in peaceful thought, once more
Be silent with the saint of yore.

JOHN VANCE CHENEY.

WITHIN

To FAIL in finding gifts, and still to give;
    To count all trouble ease, all loss as gain;
    To learn in dying as a self to live —
        This dost thou do, and seek thy joy in pain?
Rejoice that not unworthy thou art found
    For Love to touch thee with his hand divine.
Put off thy shoes,—thou art on holy ground;
    Thou standest on the threshold of his shrine.
    But canst thou wait in patience, make no sign,
And where in power thou fail'st,—oh, not in will!—
    See sore need served by other hands than thine,
And other hands the dear desires fulfill,
    Hear others gain the thanks that thou wouldst win,
    Yet be all joy? Then hast thou entered in.

ANNA CALLENDER BRACKETT.

DORIS: A PASTORAL

I SAT with Doris, the shepherd-maiden—
   Her crook was laden with wreathèd flowers;
I sat and wooed her, through sunlight wheeling
   And shadows stealing, for hours and hours.

And she, my Doris, whose lap incloses
   Wild summer-roses of sweet perfume,
The while I sued her, kept hushed and hearkened,
   Till shades had darkened from gloss to gloom.

She touched my shoulder with fearful finger;
   She said, " We linger,—we must not stay:
My flock's in danger, my sheep will wander;
   Behold them yonder, how far they stray!"

I answered bolder, "Nay, let me hear you,
   And still be near you, and still adore!
No wolf nor stranger will touch one yearling:
   Ah! stay, my darling, a moment more!"

She whispered, sighing, " There will be sorrow
   Beyond to-morrow, if I lose to-day:
My fold unguarded, my flock unfolded,
   I shall be scolded and sent away."

Said I, denying, "If they do miss you,
   They ought to kiss you when you get home;
And well rewarded by friend and neighbor
   Should be the labor from which you come."

" They might remember," she answered meekly,
   " That lambs are weakly, and sheep are wild;
But if they love me, it's none so fervent,—
   I am a servant, and not a child."

Then each hot ember glowed within me,
   And love did win me to swift reply:—
"Ah! do but prove me; and none shall bind you,
   Nor fray nor find you, until I die."

She blushed and started, and stood awaiting,
   As if debating in dreams divine:
But I did brave them; I told her plainly
   She doubted vainly,—she must be mine.

So we. twin-hearted. from all the valley
　Did rouse and rally her nibbling ewes;
And homeward drave them. we two together.
　Through blooming heather and gleaming dews.

That simple duty fresh grace did lend her.
　My Doris tender. my Doris true;
That I. her warder. did always bless her.
　And often press her to take her due.

And now in beauty she fills my dwelling
　With love excelling and undefiled;
And love doth guard her. both fast and fervent,—
　No more a servant. nor yet a child.

ARTHUR JOSEPH MUNBY.

A TRAGEDY

I

AMONG his books he sits all day
　　To think and read and write;
　He does not smell the new-mown hay.
　　The roses red and white.

I walk among them all alone,—
　His silly, stupid wife;
The world seems tasteless. dead and done—
　An empty thing is life.

At night his window casts a square
　Of light upon the lawn;
I sometimes walk and watch it there
　Until the chill of dawn.

I have no brain to understand
　The books he loves to read;
I only have a heart and hand
　He does not seem to need.

He calls me "Child" — lays on my hair
　Thin fingers, cold and mild;
O God of love, who answers prayer,
　I wish I were a child!

And no one sees and no one knows
　(He least would know or see)

That ere love gathers next year's rose,
    Death will have gathered me;

And on my grave will bindweed pink
    And round-faced daisies grow:
He still will read and write and think,
    And never, never know!

II

It's lonely in my study here alone,
    Now you are gone:
I loved to see your white gown 'mid the flowers,
    While hours on hours
I studied — toiled to weave a crown of fame
    About your name.

I liked to hear your sweet, low laughter ring;
    To hear you sing
About the house while I sat reading here,
    My child, my dear;
To know you glad with all the life-joys fair
    I dared not share.

I thought there would be time enough to show
    My love, you know,
When I could lay with laurels at your feet
    Love's roses sweet;
I thought I could taste love when fame was won —
    Now both are done!

Thank God, your child-heart knew not how to miss
    The passionate kiss
Which I dared never give, lest love should rise
    Mighty, unwise,
And bind me, with my life-work incomplete,
    Beside your feet.

You never knew, you lived and were content:
    My one chance went;
You died, my little one, and are at rest —
    And I, unblest,
Look at these broken fragments of my life,
    My child, my wife.

                 EDITH (NESBIT) BLAND.

Lightning Source UK Ltd.
Milton Keynes UK
UKHW012250140219
337323UK00011B/649/P